Love Canal Revisited

Love Canal Revisited

RACE, CLASS,

AND GENDER IN

ENVIRONMENTAL ACTIVISM

Elizabeth D. Blum

 University Press of Kansas

Published by the University Press of Kansas (Lawrence, Kansas 66045), which was organized by the Kansas Board of Regents and is operated and funded by Emporia State University, Fort Hays State University, Kansas State University, Pittsburg State University, the
University of Kansas, and Wichita State University

Library of Congress Cataloging-in-Publication Data

Blum, Elizabeth D.
    Love Canal revisited : race, class, and gender in environmental activism /
Elizabeth D. Blum.
        p.   cm.
    Includes bibliographical references and index.
    ISBN 978-0-7006-1560-5 (cloth : alk. paper)
    1. Environmental justice—New York—Niagara Falls Region—History—20th century.
2. Protest movements—New York—Niagara Falls Region—History—20th century.
3. Love Canal Chemical Waste Landfill (Niagara Falls, N.Y.) 4. Sex discrimination—New
York—Niagara Falls Region—History—20th century. 5. Race discrimination—New
York—Niagara Falls Region—History—20th century. 6. Social classes—New York—
Niagara Falls Region—History—20th century. I. Title.
    GE235.N7B58 2008
    363.72′870974799—dc22
                            2007044828

British Library Cataloguing-in-Publication Data is available.

Printed in the United States of America
10 9 8 7 6 5 4 3 2 1

The paper used in this publication is recycled and contains 50 percent postconsumer
waste. It is acid free and meets the minimum requirements of the American National
Standard for Permanence of Paper for Printed Library Materials Z39.48 1992.

To Sean

CONTENTS

List of Illustrations, *ix*

Acknowledgments, *xi*

Introduction, *1*

1 Historical Snapshots of the Love Canal Area, *9*

2 Gender at Love Canal, *31*

3 Race at Love Canal, *63*

4 Class at Love Canal, *86*

5 Historical Implications of Gender, Race, and Class at Love Canal, *120*

Notes, *151*

Selected Bibliography, *179*

Index, *187*

ILLUSTRATIONS

Map of the Love Canal neighborhood, *8*

Love Canal containment facility, *10*

La Salle neighborhood's playground complex, *11*

Vincent Morello Senior Housing Complex, *12*

Looking south down 100th Street, *13*

One of the few remaining outer-ring homes, *13*

Black Creek Village, *14*

Engraving of Niagara Falls, circa 1678, *17*

Niagara Falls in 1895, *19*

Turning the first sod at La Salle, *21*

Love Canal neighborhood in 1980, *23*

Lois Gibbs, May 1980, *32*

Richard Morris, executive director of LCARA, *45*

African American residents of Griffon Manor sign petitions, *64*

Children playing outside Griffon Manor, *65*

Marie Pozniak, Sister Margeen Hoffmann, and Luella Kenny, *87*

LCHA protest march, *99*

ACKNOWLEDGMENTS

This book began about ten years ago when my dissertation adviser, Dr. Martin V. Melosi, suggested that I combine my interest in environmental and women's history with a biography of Lois Gibbs, the primary activist at Love Canal in the late 1970s. Intrigued, I did some preliminary research and came upon the standard story that most people have heard. As I dug deeper, however, I found that large chunks of the story had not been told, despite the fact that many seemed to be familiar with it. Although Gibbs and other working-class white women were the main force in the struggle, many African Americans participated as well, as did a middle-class Christian group called the Ecumenical Task Force. I became entranced with how these groups interacted, the level of female participation and dominance, and the implications for the environmental movement. That is the tale I tell here. Although significant parts of the story remain to be told or reinterpreted, this book is the first step in a reevaluation of the message of Love Canal.

In many ways, it was a positive thing that it took me so long to finish this study (although my husband would probably disagree). It allowed me to see the material from several vantage points in my life—as a young graduate student, fresh with the ideas and theories of history; as a new professor, teaching a cadre of aspiring historians the craft that I love; and, perhaps most important, as a mother. The birth of my son, Aidan Gabriel, in August 2005 completely reinvigorated my attitude toward the material. Although I had always empathized with the women's crusade at Love Canal, I understood in a new way how they felt and their overwhelming desire to protect their children. I appreciated, at least in a small way, their concern for their children's health and future in light of the often frightening information they received during the crisis.

This book relied on many sources and influences other than my own, however. Without the help of several archivists, I would have been lost in the volume of material I encountered. Kathleen DeLaney provided invaluable guidance at both the State University of New

York (SUNY)–Buffalo and the Buffalo and Erie County Archives. She tracked down numerous names for me and even gave me a tour of the Love Canal neighborhood. Without her, my picture of the changes wrought by this environmental crisis would have been incomplete. Rodney Gorme Obien, also at SUNY–Buffalo, photocopied more pages than I care to mention, enhancing my research efforts. Sheri Kelly helped me wade through the collection of the Citizen's Clearinghouse for Hazardous Waste at Tufts University in Boston. Daniel DiLandro provided valuable assistance as well, first at SUNY–Buffalo and later at Buffalo State College.

Many of the participants at Love Canal graciously agreed to be interviewed. Lois Gibbs and the Center for Health, Environment, and Justice provided support and copious information. I would also like to thank the Reverend Dr. James Brewster, Norman Cerrillo, Roger Cook, Debbie Curry (formerly Cerrillo), Patricia Grenzy, Joann Hale, Ann Hillis, Sister Margeen Hoffmann, Luella Kenny, David Koepcke, Dr. Adeline Levine, Richard Lippes, Terri Mudd, Donna Ogg, Edmund Pozniak, Barbara Quimby, Sarah Rich, and Susan Wattle for their time and participation. I am indebted to each of them for their kindness and generosity, and hope I have done their stories justice.

The staff of the University Press of Kansas was supportive and patient, especially Nancy Scott Jackson and Kalyani Fernando, my wonderful editors on the project. Allan Mazur and other anonymous reviewers provided helpful direction and comments. Martin Melosi showed me through example, in his *The Sanitary City: Urban Infrastructure in America from Colonial Times to the Present,* what an environmental history should be; I can only hope that one day I will approach his level of sophistication and skill in historical research and writing. Craig Colten provided valuable criticism on my dissertation, which greatly assisted my thinking for the book. Landon Storrs helped me understand the historical implications of feminism and the women's movement.

Most of all, I thank my husband, Sean, for his unwavering support, kindness, love, and friendship. I would have been lost many times along this path without him. He helped me make difficult decisions and endure stressful situations with his wonderful sense of perspective and humor. Aidan, at different times, has been an inspiration, a source of relaxation and happiness, and a definite work stopper. For a while he was forbidden to enter my study for fear that he would be swallowed up by the piles of paper this project generated. My parents, Ken and Larraine Oden, have been incredibly supportive throughout my academic career, as has my grandmother, Irene Bailey, and my brother and sister-in-law, Jon and Leslie Oden. I cannot begin to express my gratitude to them. Numerous colleagues and friends at the University of Houston, Troy University, and elsewhere also commiserated with me during this effort. I would especially like to thank (in no particular order) Charles Closmann, Eric Walther, Joe Pratt, Robert Gottlieb, Dianne Glave, Adam Rome, Michael Egan, Chad Montrie, Beth Peifer, Sarah Elkind, Kim Little, Allen Jones, Courtney Bentley, Tim Buckner, Bryant Shaw, Renée Michael, Carol Anne Parker, Nancy Katheryne Webb, and Nikki Webb. I hope that someday I can help them as much as they helped me. I also received a Murray Miller scholarship from the University of Houston and several grants from the Faculty Development Committee at Troy University, all of which helped defray the costs of research and travel.

Last, but certainly not least, thanks to Zoey, Rigel, Samson, Truman, and Baxter. Although they will never read this book, they know how much they mean to me.

Introduction

The standard story of Love Canal generally goes something like this: Hooker Chemical dumped large amounts of some very nasty stuff in a hole in Niagara Falls, New York, and then covered it up—literally and figuratively—before selling the property to the local school board for $1. In the 1970s, large amounts of rainfall caused some of the buried waste to leak out of its containers, flow to the surface, and contaminate homes in the area. The oozing waste generated vocal complaints, which led Michael Brown, a Niagara Falls reporter, to investigate the contamination. After reading Brown's articles, Lois Gibbs, a shy young housewife, connected the chemicals to her son's numerous illnesses. Gibbs then single-handedly began a crusade to get the entire neighborhood relocated, manipulating the media to her advantage. She became a savvy political leader, extolling the dangers the chemicals posed to children and pressing for their safety above all else. She gained the attention of the nation and the president, and as a result, the state and federal government agreed to purchase all the homes in the beleaguered neighborhood. Congress later passed the Superfund legislation to help others in similar situations.[1]

Complications are woven through the real tale of Love Canal, although the standard story contains threads of the truth. Gibbs's face certainly dominated the media during the event, but she consistently credits others with helping to obtain the residents' evacuation. In the twentieth anniversary edition of her story, Gibbs cites the "Love Canal community's fight" as an example of "how ordinary citizens can gain power to win their struggle if they are organized."[2] During the crisis, she directed her efforts toward maintaining unity among the various factions, realizing that a large group had a better chance of influencing legislators than did one individual. Dissent among the residents over goals, tactics, and methods tends to be downplayed in the telling of the story, but Gibbs says that the Love Canal Homeowners Association (LCHA) made decisions "pretty much by majority rule, and not by an executive group, but actually by 500 really unruly people."[3] Ann Hillis, another resident, concurs with the assessment that Love Canal involved far "more than Lois Gibbs. . . . I've got nothing against Lois when I say that," she notes, "but Lois was not the only one, that's for sure."[4]

The standard version of the Love Canal story also omits the complications of race,[5] gender, and class in grassroots activism. For instance, it fails to mention the plight of the mostly black renters in the neighborhood, who faced both class and racial discrimination. It neglects the "outsiders," or nonresidents, who played an integral but secondary role in the struggle. In addition, the standard story generally neglects to explain why women, as opposed to men, became the primary public faces at Love Canal. Accounts that touch on this issue tend to rely on the superficial and essentialistic argument that "the men had to work" or that "women protect their children" to explain the gender imbalance in public activism during Love Canal.[6]

The standard account also completely disregards the deep historical context of Love Canal. Modern environmental attitudes and women's involvement in pollution-related issues date back to the turn of the twentieth century. Each group present at Love Canal had close but often unconscious connections with and similarities to historical actors in comparable situations. Love Canal's activism must be placed in this context to recognize how history paved the way for what many consider a watershed event. The events and activism of Love Canal constitute far more than a simple, limited case study; they had implications for the paths of the environmental movement, the women's movement, and the civil rights movement in the United States. In this case, environmental activism serves as a lens through which historians can examine the extent to which different segments of the population absorbed the ideas, goals, and attitudes of other social movements.

In reality, gender, race, and class played a vital role in how the residents of Love Canal experienced and dealt with the environmental crisis. There is no standard story of Love Canal. Each group, and even each person within each group, had a different, equally valid perspective and told a different version of the truth about what really happened. However, some generalizations can be made. An examination of the rhetoric of each group reveals why they became involved and what they sought to accomplish, as well as how they perceived the world around them. In addition, their language illustrates their sense of entitlement to health, to property, and to be valued and protected as American citizens, along with their attitudes about their gender, race, and class status in society.

Language, tactics, and goals play an important role in the environmental movement, yet they remain fairly underdeveloped topics in environmental research. Activists use a wide variety of rhetoric to achieve their goals—some more common than others. One of the earliest justifications for environmentalism was aesthetic or spiritual: people sought to preserve the places they found beautiful and cleansing. Others cited economic reasons, believing that resources should be protected so that they can be used by current and future generations. Environmental activism has often been justified for health reasons as well, most commonly as a type of maternalism, whereby women stress the potential dangers of pollution to children. Others see environmental activism as part of the continuing struggle to obtain justice for different racial or ethnic groups and to nurture class equality. These justifications and their accompanying rhetoric are not exclusive; activists pick and choose from among the many different rationales (not all of which are described here) to explain their actions. These combinations of justifications reveal much about a person's mind-set on the issues of class, race, and gender.

This book examines some of these issues in more detail. Rather than taking a simple chronological approach, the chapters present "snapshots" of representative facets of the Love Canal saga. The first chapter briefly explores four historical episodes in the Love Canal area, demonstrating that it has long been a site of environmental use (and overuse) and a place where human beings exploit others. Like the rest of the story, however, the explanations are rarely simple, and Love Canal has also witnessed the empowerment of marginalized populations.

Chapter 2 turns to the issue of gender and reveals distinct gendered reactions to the Love Canal crisis of the late 1970s. Led by Lois Gibbs, the

working-class white women pressed for a way out of the neighborhood, using health-centered language that stressed concern for their families—specifically, the effects of pervasive chemical contamination on the health of
their children and their own reproductive health. In contrast, the working-
class men and political elites tended to focus on economic problems. They
worried about paying taxes and mortgages on worthless homes, the loss of
tax revenue to the city, and damage to the city's image as a tourist destina-
tion. Gender distinctions were much more fluid than many realize, however:
some businesswomen and single mothers stressed economic concerns, and
some men worried about health issues.

The third chapter explores the often rocky relationship between whites
and blacks in the neighborhood. Although almost completely invisible
throughout the struggle, black women constituted a majority of the low-
income residents at Griffon Manor, the federal housing project adjacent to
Love Canal.[7] Marginalized by their race, class, and gender, these black women
fought to be heard as they defined their environmental activism as an ongoing part of the civil rights struggle against the racism and classism inherent
in American society.

Chapter 4 turns to a comparison of class at Love Canal, examining several
snapshots of the LCHA, the working-class organization led by Gibbs, and
the Ecumenical Task Force (ETF), a solidly middle-class group. The middle
class, having absorbed more of the values of the burgeoning environmental
movement, took a broader view of the problem at Love Canal and the possible solutions. They also enlisted a more complicated, layered rationale for
involvement than that seen among the working class.

The final chapter examines the historical implications of activism at Love
Canal. Three snapshots of the environmental movement over the course of
the twentieth century parallel the snapshots at Love Canal. First, men's and
women's environmental activism during the Progressive Era exhibits similar rhetorical dichotomies, yet it also demonstrates that gendered language
can be fluid. Second, black women's environmental activism during the Progressive Era and the 1950s reveals the marginalization of African American
women and their constant connection between environmental activism and
the ongoing struggle for civil rights and equality. Finally, to make class comparisons, the chapter ends with an examination of an antinuclear women's
group from the 1960s: Women Strike for Peace (WSP). WSP and the ETF

shared a predominantly white, middle-class membership, as well as a wide focus on global or national environmental issues rather than local ones. But whereas WSP showed no interest in issues of race and class, the ETF, having the benefit of a longer exposure to the civil rights movement, made racial and class justice one of its primary goals.

In many ways, the organization of this book into discrete sections on race, class, and gender alone is misleading and forced. The variables discussed cannot be removed and analyzed separately. A person is defined not by his or her race, class, or gender alone, but by a combination of all three (and other factors as well). However, an examination of how certain groups acted reveals vital comparisons and dichotomies. Of course, the picture is rarely simplistic, and examples abound of individuals moving outside the confines of the general characteristics of their group: men adopted the concerns of women, whites worked with marginalized blacks rather than against them, and members of the working class embraced the environmental goals and ethics of the middle class.

Race, class, and gender play other roles as well. Status can marginalize one group, affecting its activism. For example, with the high level of racism in Niagara Falls in the late 1970s, black women's views melted into the background. This forced them to turn to more middle-class, established groups to help with their relocation. The working-class group, desperate to escape the area, resorted to more radical tactics over time, culminating in the kidnapping of two officials from the Environmental Protection Agency. The middle-class group, more firmly entrenched in the power structure, emphatically disapproved of such actions and continued to work within the system for change.

Although certain groups demonstrated dominant concerns, environmental rhetoric and justifications for involvement are fluid concepts that change over time, from group to group, and in different situations. Perhaps more important, however, the examples at Love Canal reveal that environmental activism can be used to measure the acceptance of other major social movements and general ideas about race, class, and gender by different groups over time. For instance, this 1970s case study reveals how segments of society perceived the values of the second-wave women's movement, the civil rights movement, and the environmental movement. Reflecting the emerging New Right coalition, and tempered by the inherent threat to masculine domination, many working-class white men rejected the goals of both the civil rights movement and the women's movement. They resented women's public role in the Love Canal crisis and pressed for a return to "normalcy"—which meant a clean house and dinner on the table when they arrived home from work. Many also resented their black neighbors' attempts to be included in the solution to the problem, because they considered blacks less deserving of the benefits of a healthy neighborhood. Working-class women's reactions to the ongoing social movements tended to be less straightforward. Many of them accepted some of the ideas of the women's movement—citizenship and the right to a public voice, for example—but rejected others. Most of the women at Love Canal defined themselves and their activism as antifeminist: in their minds, they worked to affirm their worth as mothers and house-wives, something for which they felt the women's movement lacked respect. In addition, many women searched for a solution to the crisis that would benefit African Americans as well as whites. For their part, black women framed the struggle as part of the inherent racism and classism of American society, taking cues from the civil rights movement and working within its main premises: citizenship rights and equality regardless of skin color. Their activism became part of the movement to extend and develop the right to a clean environment shortly before the emergence of the national environmental justice movement.

Neither working-class whites nor African Americans articulated an explicit view of the environmental movement through their activism at Love Canal. They certainly added their opinions and versions of environmentalism to the crisis, but their actions rarely had any context outside of local concerns. The middle class group, however, with a higher level of education and social activism prior to Love Canal, adopted concepts embedded within the mainstream environmental movement. In contrast to the working class's not-in-my-backyard (NIMBY) concerns, the middle class saw a bigger picture, with a specifically environmental rationale. They incorporated diverse elements of Protestant theology, pagan concepts and theories, ecofeminism, Native American beliefs, and popular culture into their arguments. Middle-class beliefs stressed the value of the earth for aesthetic reasons; the need for humans, as the dominant species on the planet, to protect the earth; and the widespread, interconnected nature of environmental problems. Through these concerns, the middle class became involved in other environmental problems and pushed for the greatest level of inclusion and entitlement to aid among the groups at Love Canal.

As a final note, I want to point out that this work is not an exhaustive study of Love Canal or even of the gender, race, and class issues associated with it. In particular, I omitted, for the most part, a discussion of the gendered implications of the scientific arguments at Love Canal. Women's health studies were often denigrated as unscientific or invalid because of improper methods using community knowledge, whereas decision makers gave greater currency to male-based scientific reports. This topic alone could encompass an entire study, and several scholars are currently working on it.[8]

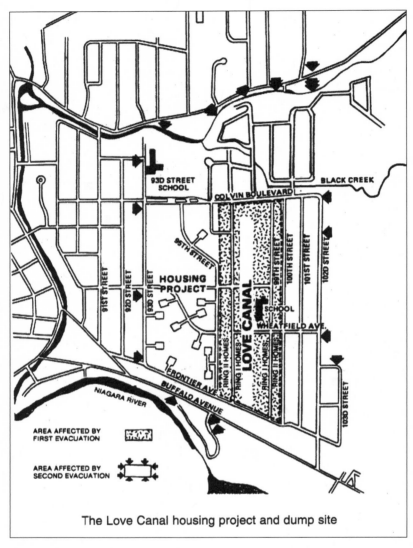

The Love Canal housing project and dump site

Map of the Love Canal neighborhood, indicating the "inner ring" (dotted area) and "outer ring" (inside the arrows) relocation areas. (Courtesy of Lois Gibbs and the Center for Health, Environment, and Justice)

1

Historical Snapshots of the Love Canal Area

Love Canal, July 2006

A crisp American flag flaps in the hot breeze over a squat, red-brick building. Somewhat lonely looking, the building sits on a roughly rectangular piece of open land surrounded by a high chain-link fence, like a dangerous beast. On the 70 acres of territory enclosed by the fence, pipes sprout from the green grass at seemingly random points. At the northwestern end, outside the fence and directly across the street, several children play on a neatly landscaped playground while being monitored by a young woman. The colorful playground equipment includes an elaborate blue, purple, and yellow tunnel slide, swings, and climbing bars. A small, covered pavilion sits nearby, looking like a pleasant spot for a family reunion, a Boy Scout cookout, or a summer picnic. Visitors driving through the neighborhood might notice people walking their dogs along the almost empty streets, stopping to chat with neighbors, or jogging in an attempt to burn a few calories.

On the southeastern edge of the chain-link fence, within walking distance of the playground, the Vincent Morello Senior Housing Complex beckons with a half-empty parking lot. Sparsely landscaped, the center appears just as sparsely populated, which is not surprising in the high heat of a July afternoon in Niagara Falls. The buildings that make up the complex look inexpensively put together, multiple versions of unimaginative square, two-story, cream-colored edifices. Some of the upper-level rooms have small balconies, with enough room for a lawn chair. Several of these balconies have a good view of the chain-link fence and its interior.

Love Canal containment facility. The containment facility sits in the middle of a fenced-in area in the inner-ring neighborhood, not far from where the 99th Street School stood in the 1970s. (Photo by author, 2001)

In contrast to the inviting, colorful playground, the eastern side of the enclosed area has more of a feel of abandonment. Some of the eastern area seems pleasant enough at first glance, with lots of shade trees, grass, and small shrubs growing in profusion. However, where a vibrant neighborhood of small, neat houses and lawns once stood in the 1970s, only a few scattered homes remain. Owners have boarded up some of the houses completely, adding to the air of desolation. Other still-existing homes stand out even more, odd islands of neatly mowed lawns and manicured landscaping, with prominent pools or vegetable gardens. The streets have been heavily patched, with evidence of large cracks and other disrepair. Vegetation threatens to consume the broken curbs and abandoned fire hydrants. Driveways lead to nowhere, although digging beneath the tranquil surface would reveal hundreds of homes demolished into their basements. At the far southeastern corner of the area, a tattered American flag hangs above the abandoned Frontier Fire Station, which displays a prominent "Now Leasing" sign and promises to "renovate to suit."

The La Salle neighborhood's playground complex, located near Colvin Boulevard and 95th Street, was constructed after the crisis. (Photo by author, 2001)

Evidence of the area's renewal begins with the Black Creek neighborhood directly north of the fenced-in acreage. Hundreds of small starter homes stretch north to Bergholz Creek, and others line the curved streets around the creek's banks. Children ride their bikes and splash in pools, teenagers cruise in their parents' cars, and fathers tend to lawns. A large, well-kept baseball facility sits empty; the players perhaps wait for a respite from the heat of the day.

Little remains at Love Canal to remind visitors of the crisis that gripped the area almost thirty years ago. Only a small sign adorns the entrance to the containment area, surrounded by the chain-link fence, barely noticeable to passersby. No evidence exists of the former homes, gardens, pools, or family life inside the fence. Certainly no one would guess that a large school once stood in the center of the area.

The senior citizen center, serving a marginalized population of elderly New Yorkers, sits on the spot where Griffon Manor once housed hundreds of low-income families (mostly African Americans) for several decades. The Frontier Fire Station was a prominent meeting place for Lois Gibbs and

Vincent Morello Senior Housing Complex. This senior citizens' residence was constructed in 2000 on the site of the Griffon Manor development, where many of the African American renters lived during the crisis. (Photo by author, 2001)

her fellow protesters. President Jimmy Carter pronounced the Black Creek neighborhood, north of the containment area, part of the Emergency Declaration Area in the early 1980s, and most of the residents subsequently abandoned the area.

The place remains a contested site. Suggestions to create a museum or an interpretive center began as early as 1982, contained in a residents' report presented to the Love Canal Area Revitalization Agency (LCARA), the authority responsible for rehabilitating the area. Nothing came of the idea at the time, but in 1998, Susan Wattle, then executive director of LCARA, formed an ad hoc group to develop plans for an interpretive center. The board of LCARA became disenchanted with the idea of the center and "disowned the group early on," according to Wattle.[1] Nevertheless, it continued its mission as "Love Canal 2000," a "bi-partisan group of former and current residents of Black Creek Village, politicians, urban planners, and a retired journalist whose beat for more than two decades included Love Canal." Love

Looking south down 100th Street. The edge of the containment facility is on the right. (Photo by author, 2006)

One of the few remaining homes at the western edge of the outer ring. (Photo by author, 2006)

Black Creek Village, looking north up 98th Street. Although it was part of the outer ring, and families were relocated from this area, the neighborhood was "revitalized" through the efforts of LCARA in the 1990s. (Photo by author, 2006)

Canal 2000 received a grant from the Niagara County Environmental Fund to conduct a feasibility study for a museum. When the study yielded positive results, the group hired the environmental consulting firm AKRF to design a "tourist center to commemorate environmental disaster."[2] The plan included both a "landscape interpretation and a small building that would tell the story of the event and the history of citizen based environmental activism."[3]

Despite the detailed planning, Love Canal 2000 encountered significant opposition from residents in both Niagara Falls and the local neighborhood. In the summer of 2001, opponents collected more than 2,000 signatures from angry Niagara Falls residents. Some saw the project as a continuation of pork-barrel politics; others considered it a waste of taxpayer and county money. Some worried about the effect on tourism. One resident angrily told Sam Granieri, Love Canal 2000's chairman of the board, "You're going to put the stigma back on Niagara Falls." Others simply felt that all history should be pleasant and happy. Voicing this position, freelance writer S. K. Brown noted caustically, "There are Holocaust museums everywhere to remind people they must never forget such a blatant crime. . . . I've never been to a Holocaust museum and don't plan a visit. I don't forgive crimes against mankind, much less forget them, and I don't need a museum to remind me. . . . Clearly, I won't be lining up to see photos of Love Canal's dead children."[4]

Paradoxically, others feared that the center might actually increase tourism in the area, transforming residents into some type of zoo animals. Wattle noted, "The current residents are not in favor of it. The reasons vary; mostly it's that they don't want to be put on display. And discussions about the fact that people will come to the facility. [But] the [proposed site for the] facility is away from their residential streets. There's a lot of people who travel through the area. Buses go through there, people on their own. And they don't like that. . . . [Residents say] 'We're tired of being on display and we want you to go away.'"[5]

With such fierce opposition, the movement to build the interpretive center withered fairly quickly. Wiping out the memory of the events of Love Canal may be easier said than done, however. For more than 350 years, the Niagara Falls area has been used and exploited by various groups of people, but it has also been the site of empowerment by groups working against established power structures. Several snapshots of the area over time demonstrate vivid changes in the landscape, as well as in the relationships among its people. The Love Canal crisis magnified these relationships and themes, culminating in the late 1970s.

Niagara Falls, Late 1600s

Flowing via a circuitous route from Lake Erie to Lake Ontario, the Niagara River drops hundreds of thousands of gallons of water over its banks at the famous falls each second. From earliest recorded history, the river's power served human interests in various ways. For example, the Seneca Nation, part of the Iroquois Confederation, used the tremendous force of the falls as a food source in the 1600s and 1700s. Frenchman Baron La Hontan noted, "All the Beasts that cross the Water within half a quarter of a League above this unfortunate Island [Goat Island, which separates the falls], are suck'd in by force of the Stream. And the Beasts and Fish that are thus kill'd by the prodigious fall, serve for food to fifty Iroquese, who are settled about two Leagues off, and take 'em out of the water with their Canows."[6]

Father Louis Hennepin, a French priest, documented the falls and the surrounding area for Europeans in a book entitled *A New Discovery of a Vast Country in America,* published in 1678. The natural wonder that Hennepin witnessed at Niagara Falls captivated him. The falls, he wrote, cascade "down after a surprising and astonishing manner, insomuch that the Universe does not afford its Parallel." The falls made "an outrageous Noise, more terrible than that of Thunder; for when the Wind blows from off the South, their dismal roaring may be heard about fifteen Leagues off."[7]

Hennepin, a member of the expedition led by explorer René-Robert Cavelier, Sieur de La Salle, included copious descriptions of the countryside as well as his interactions with the local Indian tribes. Generally, he focused on the lack of noticeable human development in the area. He traveled with the Indians through "the wild Forests that their country is full of." He repeatedly noted the alien nature of the territory to European habits. For example, on one expedition, Hennepin and his group "pass'd through Ways that were overflown with Water, and such as wou'd have been unpassable by any European: For when we came at vast Marshes and overflowing Brooks, we were oblig'd to crawl along by the Trees."[8] Engravings that accompanied Hennepin's writings, and subsequent paintings by later artists, showed an area covered by forests and heavy vegetation as far as the eye could see.

Hennepin's descriptions also acknowledged the abundance of natural resources. Near Fort Frontenac, he noted that the Seneca Indians "manure a great deal of Ground for sowing their Indian Corn in, of which they reap ordinarily in one Harvest as much as serves 'em for two Years." The region also hosted a variety of fish. On the Niagara River, Hennepin noted, "they take an infinite quantity of Whitings, Sturgeons, and all other sorts of Fishes, which are incomparably good and sweet . . . they might furnish the greatest City in Europe with plenty of Fish." In addition to fish, Hennepin reported abundant elk, deer, beaver, and other animals.[9]

The French expressed an interest in the Niagara Falls area as a trade route for furs. Hennepin observed that the presence of Frenchmen in the region was a way to control the fur trade with the Indians. Fort Frontenac, Hennepin noted, served "to interrupt the Trade of Skins that these Savages maintain with the Inhabitants of New York . . . for they furnish the Savages with

Engraving of Niagara Falls from Father Louis Hennepin's *A New Discovery of a Vast Country in America* (1678). (Courtesy of Buffalo and Erie County Historical Society)

Commodities at cheaper Rates than the French."[10] The falls interrupted the transportation of goods and men between Lakes Erie and Ontario and therefore deeper into New France. The French, therefore, continued to consolidate their position within the region and to control as much of the trade, and the local population, as possible.

Hennepin and his fellow Europeans thought little of the Indians. He variously described them as barbarous, warlike, cruel, and even cannibalistic. However, in seventeenth-century North America, they still constituted a significant force—and one with which the French had to negotiate. In early 1679, for example, Hennepin accompanied a group of Frenchmen to talk to Seneca leaders. The French, after presenting numerous gifts to the Indians, informed them of the French desire to build two things: a "great Hangar or Store-house, to keep the commodities we had brought to supply their Occasions," and "a ship, or great wooden Canow . . . to go fetch European Commodities by a more convenient passage." Although they tried to convince the tribe that the building and the ship would be used only for trade purposes with the Seneca, the Indians remained justifiably suspicious.[11]

Certainly, the French intended the "great Hangar" to be a fort to consolidate French control of the area and possibly to prepare for war against either the Indians or the British. The "great wooden Canow" was no less incendiary and drew the ire of the Seneca. At 60 tons and armed with guns, the ship, named the *Griffon,* seemed to have more sinister purposes than trade. The Seneca soon stopped selling food to the French at the construction site, located on the Niagara River above the falls (directly south—and within walking distance—of the future site of Love Canal). In addition, they attempted to kill some of the workers and unsuccessfully plotted to burn the ship before the French launched it.[12] The Indians' suspicions turned out to be justified when fighting between the British and the French ensued, culminating in the Seven Years' War.

Early French settlers and explorers proved adept in manipulating the local tribes and using the Niagara area to enhance their financial gain and their nation's power. Yet the Seneca, hardly powerless, forced concessions and gifts from the French and even dictated their work patterns.[13] The European successors to the French, the British, demonstrated far more mastery of these tactics. As disease and alcoholism spread among the Iroquois in the next century, the British consolidated control of the Niagara area, manipulated land gains from the Indians, and began settling the area in large numbers. With control of the area came control of the Niagara River and the falls themselves, which later passed to the United States of America.

This early period saw the beginning of the themes of oppression extant in the Niagara Falls area over the next 350 years. Groups attempted to establish dominance over one another, with varying degrees of success. In addition, people exploited the region for its natural resources—food, lumber, and fur.

Niagara Falls, Late 1800s

Since their "discovery" by Europeans, the falls have been admired not only for their natural beauty and magnificence but also for their potential to generate power for various types of industry. Daniel Joncaire constructed a mill near the American falls in the mid-1700s, using the tremendous flow of the Niagara River to produce lumber. The tradition of using the water flow for

Niagara Falls in 1895. At around the turn of the century, the city became more heavily industrialized, utilizing the great power of the Niagara River for electricity. (Courtesy of Buffalo and Erie County Historical Society)

industry continued throughout the eighteenth and nineteenth centuries and became especially important with the development of electricity in the late nineteenth century.[14]

Enterprising businessman Jacob Schoellkopf opened the first hydroelectric station in 1881, to instant success. In fact, demand for the amazing electrical lights it powered quickly outstripped the capability of the small enterprise, since no technology for supplying electricity at a distance existed at the time. Thomas Edison wrote a proposal in 1886 to deliver direct current to nearby Buffalo from the falls, but the town fathers thought the cost was far too high. Fortunately, the development of alternating current allowed Schoellkopf to build a large power station to supply the town of Niagara Falls with electricity in 1895. With additional technological advances, the Schoellkopf family built more and larger electricity-generating stations, and power from the falls reached Buffalo by the early 1900s.[15]

Thanks to this new source of power, industry sprang up along the banks of the Niagara River in the late 1800s and early 1900s. The Carborundum Company opened a plant in 1895 to produce crystals hard enough to cut diamonds, DuPont initiated the manufacture of sodium and chlorine in 1896, Shredded Wheat (later Nabisco) opened its doors in Niagara Falls in 1901, and Occidental Chemical Company (then known as Hooker Electrochemical Company) joined others along the Niagara River in 1905. The blocky warehouses, production plants, and smokestacks of heavy industry replaced the shoreline trees and vegetation of Father Hennepin's time. Tunnels and canals of various widths and depths sliced across the territory to reroute water and supply power to these flourishing businesses.[16]

The spectacle of the falls themselves succumbed to this enterprising, capitalistic spirit. By the mid-1800s, the falls, widely hailed as the most breathtaking sight in North America, drew tens of thousands of visitors each year. With the property surrounding the falls in private hands, however, the site was soon choked with billboards, fences, and tourist stands. Visitors from Europe decried such blatant commercialism. With exasperation and despair, an English traveler noted in 1849 that "the Yankees put an ugly shot tower on the brink of the Horseshoe and they are about to consummate the barbarism by throwing a wire bridge over the river . . . it requires very little more to show that patriotism, taste, and self-esteem, are not the leading features in the character of the inhabitants of this part of the world."[17] Embarrassed by such comments, some Americans took action to protect and restore the falls. Frederick Law Olmsted, among others, initiated a campaign to help "the state of New York to restore the cataract and its environs to their national condition." Olmsted succeeded in 1885, and the memory of uncontrolled capitalism at Niagara Falls helped inform the nascent national park movement.[18]

In the 1890s, William T. Love joined the tradition of rampant capitalism with his plan to build a canal connecting the Niagara River to Lake Ontario. Love's goal was to create a navigable route along the Niagara as well as to provide abundant electrical power for the area. He also planned a "model city" for the northern end of the canal, along the banks of Lake Ontario.[19] Little information exists about the workers Love employed, but based on past examples of canal labor, those who toiled at Love Canal faced incredibly dirty, tiring, and often dangerous work. Industrialists generally hired recent immigrants to perform the basic work of digging canals; first, however, they

Turning the first sod at La Salle. A group of interested citizens turned out on 23 May 1894 to see the beginning of Love's canal. (Photo by H. C. Percy, courtesy of Buffalo and Erie County Historical Society)

had to clear the area of tress and other obstacles. Lore has it that the Irish immigrants who built the Erie Canal worked in degrading conditions for $1 a day plus shots of liquor. Disease ran rampant in the workers' quarters, a result of spending most of the day laboring in murky, standing water.[20]

Love's grand scheme, however, fell victim to economic misfortune. The Panic of 1893 hit the country with unusual severity, forcing investors to pull out of the canal project after the initial work had begun. When Love abandoned his idea, approximately a mile-long section of the canal, about fifty feet wide and ten to forty feet deep, had been completed.[21]

A little more than a decade later, Hooker Electrochemical Company (later Hooker Chemical Company), founded by Elon Hooker, began to produce chemicals in the Niagara Falls area. Over the next seventy years, Hooker Chemical became an integral part of the community, providing jobs to residents and tax revenue to the local government. In 1942, Hooker Chemical obtained the right to dispose of its chemical wastes in the old Love Canal, and it later purchased the property from the city.[22] This development continued the long-standing tradition of exploiting the land in Niagara Falls. In

addition, with callous disregard for the health and safety of the neighborhood, Hooker Chemical perpetuated the theme of human oppression.

Love Canal, Late 1900s

Hooker Chemical eventually realized that its method of disposing of chemicals constituted at least a fire hazard to the growing number of buildings, including homes, in the area. Aileen Voorhees, a longtime resident whose yard
abutted the canal area, remembered, "If a drum containing a certain material
would break, the air would hit it and it would catch on fire. It seemed Hooker
was always out there putting out fires."[23] Her daughter, Karen Schroeder, a
lifelong resident of Love Canal, recalled more dramatic examples of the danger. She said that "workers would run screaming into her yard when some
of the toxic chemicals they were dumping would spill down on their skin
or clothes. She remembers her mother washing them down with a garden
hose until the first aid could arrive."[24] The company used the property until
1952, dumping at least 21,000 tons of chemicals, including "caustics, alka-
lies, fatty acids, and chlorinated hydrocarbons from the manufacture of dyes,
perfumes, solvents for rubber and synthetic resins."[25]

After covering the entire area with dirt, the chemical company sold the
plot of land to the Niagara Falls School Board for $1 in 1953. The board in-
tended to build an elementary school on the newly acquired property, and
although numerous warnings surfaced—some veiled and some direct—they
failed to dissuade school district officials from their construction plans. For
example, Hooker alluded to the potentially dangerous nature of the property in the deed that transferred its ownership. In that document, Hooker
stated, "prior to the delivery of this instrument by conveyance, the grantee
[school board] herein has been advised by the grantor [Hooker] that the
premises above described have been filled, in whole or in part, to the present
grade level thereof with waste products resulting from the manufacturing of
chemicals by the grantor at its plant in the City of Niagara Falls, New York,
and the grantee assumes all risk and liability incident to the use thereof."[26]
The deed also contained a clause releasing Hooker from all legal obligations
should any lawsuits arise.

Despite the somewhat cryptic warning from Hooker, and despite a city
attorney's advice not to accept liability for the chemical waste, work on the

The Love Canal neighborhood in May 1980, looking southeast toward the Niagara River. The 99th Street School is at the upper left, and Griffon Manor is at the upper right. (Courtesy of Buffalo State College Archives, *Courier-Express* Collection)

school continued. Construction workers later discovered a large number of drums barely below the surface, but the school board simply moved the site about 80 feet farther north along the canal and ordered construction to continue. The school opened its doors in 1955.[27]

Once workers completed the school, additional houses sprang up to accommodate the growing city, and chemical workers from the nearby plants moved their families into the modest homes. Although the area surrounding the canal had been annexed to the city in 1927, most of the neighborhood's working-class population moved in during the 1960s and 1970s, taking advantage of increasingly available government-backed and -sponsored housing loans. Few of the young families knew the entire history of the canal, and none received the benefit of information from Hooker, the local government, or their real estate agents regarding the contents of the dump site. Early on, the unfinished canal seemed to provide some benefits to the surrounding community. It quickly filled with water, and many enjoyed it as a swimming spot in the summer, an ice skating rink in the winter, and a fishing hole year-round until the 1960s.[28]

The residents who were later involved in the fight to be removed from the area almost universally found the Love Canal neighborhood aesthetically pleasing at first. In addition, many residents liked the benefits of living close to nature and the convenience of living in the city. Luella Kenny, who owned a home north of the canal, loved the view from her windows. She lived "on one acre of land, with all these oak trees . . . [and yet] still in the city. And it had the creek running through it." Edmund Pozniak cited the profusion of "trees and grass" as reasons for purchasing his home on Colvin Boulevard. Barbara Quimby's home had a large lot, and she recalled, "We were like farmers. . . . I was making my kids' baby food and we ate all our [own] veggies." Others found even the newer parts of the neighborhood visually pleasing. Debbie Cerrillo remembered "brand-new driveways, all brand-new sidewalks," and new trees in her neighborhood directly along the canal.[29]

In addition to the aesthetic advantages, a pervasive sense of family and community breathed life into the neighborhood. Pozniak expressed a common thought when he said that the area "looked like a good place for kids to grow up." Quimby emphasized a sense of continuity and family in the neighborhood that she described as "just wonderful. . . . The people that saw my mother wheeling me in my buggy were seeing me wheeling my kids in the buggy." Lois Gibbs's first impression of the neighborhood was "delightful. I mean, it was a young neighborhood. There were lots of young people who had young children with buggies and Big Wheels. It was vibrant and it was alive and people had little yards with manicured little flower boxes. And it was exactly what I wanted. And the school was within walking distance, so that when Michael [her eldest child] got old enough, . . . I felt we could walk over there to school every day, and he could come home for lunch. It was very romantic, the way I looked at it. I didn't know it was going to be a nightmare!"[30]

In the late 1970s, journalists from the *Niagara Gazette* began to investigate complaints from several residents in the Love Canal neighborhood.[31] Owing to an usually high level of rain and snowfall during the mid to late 1970s, the ground in the Niagara Falls area became saturated. This caused many of the drums of waste, already deteriorating because of age and rust, to burst or be pushed to the surface. Residents began to notice puddles of oily, colored residue in their yards or seeping into their basements. Samples from several basement sump pumps revealed chemicals produced by Hooker.[32]

Michael Brown, a young reporter for the *Niagara Gazette,* became interested in Love Canal in 1977. He witnessed firsthand "homes where dogs had lost their fur . . . children with serious birth defects . . . entire families in inexplicably poor health." He wrote a series of probing articles, using Tim and Karen Schroeder as his main contacts. The Schroeders' problems with Love Canal began with the strange behavior of their swimming pool, which, one day in 1974, "had suddenly risen two feet above the ground." When they removed the pool, the resulting hole filled with "rancid liquids of yellow and orchid and blue." The waste overflowed into the Schroeders' yard, destroying plants and eating through their fence.[33]

These were not the only problems that the Schroeders later connected to the chemicals. Their daughter, born in 1968, suffered from mental retardation and numerous deformities. Karen's parents, Aileen and Edwin Voorhees, also canal residents, had chemical problems as well. The Schroeders, however, felt compelled to stay in the neighborhood because they could not afford to move if no one would buy their home. For the most part, the Schroeders kept their struggle a private one, discussing the matter with Brown but failing to communicate widely with their neighbors. One neighbor with whom they did share their troubles was Tom Heisner, who had also experienced problems. Both the Heisners and the Schroeders hoped that Hooker would pay to remove them from their contaminated homes.[34]

The city of Niagara Falls hired Calspan Corporation to report on the extent of the pollution in the area and to suggest methods for cleanup. Calspan found, among other things, "that 21 of the 188 homes adjacent to the canal had varying degrees of chemical residue in their sump pumps and strong odors, with 75 percent of the affected homes clustered at the southern section of the Love Canal site." The consultants recommended a cleanup project that would cost almost half a million dollars to "seal off home sump pumps, install a tile drainage system, and partially cover the canal site."[35] The city refused to follow Calspan's recommendations. Congressman John LaFalce (D-N.Y.) urged the Environmental Protection Agency (EPA) to become involved in the growing controversy. The EPA and state environmental agencies soon began to sample air, water, and soil in the neighborhood, providing additional evidence of chemical contamination. In addition, state officials began to test the residents' blood during the summer of 1978. Initially limited to those families closest to the canal, the blood testing eventually encompassed about 4,000 people in the area.[36]

Once the city began its initial studies, more and more residents became aware of the situation through the growing news coverage. One of these residents, a self-described "news junkie" named Lois Gibbs, connected the chemical waste to her son's recent spate of illnesses. Michael had started school in September 1977 and developed epilepsy in December. Doctors also discovered a low white blood cell count the following February, and the boy had surgery twice for urethral strictures. In June 1978, Gibbs began reading Brown's articles on the history of the canal. After reading other articles and talking with her brother-in-law, a biologist, Gibbs connected her son's recent health problems with his attendance at the 99th Street School, which had been built directly on the canal.[37]

Gibbs quickly became convinced that she had to remove her son from the presence of the harmful chemicals. "When I started," she said, "I was interested only in myself and my child. I didn't stop to think about the other children in the neighborhood." Furious when the superintendent refused her request to move Michael to another school, Gibbs decided to discuss the issue with other parents. She began on her own street, since she found contacting her friends and neighbors less intimidating than knocking on the doors of complete strangers. At house after house, Gibbs heard stories similar to her own. Many children suffered from unexplained illnesses. Other women related stories of miscarriages, deformed or retarded children, or crib deaths. She also witnessed physical damage to property, including foundations sinking, basements filling with unknown substances, and landscape vegetation dying.[38] Alarmed by the reports from her neighbors, and frustrated in her attempt to obtain information from public officials, Gibbs enlisted the help of Debbie Cerrillo, who became her close friend and organizing cohort.[39]

In response to the initial studies and the residents' outcry, Robert Whalen, New York's health commissioner, issued a dramatic announcement from the state capital. On 2 August 1978, he stated that residents near the canal showed evidence of higher than normal levels of spontaneous abortions and birth defects and that at least one human carcinogen had been located in the area. In declaring "the existence of an emergency" at Love Canal, he stated, the

"Love Canal Chemical Waste Landfill constitutes a public nuisance and an extremely serious threat and danger to the health, safety, and welfare of those using it, living near it, or exposed to the conditions emanating from it, consisting, among other things, of chemical wastes lying exposed on the surface in numerous places and pervasive, pernicious, and obnoxious chemical vapors and fumes affecting both the ambient air and the homes of certain residents living near such sites."[40] Whalen cautioned all residents to avoid their basements and not to eat food grown in home gardens. In addition, he recommended the temporary relocation of all pregnant women and children younger than two years living in the ring of homes bordering the canal.[41]

Gibbs, her husband, and Cerrillo made the 300-mile trip to Albany to attend Whalen's announcement. Beforehand, Cerrillo and Gibbs read as much information as they could to prepare for their confrontation. The announcement itself only increased their anger and frustration. Gibbs remembered, "I was furious. I jumped up and said to Commissioner Whalen, 'If the dump will hurt pregnant women and children under two, what, for God's sake, is it going to do to the rest of us!? What do you think you're doing?' Now very emotional, I said, 'You can't do that! That would be murder!'" The two women were extremely wary of the state bureaucrats. "These guys were giving us a bunch of baloney," Gibbs said. "I had a list of fifty questions, but all I got was engineering jargon and political answers that made no sense."[42]

Gibbs returned home to find a spontaneous neighborhood meeting in Heisner's front yard. Regarded as an authority because of her presence at the commissioner's announcement, Gibbs nervously stepped up to speak to the angry, frightened crowd. She explained what Whalen had said and encouraged everyone to notify the state health department of any problems. She also urged them to attend a meeting with state officials, scheduled for the next day, and to be prepared with questions. The crowd's emotions overflowed. Gibbs recalled, "One man stood up, grabbed his wife's arm, stood her up and started yelling, 'What does it mean for my wife who is eight months pregnant? What does that mean for her? It's too late for her?' This man actually had tears in his eyes." Other residents echoed the man's concern.[43]

Frustrated by the lack of information, Gibbs consulted with attorney Richard Lippes, and the pair decided to form a home owners' association. More than 550 residents met at the Frontier Fire Station and pledged their support, thus transforming the angry crowd into the Love Canal Homeowners

Association (LCHA). They elected Lois Gibbs president, Tom Heisner vice president, Karen Schroeder secretary, and Debbie Cerrillo treasurer.[44] The LCHA became the most visible and most vocal residents' organization pressing for remedies to the chemical contamination.

In response to the residents' growing agitation, state and federal officials acted quickly, at least verbally. They closed the 99th Street School, whose grounds included substantial portions of the canal.[45] Governor Hugh Carey announced on 7 August that the state planned to purchase the homes of the inner-ring families so that they could leave the area.[46] To coordinate the purchase of these homes and to deal with the residents' problems, Mayor Michael O'Laughlin developed the Love Canal Task Force, headed on-site by Michael Cuddy from the New York State Department of Transportation. The next day, President Jimmy Carter declared a federal health emergency at Love Canal. Concerned about the continued seepage of chemicals into area homes, state officials initiated a cleanup plan that differed only slightly from that proposed by Calspan a few months earlier. It involved the installation of a tile drainage system and numerous trenches to move the waste to the city's sewer system. In addition, construction crews intended to "cap" the canal with an eight-foot-thick clay ceiling to keep rainwater from entering the site.[47]

Meanwhile, additional results of blood work and physical samples filtered in, further alarming residents almost to the point of panic. Water samples from nearby streams showed the presence of dioxin, an extremely dangerous chemical.[48] So toxic that it is usually measured in parts per *trillion,* dioxin levels in the Love Canal samples registered 5.3 parts per *billion.* In addition, chromosome studies performed on some residents showed that an alarming 33 percent had some damage, compared with a rate of 1 percent expected among the general population. These and other health studies, a congressional investigation, and constant pressure from residents' groups prompted President Carter to widen his emergency declaration on 21 May 1980 and order the temporary relocation of 700 outer-ring families around Love Canal. By the summer of 1981, more than 500 families had abandoned their homes, and the Griffon Manor housing project at the western edge of the neighborhood stood half empty. Less than 10 percent of the original 900 families chose to stay permanently.[49] Love Canal had become a virtual ghost town.

Science failed to take a definitive role during the Love Canal situation, tending to operate on both sides of the fence. For instance, Governor Carey commissioned a panel to review the Love Canal scientific findings, and in a report issued in October 1980, the panel criticized the numerous health studies to date. It found no evidence of acute or chronic health problems due to chemicals in the area.[50]

In addition to contradictory reports on the health effects of the chemicals, arguments continued over the safety of the neighborhood. State and local officials moved quickly to turn the Love Canal area into a viable neighborhood. Formed in June 1980, the Love Canal Area Revitalization Agency (LCARA) was entrusted with the dual tasks of purchasing homes from residents and restoring the area. In September 1988, LCARA declared parts of Love Canal "habitable," which prompted Gibbs, then living in Virginia and active at the national level in her own organization, to return to the area to fight the action. Although LCARA demolished many of the homes immediately surrounding the canal, the area north of the canal became a thriving neighborhood known as Black Creek Village.[51]

Just as the Love Canal situation was resolved slowly, so was the legal action against Hooker. In 1988, Judge John Curtin found Occidental Petroleum Corporation (Hooker's successor) responsible for the environmental contamination and ordered the company to pay $98 million to New York State.[52] The federal government settled with Occidental for $129 million later that year. Residents' individual lawsuits were eventually settled as well, with the last cases ending in 1997, almost twenty years after the fact.[53] Thus, the grassroots activism at Love Canal proved successful, eventually prompting state and federal action to remove residents from the neighborhood and giving them some belated financial restitution for their health and property losses.

Over the course of history, the Niagara Falls area has seen its share of exploitation of both land and population. Early Native Americans used the falls as a source of food. The French and later the British used the area to consolidate their power in North America and to dominate the local fur trade. These efforts were successful to varying degrees, depending primarily on how well the Europeans manipulated or misled the Indian population. With the emergence of the Industrial Revolution and the need for power sources,

Americans attempted to harness the rushing waters of the river to serve their own ends. This gushing capitalistic spirit had its consequences, however. Waste produced by those industries had to go somewhere, and much of it generated by Hooker Chemical found its way into an unfinished canal located nearby. The waste percolated to the surface, affecting the health of hundreds of people in the small working-class neighborhood. Workers faced hazardous conditions both on the job and at home with their families.

The area also gave a sense of empowerment to those traditionally seen as victims in environmental tales. The Seneca, for example, proved to be adept and intuitive adversaries in their dealings with the French. Likewise, the working-class neighborhood of Love Canal gained political success and spread its ideas beyond the traditional extent of its influence.

Love Canal's transformation from heavy forests and vegetation to heavy industry and back to vegetation is only part of the story. This case study raises numerous questions concerning ethnicity, class, and gender in environmental activism. In addition, we can use environmental activism as a lens to examine certain attitudes about race, class, and gender in the wake of other social movements of the time—the women's movement and the civil rights movement.

2

Gender at Love Canal

Even cursory studies of the Love Canal crisis note the pivotal leadership of Lois Gibbs and other women and the notable absence of men from public activism. A simplified explanation relies on traditional gender roles: Men, afraid of losing their jobs with local industries, maintained a stony silence. Women, because the threat involved harm to children, were vocal and active. However, this reasoning minimizes the agency of both the men and women involved. The threat at Love Canal centered on children because the women consciously chose to emphasize that concern. Men played a public role as well, involving their local unions and expressing concern over family economics.

A more layered picture emerges on closer examination. Women formed the most visible corps of activism, and they certainly focused on maternalistic concerns, especially as the story of Love Canal gained the attention of the national press. This gendered rhetoric, however, was somewhat fluid, especially early on. Women also expressed economic concerns, and some men echoed the women's health concerns. Activism at Love Canal clearly shows how the working-class whites of the neighborhood interpreted the values of equity, entitlement, and rights expressed by the women's movement, the civil rights movement, and the environmental movement of the 1960s and 1970s.

Led by Lois Gibbs, the working-class women adopted a language that stressed a solution to the problem based on their status as wives and mothers. Historians have a long-standing argument over the meaning of this commonly used maternalistic language. Some historians see it as inherently conservative, meaning that it reinforced subordinate roles for women. Others argue that it provided a safe avenue for activism in a society that saw

Lois Gibbs, the most well-known face from the Love Canal crisis. This photograph was taken in May 1980, shortly after two EPA officials were taken hostage by the LCHA. (Courtesy of Buffalo State College Archives, *Courier-Express* Collection)

women as second-class citizens whose proper place lay in the home. Generally, though, historians agree that such language must be interpreted within the context of the times and historical events.[1] Since the activism of working-class men and women at Love Canal involved highly gendered language and occurred in the wake of the second-wave women's movement, it tells us much about how they interpreted gender roles for men and women as well as how they interpreted the women's movement.

The working-class women at Love Canal adopted some elements of the struggle for women's rights and chose to eschew others. Their interpretation of the movement itself proved to be pivotal to their activism. They easily accepted the notions of women's citizenship and public roles and believed that women had a right to speak publicly and to demand action from the government. They also accepted an expansive definition of who should benefit from governmental action. Yet most of them interpreted the feminism of the 1970s as being antifamily, and rather than locating their activism within that realm, most of them consciously chose to use language and actions that reinforced the value of women as mothers and housewives. Thus, most women's activism at Love Canal reflected a complicated legacy for gender roles and the women's movement. On one hand, the women consciously rejected the idea of feminism; on the other hand, they embraced some of its core ideals.

The working-class men more blatantly rejected the goals of the women's movement. Many resented their wives' activism and involvement with issues outside the home. Some hoped for a return to "normalcy" in family relations once the crisis ended, which meant a wife who stayed home with the children and a husband who provided for his family. In keeping with that role as provider, more men stressed economic concerns, in contrast to the women's articulation of health issues as being foremost. In addition, the men often had a far narrower view of citizenship rights and who should benefit from governmental action. Men from many groups expressed a latent racism as well, directed against the black renters in the neighborhood. Of course, a historical picture rarely reflects a clear dichotomy. Men and women overlapped and contrasted in their concerns, their rhetoric, and their actions throughout the crisis.

Two snapshots from Love Canal illustrate these points. First, the early struggle for leadership among the working-class whites of the neighborhood reflects the differing concerns of the sexes: health issues for women and economic issues for men. This early power struggle also illustrates the gender-related differences in defining the scope of the problem and who should receive benefits. The male-dominated resident group (led by Tom Heisner) focused on a smaller, more exclusive section of the neighborhood, while the female-dominated group (the LCHA, led by Gibbs) stressed a larger area. The second snapshot, taken at the end of the story, focuses on the contrasting goals for the future of the area. For LCARA, tourist revenue and tax dollars took center stage. LCARA forced the "revitalization" of Love Canal by returning families to the area; it silenced opponents who raised the issue of potential health problems, demonstrating a callous indifference to the citizenship rights of residents along the way. The LCHA, in contrast, pushed for nonuse, or at least no residential use, out of an overriding concern for health issues. Although the LCHA had used this argument successfully to force the government to relocate residents, LCARA's language dominated the long-term solutions to the problem.

Early Leadership at Love Canal: Heisner versus Gibbs

When the national media descended on Love Canal in the summer of 1978, male leadership dominated, and most of the concerns reported by the media involved economics and finances. Thomas Heisner, an inner-ring resident, briefly emerged as a local leader, along with Tim and Karen Schroeder, in the weeks immediately following the 2 August announcement by health commissioner Whalen. Heisner and the Schroeders both had children with birth defects and had been negotiating with the city and Hooker Chemical to leave the neighborhood for some time.[2] The Schroeders' story captured the attention of *Niagara Gazette* reporter Mike Brown and prompted him to look into the matter more deeply.[3]

Heisner's rhetoric illustrated the extreme economic concerns of the residents. He first organized a tax and mortgage boycott, believing that his property value had diminished to the point where he could no longer sell his house. Approximately 200 other residents joined him in an impromptu meeting on his front lawn on the evening of 2 August, and Lois Gibbs spoke to the group when she returned from her trip to Albany. Resident Gerald Snyder asserted, "I'm not paying any more taxes. I don't know how I'll pay the mortgage, but I won't pay the taxes." Several other residents agreed, slipping mortgage payment envelopes into a basket on Heisner's fence that evening as a protest.[4]

Heisner also responded negatively to Whalen's recommendation that small children leave the area. "I don't see the day when they'll move my kids out and not me," he told a reporter. Heisner's reaction indicated a stubborn determination to keep his family together and under his control, regardless of the health consequences—a direct contrast to many women's primary concern about their children's health.[5] Yet even Heisner, the most outspoken man regarding economic issues, did not ignore the importance of health and children. At a 4 August meeting with state health officials, Heisner stood up and angrily remarked, "My child has a birth defect. We're not giving up. We want to live. We're going to fight the stinking Hooker chemicals."[6]

This economic rhetoric extended to some women as well. In an early interview, even Gibbs stressed financial concerns and obligations as part of her justification for activism. Three weeks into the struggle, Gibbs told a *Niagara Gazette* reporter that she had first learned of the chemicals when she tried to put her home on the market in June 1978. The Gibbs family hoped to "buy a home with a large garage, so [Harry Gibbs] could start his own business." But a realtor told her that she would not be able to sell the house for the price she expected because of possible chemical contamination. It was this discovery and her subsequent research that initially prompted her to take action. However, she emphasized that financial considerations remained secondary to concern for the health of her children.[7] Later, these financial issues completely disappeared from Gibbs's language, allowing the maternalistic language to emerge loud and clear.

When Heisner made his plea for tax and mortgage payment boycotts, he also stressed a need for community support, stating, "We've done nothing as a unit. . . . It's get acquainted night and it's united we stand. If we don't, we'll fall."[8] Heisner's definition of unity, however, proved to be rather limited. As the days moved on, Heisner failed to press for expansion of the area to be evacuated. He expressed concern for himself and little else, especially in the face of limited financial resources to help with relocation. Snyder joined Heisner to push the newly formed LCHA to set up priority lists for aid, aimed at getting the "ring one" people out first. They also planned to stop paying water bills and expanded the tax and mortgage boycott, obtaining assurances from the Federal Disaster Assistance Administration and several area banks that no one would be evicted for participating.[9] Heisner and his supporters displayed a sense of entitlement to assistance that excluded all but those who lived closest to the canal.

With their exclusionary, finance-based arguments, Heisner and Snyder quickly ran into significant opposition from others in the LCHA, especially as Gibbs gained stature as the group's leader. Most members of the LCHA, which included residents from 93rd to 103rd streets, hoped to act together and to be evacuated as a group; they refused to accept Heisner's suggestion that the "most affected" families be placed ahead of the others.[10] One man responded to the idea of a priority list with the angry comment, "We're not going to let you get out and stand and laugh at us at the other end of the street."[11] For those outside the inner rings, unity and a sense of entitlement to help had very different meanings than they did for Heisner.

This vast gulf that separated Heisner and his followers from the bulk of the other residents led to quick changes in the LCHA. On 12 August, Heisner attempted to form a separate group composed solely of ring-one residents. His obvious lack of concern for the area as a whole led to swift repercussions: the LCHA voted to remove Heisner as vice president and Karen Schroeder, who supported him, as secretary. After the change, Gibbs asserted that a "good 95 percent" of residents remained with the LCHA rather than go with Heisner.[12]

Heisner continued to stress economic considerations and to focus on his own situation after his ouster from the LCHA. The state purchased his property, but he refused to simply leave the house, as almost all the other residents did. In October 1978, the Heisners physically moved their house from the Love Canal neighborhood to "a safer part of the LaSalle neighborhood," only half a mile from its old location. The Heisner home was the only one moved from Love Canal, as other neighborhoods quickly expressed concerns about moving "contaminated" houses to or through their areas.[13] With his family evacuated and his financial situation secured, Heisner completely disappeared from Love Canal activism, as did Karen Schroeder.

Soon after the split, Gibbs began to emphasize maternalistic and health concerns over financial concerns, further distinguishing her from Heisner and Schroeder. Several days after their break with the LCHA, Heisner and Schroeder told a state task force that they would not allow any type of cleanup plan to proceed until they had firm offers on their homes. Reporter Gary Spencer found this surprising and noted, "Health fears moved into the background, and economic considerations into the forefront in the troubled Love Canal area." Gibbs moved quickly to distance herself from the splinter group's demands. In a letter to the editor of the *Buffalo Courier-Express,* Gibbs wrote that the LCHA "has always held as its first priority the health and safety of the people.... [Heisner's and Schroeder's views] represent only individual priorities, and [this] in no way influences or reflects the concerns"

of the group as a whole.[14] Emphasizing the health and safety of children provided a way for Gibbs to unify the majority of the community behind her
and to take the moral high ground in the press as she attempted to solidify
her leadership.

The early struggle over leadership yields two main points. First, early
gendered language was somewhat fluid. Both Heisner and Gibbs expressed
a combination of economic and health motivations in the first few weeks,
although even then, they had begun to establish a dichotomy for their respective followers. Gibbs's health concerns proved to be more captivating
to the neighborhood and to the press as she established her leadership. Second, Gibbs's language stressed a more inclusive, wider geographic view of
who should benefit than that expressed by the men. This wider view was also
more inclusive racially: Gibbs's definition included the mostly black Griffon
Manor residents as well (see chapter 3).

Gendered Goals at Love Canal: The Struggle over Its Future

The second snapshot comes from the end of the story and illustrates the respective goals and solutions of the female-dominated LCHA and the male-
dominated LCARA. Charged with selling the homes of outer-ring residents
and developing a plan for the future, LCARA provides the greatest contrast
to the health- and child-centered language of the LCHA. Even so, the organization lacked unity in its justifications; despite the dominance of economic
concerns, some of the men vocally championed the women's goal of protecting health.

Plans to establish an agency to deal with the future of the Love Canal
neighborhood unfolded soon after the crisis began. LCARA grew out of the
task force formed to handle the relocation of inner-ring residents and the
initial cleanup efforts. The Department of Transportation, headed by William Hennessey, led the task force, with on-site coordination provided by
Michael Cuddy. The task force pursued a goal of revitalizing the area for human habitation. In August 1978, Cuddy stated that the purpose of the cleanup
was "to return it [Love Canal] to a liveable area." Despite a rather limited focus on the economic facets of the situation, he remained fairly open-minded,
acknowledging that because this was uncharted territory, "all of the data is
not yet in on the extent of toxins in the area. . . . After the work is done, it

may be some time until the area is stabilized."[15] A week later, both state and federal officials reiterated that the prime motivation in undertaking testing and cleanup was to make the area habitable again.[16]

In mid-December 1978, as most of the first-ring residents evacuated their homes and the remedial construction got under way, Cuddy announced the formation of the Task Force for the Future Land Use of the Love Canal (sometimes called Task Force II). This new entity would include a wide array of members, including representatives from the residents, the city, the board of education, the chamber of commerce, local environmental groups, and urban development concerns.[17]

In late January 1979, Cuddy announced that plans for the site "include everything from a chemical research center to a park and even a shopping center," and he "wouldn't rule out the possibility of even reopening the homes."[18] A week later, Mayor Michael O'Laughlin told a crowd of bureaucrats and leaders of various city organizations to "let your imaginations go wild" about potential future uses of the canal. "We might not be able to do it today," he noted optimistically, "but any plan might fit in." O'Laughlin then announced the creation of several subcommittees to study specifically targeted areas, including the 99th Street School building, ring-one and ring-two homes, and the canal itself.[19]

Some of the suggestions seem absurd today. For example, initial recommendations from the subcommittee for the canal area included a golf course, which "would involve construction of sand traps and water hazards using concrete as the floor with drainage provided to prevent the potential breaking of the clay cap" on the landfill. Other early considerations included "a large recreation center, complete with tennis and badminton courts." At the time, Gibbs thought that the school should be turned over to the state health department and converted into a hazardous waste testing center; that way, samples from the area would not have to go all the way to Albany for testing, and it would create additional jobs in the Niagara Falls area.[20]

As the discovery of chemicals outside the canal proper spread, the LCHA stopped advocating any residential or recreational uses. One of the residents, James Clark, suggested that the area be converted into a "complete waste treatment facility . . . [to] include: (a) High temperature incineration of wastes; (b) Storage—to solidify; (c) Reclaim oil and solvents; (d) Set up facilities for fair exchange—one company's waste is another company's raw material." Clark noted that such a facility would bring jobs to the area and bolster the economy of Niagara Falls. Gibbs agreed, adding that the facility could lead to new studies in environmental fields, including the use of by-products. She continued to advocate very limited use of the area and declared, "City politicians will never change the city image by arresting victims of environmental horrors and putting in golf courses."[21] Mayor O'Laughlin strongly disagreed and countered with proposals for a recreational area, a park, or a golf course on the canal itself.[22]

The mayor and other political elites associated with LCARA continued to move in the opposite direction of Gibbs and the LCHA. O'Laughlin expressed increasing levels of resentment over Love Canal and its adverse effect on the image of the tourism-dependent city of Niagara Falls. In addition, the loss of tax-generating working-class residents grated on the mayor. His ideas for the future seemed to be geared toward restoring Love Canal to its pre-1978 status, somehow revamping the image of Niagara Falls and increasing tax revenue. O'Laughlin's personal clashes with Gibbs also put him on the defensive; the media cast her in the role of heroine, leaving him to play the evil politician who cared little for his citizens.

The mayor's defensive attitude about his city crystallized with the broadcast of the ABC documentary *The Killing Ground* in March 1979. Approximately two weeks before the documentary aired, ABC issued a press release promoting the show and describing Niagara Falls as "the scene of rampant miscarriages, nervous disorders, suicides and a host of other physical and mental ailments."[23] O'Laughlin strongly objected to the network's equating Love Canal with the entire city and threatened to get an injunction to prevent ABC from airing the program. One reporter who saw an advance screening described the show as "brutal . . . [it] leaves the impression that the entire city is covered with oozing chemical dumpsites. The show also hits hard at Hooker Chemicals. One former employee . . . described the company management as 'rapists.'"[24] The content of the documentary crystallized Mayor O'Laughlin's fears for the future of his city, which was dependent on tourism dollars and its reputation as a place of beauty and romance.[25]

The day after the show aired, the mayor acted quickly and defensively to counter the negative image presented by ABC. He acknowledged hazardous waste as a serious issue but strenuously objected to the insinuation that "chemical waste [was] buried all over town." O'Laughlin then went out of his way to distance the city's tourist sites from Love Canal, stating that he was worried that "the nationally televised show will prevent tourists from coming to see the Falls under the mistaken impression they will be subject to chemical contamination . . . [since] the problem," he noted, "is located in neighborhoods far from the falls."[26]

O'Laughlin and the majority of the task force continued to be preoccupied with financial concerns, sometimes demonstrating a callous attitude toward the health dangers faced by Love Canal residents. In April 1979, the task force decided to test the market by attempting to sell the abandoned houses in the first ring, having the buyers pay for the expense of moving the structures out of the neighborhood and collapsing the basements. One official with the task force estimated the homes' values at between $26,000 and $34,000, noting that "there is nothing structurally wrong with the houses" and that they needed only "washing and painting." Nevertheless, the task force intended to include language in the sale contracts releasing it from liability for any future health problems experienced by the buyers.[27] No one purchased any of the 239 houses.[28]

In another action, the task force moved to hire handicapped and mentally retarded workers to perform physical labor at the site. A nonprofit group, the New York State Industries for the Handicapped, organized the effort to have these workers perform "lawn care, debris cleanup, and small maintenance repairs" on the abandoned first-ring homes. Joseph Mineo, director of the local chapter of the United Cerebral Palsy Association, thought the job experience would "provide his clients with a chance to earn a decent wage [minimum wage of $2.90 an hour] and provide them with a chance to gain the experience they'll need to be employed later in competitive industry." Although the plan was quickly scrapped when people "deluged" the agency with calls objecting to the idea, LCARA later succeeded in quietly employing other handicapped workers to perform maintenance tasks.[29] Again, its willingness to use the cheapest, most vulnerable labor, with little concern for the health of this already compromised group, indicated the task force's priorities: economics over human health.

As the residents grew louder and more oppositional, and as evidence accumulated that the chemicals had spread into surrounding areas, state politicians and bureaucrats finally acquiesced to demands that outer-ring families be relocated. In October 1979, Governor Hugh Carey accepted a plan for the state to purchase the houses and evacuate the remaining residents who wanted to leave. Carey thus created a Niagara Falls–New York State agency, the Task Force to Stabilize and Revitalize the Love Canal Community (later LCARA), to handle the complicated process of purchasing the homes and overseeing the residents' relocation. The state found $5 million within the existing budget to assist with this process, but the funds had to be used for some sort of "urban renewal" project.[30]

Gibbs acted quickly to ensure her participation in the new agency, assuming that, like the earlier task force, residents would have a place at the table. However, initial plans for the agency failed to include residents; members of the present task force would appoint a "community board" that, O'Laughlin noted, would have no voting power and would function only in an "advisory capacity." Thus, the task force, led by the state's Urban Development Corporation, was composed entirely of white male politicians and bureaucrats: Angelo Massaro, director of the Niagara Falls Urban Renewal Agency; Michael Raymond, director of the Niagara Falls Housing Authority; Stanley Brzezinski, supervisor of the town of Wheatfield (which included part of the affected area); Russell Parker, chairman of the Niagara County legislature; James Jones, assistant secretary to the governor for minority affairs; Brad Johnson, head of the governor's Washington office; and others representing several state agencies.[31]

The move to eliminate residents from the decision-making process infuriated Gibbs and others from the LCHA. Gibbs blasted O'Laughlin, who stated that the task force had a "mission" to arrange for the purchase of the homes and to encourage "the survival of the neighborhood." Upset with his emphasis on economics over health, Gibbs queried emphatically, "How can you in good conscience talk about revitalization of the Love Canal neighborhood? . . . To attempt to repopulate the area could be negligent, irresponsible, and murder." The committee ignored Gibbs's harangues and turned to other matters—namely, requesting the state to supply appraisers for the homes.[32]

Not everyone shared Gibbs's eagerness to be a part of LCARA. The state had been asked to participate but declined, stating that it would act only as an adviser in what it considered a local issue.[33] Niagara County's—specifically, county attorney John Simon's—reluctance stemmed not from health concerns but from legal and financial ones. Simon pessimistically described LCARA as "a paper corporation that has no means of raising the money that may be necessary to buy all these homes."[34] With only $5 million appropriated, he also worried that the county would be liable for any uncovered expenses associated with purchasing the houses. In addition, he believed that, under state law, only an urban entity—namely, a town or a city—could be part of an urban renewal project; therefore, LCARA did not qualify. Finally, Simon argued that there was no need for the county to become involved; he suggested that the state, which had already purchased the inner ring of homes, simply continue doing its job.[35] The town of Wheatfield reluctantly signed on as well. Town officials expressed similar financial concerns as the county, but they fell into line once state senator John Daly persuaded them that they would not have to contribute any funds.[36]

Armed with these loud complaints, state legislators eventually submitted amendments to the LCARA formation bill. Under the final proposal, three representatives from each of three segments constituted the agency: the city of Niagara Falls, the town of Wheatfield, and the residents. The state legislature passed the LCARA proposal in June 1980.

Soon, however, conflict arose over the method of choosing the residents to sit on the panel. The six representatives from Niagara Falls and Wheatfield were empowered to select the resident representatives.[37] The residents feared that nonresidents of the Love Canal area would be appointed to represent them and that the selection process would allow the political elite to squelch any opposition. These fears quickly proved to be well-founded. O'Laughlin moved to severely limit the list of potential candidates when he proposed that no one involved in a suit against Hooker Chemical or the federal, state, or local government be allowed to sit on the agency. Residents quashed that proposal when they pointed out that O'Laughlin himself had been named as a defendant in several lawsuits.[38] In another attempt to block citizens' voices, O'Laughlin moved to hold a closed session while members discussed the nominees, but residents cited possible violations of the New York Open Meeting Act.[39]

The agency finally chose three men—John Lynch, a board member of the Ecumenical Task Force (ETF) and executive director of Catholic Charities; the Reverend Leotis Belk, a local African American minister from the New Hope Baptist Church; and William Waggoner, the only actual resident of the area—to be the resident representatives. Both Lois Gibbs and Barbara Quimby had been on the list of candidates, and a number of people expressed their dissatisfaction with the choices. LCHA member Grace Mc-Coulf stated bluntly, "I think this whole thing stinks."[40]

Many of the LCHA activists maintained that the three resident representatives were unacceptable not only because of the exclusion of "real" residents but also because of the lack of a female voice in the new agency. Women had been prominent in the struggle up to that point, and Quimby noted that the agency needed a "woman's point of view. . . . I'm not saying that men cannot do the job. But I think that women have an advantage in this case. We can look, not only with our eyes, but with our hearts. We know who has children with birth defects. . . . We have so much more personal contact day-to-day than the people who are on the board now that we could do a superior job if we had been allowed on the agency."[41] Massaro responded to Quimby's criticism with an emphatic statement that "to raise the flag of discrimination is improper. . . . There were a number of women who were considered for seats on the agency." He then added weakly, "It just didn't turn out that any were finally chosen."[42]

With no women on LCARA, the LCHA leaders worried that their concerns would be neglected entirely. Initially, however, the resident representatives vocally opposed O'Laughlin and Massaro's plans to revitalize the area quickly. They expressed sympathy with the residents' demands and their focus on health issues. At the first meeting of the newly constituted agency, Lynch stated, "Social justice demands that those who want to be permanently relocated should be and that they should be able to get full market value for their homes. We can't be concerned with industry, tourism, and property. The main concern has got to be people."[43] Thus, the three male resident representatives took up the dominant concerns of the LCHA women as their cause within LCARA.

These basic philosophical differences between the three resident representatives and the other six members of LCARA intensified with the appointment of Richard Morris as the agency's first executive director. Morris, a Department of Transportation employee who specialized in the acquisition of property, assumed the position on a temporary basis. The board approved his appointment on 27 August and named him permanent director on 1 October. O'Laughlin backed Morris for the position over longtime task force director Michael Cuddy and an official from the Housing Department. Morris fervently believed in the concept of revitalization as defined by the majority group in LCARA. Repopulating the area and attempting to return it to its pre-1978 neighborhood status constituted his rather limited definition of revitalization.[44]

Morris's commitment to revitalization took a surprising turn in mid-May 1981. To the horror of LCARA's resident representatives, Morris announced that he planned to move his family into a home in the Love Canal neighborhood. Tired of being separated from his wife and two daughters, who lived in Rochester at the time, Morris felt that his decision was completely appropriate. He told one reporter, "Why shouldn't the people who are responsible for revitalizing the area do something like this?" Numerous reports had convinced him that no significant health risks existed in the neighborhood, and he wanted to move his own family there to illustrate his point.[45] He hoped to lead by example, demonstrating by his presence alone that others could move back as well.

Residents and others criticized Morris's move on a variety of levels.[46] The EPA called Morris's decision "premature," without revealing the contents of its upcoming report on the habitability of the Love Canal area.[47] In addition, since Morris held only a temporary position at LCARA at the time, and since he had no intention of actually purchasing the home in Love Canal, residents considered the act little more than a publicity stunt. Morris and LCARA agreed that he would live in the house rent free, paying only for utilities and any upgrades. His choice of a home, a "rambling ranch" at 9714 Greenwald Avenue, north of the canal, also raised eyebrows. The former residents, Eileen and Albert Matsulvage, had experienced numerous illnesses and reported high levels of chemicals in their basement. They stated, "It's not a safe house. . . . If he's crazy enough to live there, God bless them." Morris dismissed the Matsulvages' claims, observing that their liver damage, lung irregularities, and frequent nausea had "never been conclusively linked to their exposure to chemicals." By the time of the move, Morris's wife, Anne, had stepped into line with her husband, defensively asserting to reporters, "People ought to pay us for living here. We're going to be the eyes and ears of this neighborhood and if there's a problem anywhere, we'll be here to report it."[48]

The resident representatives expressed little support for Morris's decision, and reports of a division within LCARA surfaced slowly. Lynch and Waggoner led the criticism. Waggoner called the move a "breach of public trust,"

Richard Morris, first executive director of LCARA, July 1981. Here, Morris is walking through the neighborhood after deciding to move his family into 9714 Greenwald Avenue, one of the abandoned Love Canal homes. (Courtesy of Buffalo State College Archives, *Courier-Express* Collection)

and both he and Lynch reiterated their belief that no one should be returned to the neighborhood until the EPA declared the area safe. Waggoner believed that Morris's move required explicit board approval, but O'Laughlin and LCARA's attorney countered that the agency would have no legal liability for any health problems suffered by the Morris family during their stay. Morris noted that he fully expected the EPA report to sanction the area's habitability, but he decided not to wait.[49]

Others in LCARA had also grown tired of waiting for the EPA study, which had originally been promised for the beginning of 1981. However, in light of the numerous scientific controversies, the EPA had decided to err on the side of caution.[50] O'Laughlin interpreted the delay, and the lack of alarming information, to mean that the outer rings of the neighborhood were suitable for habitation, and he pressed forward with revitalization before the EPA issued its report. He envisioned the area returning to "its previous status, a generally residential area consisting mainly of single-family homes."[51] Thus, the majority of men in LCARA, led by O'Laughlin, continued to have a very limited view of the area's future, hoping to restore it to its previous state. The resident representatives continued in their minority opinion, stressing health concerns.

Furious about the rush to repopulate the area, the resident representatives on LCARA decided to use the group's structure to their advantage in an attempt to delay revitalization until the EPA issued its report. Under the agency's rules, passage of any action or motion required a majority vote from each of the three segments, rather than a simple majority of the group as a whole. In August, the resident representatives refused to approve payments to the navy for rental costs, damages, and thefts by displaced Love Canal residents who had been housed temporarily at Falcon Manor, a military base. They also refused to grant approval to obtain bids to demolish the inner-ring properties and to approve insurance policies for the purchased homes.[52] Although publicly stating that they simply disagreed with the amounts of such payments, the resident representatives hoped to bring the business of the agency to a grinding halt until the others listened to their concerns.[53]

Mayor O'Laughlin, annoyed by the resident representatives' tactics, decided to end the roadblock and stymie the residents' efforts entirely. Initially, O'Laughlin considered simply replacing the resident representatives, since, as he put it, "we've had some extreme difficulty with them." Some of the residents who had chosen to remain in the area wholeheartedly supported O'Laughlin's efforts. Nunzio LoVerdi, head of the Concerned Area Residents, requested that LCARA forcibly remove the three "obstructionists" from their positions.[54] O'Laughlin found a far more effective solution, however. In January 1982, he reorganized the agency, making Waggoner a city of Niagara Falls representative and Lynch a town of Wheatfield representative. Belk, the least vocal of the three, remained a resident representative. O'Laughlin then named the two displaced Niagara Falls and Wheatfield representatives to serve as resident representatives.[55] This effectively silenced the resident opposition and paved the way for revitalization to proceed unobstructed. Since they no longer constituted a majority of any group, Waggoner, Lynch, and Belk lacked the power to force the consideration of health issues.

With the political marginalization of these men, the process of revitalization, as defined by LCARA, moved ahead. The agency completed the destruction of the inner-ring homes in the summer of 1982, collapsing the structures into their basements. New occupants began moving into the Black Creek Village neighborhood in 1990. Griffon Manor was completely destroyed and replaced by a senior citizens' center by 2000.[56] Although the women's health concerns gained them national media attention and promoted the resident's evacuation, LCARA's economic concerns ruled in the long term.

The example of the debate over the future of the Love Canal neighborhood provides some useful information about gender and environmental activism. First, the LCHA continued to focus on the health risks for children as a prime motivator in their efforts both to relocate residents and to determine the future of the area. In other words, their maternalistic language spread to peripheral concerns. The LCHA consistently pressed for a non-residential use of the area, although it seemed willing to accept some type of human occupation as a workplace. The male-dominated LCARA, however, under the control of the mayor, polarized around the issue of a return to human habitation. In opposing the LCHA's suggestions, the agency deliberately eschewed health concerns in a variety of ways and placed more importance on the city's economic status. Those men who expressed opposing views within the agency were labeled "obstructionist" and were deftly silenced by the mayor. Finally, the snapshot also reveals an increasingly exclusionary attitude toward the acceptable range of opinion within the male-dominated group. Like Heisner, O'Laughlin clearly had a severely limited notion of inclusion and democracy.

The Role of the Women's Movement and the Limits of Entitlement

In the previous examples, the working-class white women of Love Canal ventured from their homes and into the public sphere, yet they used a language centered around their roles as wives and mothers. Although the right to a public voice represented a cornerstone of the women's movement, the women of the LCHA did not define their activism as "feminist." They saw the feminist movement of the 1970s as exclusive and unrepresentative, but they borrowed certain elements of feminism while deliberately abandoning the parts they found objectionable. Certainly, the women believed that their voices should carry equal political weight to men's. They also believed in their rights as citizens and taxpayers and that this status entitled them to a certain amount of action and attention from the government. Their rejection of feminism and their subsequent activism yielded a sense of empowerment and agency and, ironically, roles outside the home. They became feminists while vocally rejecting the movement itself.

Women and Feminism

Their adoption of the ideal of political equality notwithstanding, the working-class white women of Love Canal explicitly rejected feminism.[57] To them, feminism either had very negative connotations of being "antifamily" or was irrelevant to their lives because they were wives and mothers. Debbie Cerrillo, who described herself as a "Suzy Homemaker" prior to Love Canal, stated that she "wasn't interested" in the women's movement, since "that wasn't the warm, fuzzy, do cooking and cleaning and taking care of your baby thing." Patti Grenzy also had no interest in the women's movement prior to Love Canal. "That didn't involve me because I was a family mother," she noted. Luella Kenny, who had experienced sex discrimination firsthand as a natural science major in college, stated that the term *activist* had negative connotations in the 1970s. Kenny said, "I didn't consider myself a feminist."[58]

In contrast to some of the other working-class women in the area, Lois Gibbs had some contact with young college women interested in the women's movement through her sister Kathleen. Although Gibbs "supported what they wanted, in reference to equal pay for equal jobs and those sorts of things," she did not always see eye to eye with her sister's friends. Gibbs noted that she was "very turned off" by the attitudes of some young feminists who considered her "pond scum" because she was "just a housewife." Feminists, Gibbs perceived, failed to recognize that being a homemaker was "a profession in and of itself," requiring hard work and expertise. She also resented the attitude that "anytime a woman has a relationship with a man, she's somehow subordinate to him . . . that's just not so." Despite her highly successful role as activist, Gibbs never thought of herself as a feminist.[59]

The women of the LCHA thus saw their activism not as part of the feminist movement but as a reaction against it, which reinforced the value and importance of women's roles as wives and mothers. Their environmental activism provided a way for them to comment on gender roles in society during the 1970s.

Women and the Rights of Citizenship

Despite the use of language that seemed to stress conservative or traditional roles for women, the working-class women seized on the feminist concept of women as equal political actors. They consistently stressed their citizenship rights and their rights as taxpaying Americans to justify the provision of environmental health and safety.

The events surrounding the EPA's release of the results of a chromosome study to the media in mid-May 1980 provide a useful snapshot of this emphasis on citizenship. The EPA intended the study, performed by Houston scientist Dante Picciano, to be used for ongoing litigation against Hooker Chemical to support allegations of serious health effects on the residents of Love Canal. Picciano's study, performed on thirty-six of the most ill residents, revealed a startling trend: eleven of the thirty-six had chromosome abnormalities. On average, only 1 percent of the population would be expected to possess such defects. One reporter cited a source that described the results as "alarming," noting that such damage could lead to a "higher-than-usual incidence of miscarriages, birth defects and cancer."[60]

In many cases, the press received the results of the study before the residents who had been tested, and the EPA failed to explain the findings carefully to them. Told only that they may have "genetic damage," many reacted with anger and panic. The media reported that "the chromosome break meant an increased risk of miscarriages, stillbirths, birth defects, cancer, or genetic damage, which could affect their children's children." Barbara Quimby, one of those told that she had damage, reacted with fear when she learned that no further chromosome testing would be done, not even for her children. As the EPA doctors notified each family, Gibbs witnessed their array of reactions. "They were frightened and depressed. . . . Some arrived at the office crying. . . . Others were so nervous they couldn't sit; they just paced back and forth. . . . The tension in the office increased as people went in and out of the doctor's rooms. . . . Tempers grew shorter."[61]

Gibbs reacted quickly to the results of the chromosome study, seizing on the opportunity to send a message to President Carter. Rather than focusing exclusively on maternalism, Gibbs chose to discuss citizenship rights, perhaps influenced by news reports about the influx of Vietnamese and Cuban refugees into the United States.[62] Gibbs's statement demanded action and the relocation of the remaining residents of Love Canal; she asked the U.S. government to help "tax-paying American citizens" just as it did foreigners. Gibbs noted, "Our government has gone out of its way to assist the boat people and the Cuban refugees. Please, President Carter, help your loyal tax-paying United States citizens. Don't let our people get lost in a sea of red tape as we watch our babies fighting sickness and growing up into an uncertain future. Please save our suffering babies. And please let my people go."[63] One angry resident, Eva Lynch, wrote to a local official and stated bluntly, "If we were starving 'Boat People' the government would come save us, but we are only hardworking, taxpaying CITIZENS of the U.S.A., who . . . are only needed for our tax dollar[s]."[64] These working-class women used their citizenship rights to press for the governmental assistance to which they felt entitled. Their pleas also expressed an intrinsic belief that citizenship includes the right to a healthy environment.

This sense of entitlement based on citizenship emerged clearly in a document produced by resident Ann Hillis. In October 1979, Hillis drafted a petition to the Canadian government requesting foreign aid for the citizens of Love Canal. After quoting the preamble to the U.S. Constitution, Hillis asserted that Love Canal residents "have lived up to our Constitutional responsibilities by: abiding by the laws of the land, serving our country in times of war, participating in democratic elections, and financing our government through the payment of taxes." The federal government, however, "failed to live up to its *Constitutional* responsibilities, thereby [not] honoring our basic *human rights,* to wit, the right to justice, domestic tranquility, welfare, and the blessings of liberty to ourselves and our future generations."[65] The precepts of the Constitution and the rights of citizenship embodied in it, according to Hillis, required that the U.S. government relocate Love Canal residents.

In addition to the Constitution, the women cited the Declaration of Independence as a source of rights. In a letter to area newspapers, Gibbs stated, "According to the Declaration of Independence we at Love Canal, Niagara Falls, New York should be taken care of. We should be able to use our rights to protect our families and we should be able to accomplish this with the help of the government. This has not happened in Love Canal, all our rights have been taken away by Government and Industry, our safety and happiness have been affected."[66] The very core of American values, according to the women, required that the government help the citizens of Love Canal.

The citizenship language employed by the women as an auxiliary to maternalism could be both empowering and exclusionary. They certainly accepted and demanded their rights as political citizens of the United States on an equal level with men. However, some residents, including Lynch, believed that citizens—and, more importantly, taxpayers—deserved special rights over others, including the "boat people" and, closer to home, poor African Americans. As discussed in the next chapter, African Americans in the neighborhood lacked resources, and the elites marginalized their concerns, sometimes aggressively. The consistent references to the rights of taxpayers constituted a veiled attempt to limit the rights and benefits of those African Americans surviving on welfare in Griffon Manor.

Men and Family Roles

While working-class white women embraced some facets of feminism and rejected others, their male counterparts adopted a far stricter interpretation of gender roles. Rejecting many elements of the women's movement, most working-class white men acted to reinforce traditional gender roles. Men's reactions to the larger women's movement can be seen in their reactions to the dramatic changes in family roles over the course of the Love Canal crisis. When the women became active, the traditional gender roles were partially reversed. Indeed, for some men, housework and child care constituted their primary form of activism. The fact that this male activism was invisible serves as a testament to the difficulty of overcoming gender stereotypes. "Women's work" had been devalued in society, and it continued to be so, even when men took over.

Before the activism inspired by Love Canal, local couples displayed a wide range of gender roles within the family structure. Norman and Debbie Cerrillo exemplified the most authoritarian gender breakdown. Norman, the product of a broken home, strove to maintain the family relationship that his parents had failed to achieve. Debbie's activism, however, took her away from her "proper role." "After work, I would take care of my children. And she was always gone," Norman recalled. "Her worth in this world was to be a good wife and a good mother."[67] Debbie's absence from the family when she attended LCHA activities and meetings frustrated Norman's attempt to maintain a "stable" family atmosphere. Debbie also felt that her role as an activist conflicted with her definition of a "good" wife and mother. She observed, "Women were standing up for their rights, instead of cowering, standing there, being the good little housewife."[68] For both Debbie and Norman, a "good" housewife meant someone who was submissive to her husband and wholly devoted to her home and children, without any interference from outside issues or concerns.

Most husbands and wives had a somewhat more equal relationship, although the wives generally stayed home with the children. Husbands occasionally helped with housework or child care when asked to do so. Lois Gibbs, for one, felt that her marriage to Harry was far different from her parents' union, although it was still a "traditional blue-collar" marriage. "We really sort of shared responsibilities," she stated, with both contributing to "decisions about where to move, decisions about where to eat. In my mother's marriage, my father was the king of the castle. My father's way went whether she agreed or disagreed. . . . And in our marriage, it wasn't quite so. I mean, we would talk about things and sometimes we would do things my way, and sometimes we would do it his way."[69] In addition, Gibbs had made a conscious decision to stay home with her children. Harry would not have objected to her working outside the home.

Other women truly enjoyed the housewife experience, proudly choosing that path over one of a working mother. Joann Hale remembered, "My husband took the garbage out, and I did the rest, without complaint, because I enjoyed it. . . . He worked a full-time job, plus he worked a part-time job."[70] Patti Grenzy remembered that although her husband, Ernie, worked long hours and some nights, "when he was home, he helped with the children. He would change them, bathe them, . . . feed them. And of course, he had to [help] when they would become sick, because I couldn't do it alone." Ernie also willingly helped with housework when necessary.[71]

Still other couples shared equally in household chores. Luella and Norman Kenny, both of whom held full-time professional jobs at the Roswell Park Cancer Institute, split the housework. Luella described her husband as "great" when it came to housework. "That's one thing I could never complain about," she remembered. "He did all the ironing in the family. He always helped with the cooking and cleaning. I mean, he would grab the

vacuum cleaner from me and just do it."[72] The Kenny family, however, was
the exception; in addition, with both parents holding full-time professional
jobs, the Kennys had moved beyond the working-class status of most of their
neighbors.

For many of the other families, the wives' activism left a gaping hole in
family life, forcing their husbands to step in and assume responsibility for
some of the day-to-day chores they had previously left exclusively to women,
such as child care and housework. Many of the men saw this as their con-
tribution to getting their families out of the neighborhood. Debbie Cerrillo
noted, "They were doing what they could do, because of their hours of work.
So it was their way of doing their share, I really think."[73]

This role reversal led to varying reactions. Although Harry Gibbs "was
doing more housework," according to Lois, "he was resenting it—big time
resenting it." Ed Pozniak, Marie Pozniak's husband, worked the night shift at
General Motors and initially expressed resentment as his role changed. "We
had some arguments," he remembered, "because I wasn't seeing her much.
. . . But we got over that . . . [because] she was working for our family to get
us out of there."[74]

Some husbands supported their wives' efforts to an incredible degree. For
instance, Gary Hale quit his job to help his wife deal with the stress of Love
Canal (Joann was pregnant when Whalen made his 2 August announcement). "He had to quit to make sure I was staying sane," Joann explained.[75]
Ed Pozniak felt considerable pride and appreciation for his wife. He "definitely" became more aware of her hard work as a housewife and thought it
was "neat" that the women worked to relocate their families while the men
made money.[76] Ernie Grenzy fully backed his wife when, while eight months'
pregnant, she decided to get arrested during the picketing of the remedial
construction site.[77] Jim Quimby even supported his wife when she and Lois
Gibbs held two EPA officials hostage in May 1980.

Most husbands reluctantly accepted their new gender roles during the
temporary crisis, but they expected the family to return to "normal" after relocation. The Gibbses and Cerrillos, both of whom divorced either during or
shortly after the events at Love Canal, remembered this most clearly. Harry
took considerable flak from his coworkers about his new responsibilities at
home. Although he believed that women should receive equal pay for equal
work, he also believed that taking care of their children constituted women's

primary task. He resented being referred to as "Mr. Lois Gibbs," stating that the title "sometimes gets me bent out of shape."[78] As time went on, Lois remembered Harry complaining, "I'm tired of changing damned diapers . . . I need some help here." He also began to ask her, "When are we going to have some normalcy?" According to Lois, men saw the future as a time when "the entire environment of the household" would return to normal.[79]

Coming from a working-class culture that emphasized women staying at home and men filling the role of provider, many of the men had considerable difficulty adjusting to the change. Their attitudes indicated less acceptance of expanded gender roles than that seen among the women. Some men, notably Norman Cerrillo, even rejected a public role for his wife. Others resented the redistribution of household chores and child care, since that work had always been devalued. Even husbands who supported citizenship rights and a public voice for their wives, or the possibility of working wives, did not easily accept the "demotion" to "women's work."

In addition, the crisis at Love Canal threatened many men's roles as family leader, protector, and provider. This threat led to extreme behavior among some of the men, including outwardly emotional responses. Many sources widely criticized the display and use of emotion at Love Canal, especially among the LCHA women. Men frequently contrasted female "emotion" with "reason" or "balance." Shortly after the 2 August pronouncement, one newspaper editorialized, "We would caution against letting the emotional tensions and zeal of the moment tempt any state or federal agency into 'witchhunting.' Let us guard against overreaction; let us keep a balanced perspective."[80] Mayor O'Laughlin regularly denigrated Lois Gibbs for being "emotional." When she left Niagara Falls in 1981, he stated, "I always looked at the broader situation and tried to take into account the welfare of our whole city while remaining compassionate about the problems in that neighborhood. . . . She didn't want to deal with the facts. . . . She liked to deal with emotions."[81] Even Hooker Chemical used the term to downplay the seriousness or scientific validity of the issue. Bruce Davis, an executive vice president for Hooker in 1978, was "confident that after a while the 'emotionalism will die down and reason will prevail,' and the state and industry will continue to work on any problems."[82]

Although critics consistently labeled the women of the LCHA as "emotional" and "hysterical," their male counterparts often exhibited high levels of emotion. At one of the early meetings after the 2 August announcement, "a bearded man seated in the middle of the room stood up and cried, 'Nobody came to see my pregnant wife.' The outburst touched off a powder keg of emotion. . . . Thomas Frey [state director of operations] finally stilled the outburst by saying, 'There is no sense in persisting if this keeps up.' . . . The super-charged atmosphere of the steamy auditorium had almost become unmanageable." Another resident, with "tears filling his eyes," shouted, "The damage is done, the damage is done. It's too late for my child."[83] Such outbursts of shouting and tears indicated the lack of control these men felt. Frey's reaction, too, revealed the attitude that these emotional outbursts were inappropriate and out of place within the framework of the decision-making process.

Complicating Issues

Women with Financial Concerns

As demonstrated earlier, gender differences were striking but hardly monolithic. It would be far too simplistic to say that the women discussed only health concerns and the men expressed an interest solely in economics. Despite the early domination of maternalistic language among the LCHA, some women expressed other concerns. The roles men and women played within the family often shaped the gendered language at Love Canal. Businesswomen and single mothers in the neighborhood, for example, placed economic issues on the same level as many of the men. Maria Gogos, owner of Lewis's Bar and Restaurant, expressed a stereotypically "male" justification for activism. Gogos's establishment began to suffer soon after the 2 August 1978 emergency declaration by Whalen. People simply stopped patronizing the formerly popular restaurant, which was located slightly south of the affected neighborhood on River Street. In mid-August, the bartender, surrounded by idle waitresses and empty tables and chairs, told a reporter, "A week ago we had people standing in the hallway. Now look."[84] Problems multiplied quickly for the owner of Lewis's. A Greek immigrant, Gogos experienced health problems similar to those of some of the residents, including allergies and rashes—not surprising, considering her ten-hour days in the restaurant. As the business lost money, Gogos fought to be included in the relocation process, only to be told that the buyout was for residences, not businesses. Gogos worried constantly about her family's economic future. Before Love Canal, she noted, "We paid the bills on time and had money for other things. We could put money away." As business evaporated over the next two years, Gogos poured all her savings into the restaurant to try to keep it afloat. She attempted to sell the operation, but banks refused to issue a loan to the prospective buyer because of the proximity to Love Canal. Becoming more despondent, Gogos stated, "I feel I'm forced to come here everyday to try to earn some money in order to meet my bills."[85]

As an independent businesswoman, Gogos had primarily economic motivations for her activism, which included pressing for the inclusion of small businesses in the relocation plan and allowing residents to hold meetings and fund-raisers at her establishment.[86] Expenses soon overwhelmed her, however, and Gogos closed the restaurant at the end of June 1980. She finally received vindication in September 1980, when the Department of Transportation decided that "there is no problem with including commercial property in the relocation package." On-site coordinator Michael Cuddy said of the decision, "I can say that we've determined it would be not only legally correct but also morally right to include commercial property in the relocation program."[87]

Other women's economic concerns sprang from their dual roles as caregivers and breadwinners. Pat Pino, a single mother, worked full-time to care for her two children and their home on 100th Street. Pino sent her son to live with his grandmother when his health began to deteriorate. Although his condition improved once Pino moved him from the neighborhood, she continued to be very concerned about her daughter's health and refused to use the water in her own home. As she prepared to leave the neighborhood, she expressed considerable anger about her home's loss of value. "I'm giving up everything I've worked for. I bought this house seven years ago," she began. "I thought it was an investment for my children, but I found out that I was wrong." Her sentiments echoed those of many husbands, expressed most vividly by Thomas Heisner. Yet Pino's was a more complicated, gendered reaction that inflated her feelings about the crisis. Pino also saw Love Canal as a brutal act of violence against her family. She stated, "We've been raped. Right down to the very fiber of our lives, we've been raped." As the sole adult in the family, Pino balanced both financial and health justifications for her activism, rather than the married women's almost exclusive use of maternalism.[88]

Union Involvement

The white residents drew deeply from working-class culture at Love Canal. For the men, unionism stood as one of their strongest examples of past activism. Union involvement in the Niagara Falls area was primarily male, but it was also largely health oriented and linked to economics through the sphere of the workplace. Unions in the area had developed a sophisticated understanding of chemicals in the workplace: part of the annual bargaining process always included the acknowledgment of toxic dangers and additional compensation for those who faced them.

Male residents at Love Canal, many of whom were union members at their respective plants, began taking their concerns to their union representatives. Edmund Pozniak, a member of the United Auto Workers (UAW) at the General Motors plant in Niagara Falls, sparked interest among union leaders when he told them the Love Canal story.[89] Pozniak had good reason to expect some type of response from his union. The UAW in both Buffalo and Niagara Falls had a history of dealing with a wide variety of environmental issues, ranging from chemical exposure to toxic compounds to conservation. The UAW Amalgamated Union, the umbrella organization for local plant unions in the area, had a Conservation Committee made up of interested members. The Conservation Committee "might be more into your hunting, your fishing, any kind of conservation issues that the typical person might think of as conservation . . . like a park. . . . They might have been donating trees," Dave Koepcke, vice president of UAW Amalgamated at the time of Love Canal, remembered.[90]

In addition to the UAW, the Oil, Chemical, and Atomic Workers (OCAW) had a presence in environmental issues in the Niagara Falls area. The OCAW periodically distributed fact sheets on certain chemicals, listing the dangers of various toxic compounds along with precautionary measures, to its workers. Harry Gibbs, a member of the OCAW through his position at Goodyear Chemical, received such sheets on various chemicals, including one on vinyl chloride. His wife recalled that it explained that the OCAW was "doing a study of the workers to see if there's an abnormal number of workers in Goodyear who have this particular type of liver cancer. . . . There was a lot of information." The OCAW also negotiated higher pay for those working with certain chemicals, to compensate for the associated risks. According to Lois Gibbs, Harry received an additional twenty-five cents an hour because of his exposure to certain chemicals.[91] Roger Cook, an activist with the ETF, also noted the OCAW's concern about environmental issues, which generated significant awareness of chemicals' effects among its membership. "That union," he remembered, "generally had quite a concern about workplace safety and health. And the environment. . . . And a lot of those workers just knew from their own experience that there had been a lot of exposures in those plants. So they were fairly savvy."[92]

Concern about workplace health issues in the Love Canal area led to the creation of the West New York Council on Occupational Safety and Health, which held a conference at the Buffalo Convention Center in February 1979. A large number of union members attended the conference, stimulated by the onslaught of news about Love Canal. Cook recalled that "there were over 300 workers at that conference . . . through the workplace side of it . . . [but] we're talking basically about the same chemicals." Several Love Canal residents, including Pat Pino, also attended the conference as speakers.[93]

Through lobbying by union members, several unions—most notably the UAW, the OCAW, and the United Steelworkers (AFL-CIO)—donated time, money, space, and support to the LCHA. The strapped LCHA greatly appreciated the cash donations. In March 1979, a local OCAW chapter donated $1,000, and union president John Edwards promised more donations down the line.[94] The UAW donated $2,620 from the local and international union in August 1979 and pledged its continued support.[95] The AFL-CIO, through the local steelworkers' union, also assisted financially.[96]

Union support included more than financial contributions, however. After a request for help from Joann Hale of the LCHA, Dave Koepcke, a UAW member, donated a copy machine to the home owners so they could copy their own copious newsletters, flyers, and leaflets. Unaccustomed to such a heavy workload, the copy machine literally burned out soon afterward; Hale then brought the material over to the UAW office for copying on donated paper. "They used to go through reams and reams of paper," Koepcke remembered.[97] The donations of paper and the copier proved pivotal to the LCHA, since it communicated to the public and its members mainly through newsletters, media reports, and flyers. Several unions also participated in marches planned by the LCHA.[98]

Unions assisted with publicity for the Love Canal cause as well.[99] The UAW magazine *Solidarity* featured articles on the Love Canal residents and their problems. The Buffalo Workers' Movement (BWM), a socialist workers' group, featured the Love Canal issue in several of its newsletters. The BWM soundly criticized Hooker Chemical, stating, "Hooker is a company with a long record of environmental abuse and disregard for worker health and safety.... Love Canal lays bare in all its ugliness the fact that in this society the 'right' to corporate profit takes preference over all others—even people's lives will be sacrificed for that 'right.'"[100]

Union membership also informed the residents' tactics. As the state began a cleanup of the canal area over the winter of 1978–1979, frustrations mounted among some of the longtime union men. Charles Bryan, head of the LCHA Action Committee, thought that Gibbs's tactics lacked vigor. He had extensive union experience and decided that a direct-action demonstration at the remedial construction site might force officials to address the residents' health concerns and lead to more relocations. "I've been a union man all of my life and I've always respected picket lines. I hope they [the construction crews] respect ours," he noted.[101] Bryan also stepped up because he thought the state lacked respect for the LCHA. Some of this dissatisfaction may have come from Bryan's own lack of respect for Gibbs as a leader. Sociologist Adeline Levine recalled Bryan saying, "Oh, those government people are just walking all around that little girl. Lois is just this little skinny girl and she can't handle it. She's got to get up there and tell them to go screw themselves.... [This is the kind of thing] for a man to do."[102]

When the picketing failed to gain the desired results, newspapers reported rumors of less peaceful actions among the male members. David Shribman, a reporter with the *Buffalo Evening News*, heard "reports that so-called boobie traps had been placed along 97th and 99th streets to puncture the tires of construction workers."[103] Cook, marching alongside the residents, remembered that some of the men "had these little four-pronged nail things that you throw underneath tires."[104] The *Niagara Gazette* reported the use of inflammatory language during the picketing. "One resident said he would try to keep workmen out of the site 'even if it causes a riot,'" the paper noted in an editorial. "Another said, 'If our lives aren't worth $150 a day to the construction workers, then their lives aren't worth a nickel to the residents of the Love Canal area.'" Although the papers condemned the threats of violence, it sided with the residents, stating that their "disobedience would not have been necessary if the state officials in charge at Love Canal had treated the dioxin discovery as seriously as it deserve[d]" to be treated.[105] The men of the LCHA, reliant on their union experience, were the first members of that organization to threaten violence, a tactic informed by their knowledge of picket lines.

Although some male residents felt that union involvement and activism provided valuable assistance, other men (both union and nonunion) refused to become active publicly, fearing the loss of their jobs. Lois Gibbs recalled that several male residents expressed a desire to help in the struggle but were reluctant to do so. "They just felt they couldn't," she said. "There were a lot of them who said . . . 'I want to be on the picket line, but I can't do it, because the shop steward just told me if we're seen out there again . . . there's going to be something [bad].'" The threat of losing not only their jobs but also Niagara Falls's share of heavy industry hung over many residents' heads. Gibbs noted that many people "were very concerned about what [Love Canal] is going to do, and whether we're chasing industry out of Niagara Falls. And every union contract that came up that year, one of the big things [the company would say] is we can move to Akron, Ohio. Industry used Love Canal to fight these contract agreements." This fear did not stop all involvement, however. Many men sent "replacements"—perhaps a child or some other relative—to participate in the picket lines or marches for them.[106]

Other events revealed men's general fear to go against the companies that employed them. In April 1979, Michael Bayliss, a Hooker Chemical employee, leaked a report known as "Operation Bootstrap" to the press. The report revealed a long-standing history of dangerous chemical releases by Hooker, knowledge of the harmful effects, and, perhaps most damaging, attempts to withhold information about these releases from the public and workers. When asked about the contents of the report, union officials commented only on the condition of anonymity, and workers expressed mixed opinions about conditions at the plant, safety standards, and union efficacy. Very few attended a union-sponsored meeting about health problems held two weeks after the report's release. A general fear of reprisal should something negative be said about Hooker existed among the workers.[107]

Despite their fear to be directly involved, union activism offered men a safe alternative at Love Canal. Unions donated funds and office services, provided support, and informed tactics and protests, but they also shared a common rationale with the LCHA centered on health issues. Familiar with health concerns related to chemical exposure, the UAW, OCAW, and other unions had no qualms about extending their activism outside the workplace, just as women extended their activism outside the home.

The standard story of Love Canal simplistically equates women's activism with the effects on children and neglects the important male component. In fact, this story reverses the cause-and-effect relationship at Love Canal: rather than the children pulling the mothers in, the women of the LCHA consciously chose to emphasize the children because doing so generated the most media attention and the best results, and it helped empower them as mothers. Although working-class white men and women each expressed a dominant rationale for their involvement, gendered language at Love Canal remained somewhat fluid. Many of the women's concerns centered on the health and safety of their children, yet union men and the resident representatives on LCARA chose a similar rationale. Most male residents focused on economic concerns such as tax values and mortgage payments, while the political elite emphasized the importance of city revenue and tourist dollars in revitalizing the area. Women who ran businesses or had sole financial responsibility for their families also presented these types of concerns.

Reactions were similarly fluid. Although critics frequently denigrated the women as "emotional" or "hysterical," men's emotions also bubbled to the surface at Love Canal and were similarly castigated as inappropriate to the decision-making process. Men who followed the women's lead too closely, such as LCARA's resident representatives, faced visible repercussions. Few of the working-class men accepted the ridicule from their peers or the threats to their masculinity that came from being called "Mr. Lois Gibbs." Many men stuck to economic language, and others buried their activism within the invisible realm of the home. Just as the working-class women sought gender-appropriate behavior in their activism, the men worked within their established unions to gain results.

Women's activism reveals their judgments about or acceptance of many facets of the gender roles of the time, including citizenship rights and a public role for women. Many of the working-class women, however, explicitly rejected feminism and defined their activism as part of their identity as mothers. The women's maternalism expressed so strongly at Love Canal simultaneously reinforced standard gender roles and enlarged them. Although reactions varied, the working-class men generally rejected a more expanded gender role. Men tended to accept women's public role during the crisis but pressed for a return to "normalcy" as soon as possible.

3

Race at Love Canal

White women's maternalistic language emerged loudly during the Love Canal crisis. Lois Gibbs's effective use of the media eclipsed other types of rhetoric being used, as well as other groups' visibility, including not only male residents but also African Americans in the neighborhood. Blacks constituted a large majority of the population at Griffon Manor, a federal housing project just west of and directly across the street from Love Canal.[1] African American women headed most of the families that rented homes there, yet they never achieved a prominent voice in the media, despite their attempts to organize and gain attention. Tensions between the LCHA and renters' groups ebbed and flowed throughout the long struggle to leave the neighborhood, and many of the African American women blamed class and racial differences for their neglect by the media, politicians, bureaucrats, and the public.

Grounded in the obvious racism in the area, the African American renters believed that governmental authorities ignored their problems. Because of this, the renters clashed with the home owners on several basic issues, especially in the early stages of the crisis. Although the relationship improved over time, African Americans continued to be marginalized throughout the ordeal by both the home owners and the political elite. The examples discussed in this chapter reveal that the African Americans had internalized the values and lessons of the civil rights movement of the 1950s and 1960s, whereas many of the whites in the area decried the gain in status for blacks.

In addition to the persistence of outright racism, other indicators demonstrated whites' and blacks' attitudes toward the civil rights movement. For example, as women accepted expanded gender roles for themselves, as well as their inherent rights as citizens and taxpayers, so did African Americans.

African American residents of Griffon Manor sign petitions protesting their living conditions, May 1980. (Courtesy of Buffalo State College Archives, *Courier-Express* Collection)

Black women certainly accepted the goals of the civil rights movement in terms of giving a political voice and status to blacks. Black women spoke up for their families and children, believing that their voices had equal legitimacy to the white voices asking for assistance.

Many whites—both men and women, working class and elite—had a more limited view of the civil rights movement and tended to reject more of its values. Many white men, for example, limited the definition of those who should receive benefits to "home owners," minimizing the problems of the mostly black renters. In addition, white men reluctantly helped the renters evacuate and often exhibited negative, stereotypical attitudes about African Americans. Several of the white women were notable exceptions to this tendency, especially those who had firsthand experience with the more visible racism of the South. Faced with this racism and their subsequent marginalization during the crisis, and lacking a charismatic local leader, African

Children playing outside Griffon Manor, July 1982.
Several of the Griffon Manor complexes were boarded
up as the renters found other accommodations, but
some residents remained until the mid-1980s.
(Courtesy of Buffalo State College Archives, *Courier-
Express* Collection)

Americans turned to the local branch of the National Association for the
Advancement of Colored People (NAACP) and the Ecumenical Task Force
(ETF), a religious group in the area, for help. The following snapshots illu-
minate the marginalization of the black residents and the avenues of their
empowerment in the struggle over race at Love Canal.

Racial Tension

The black women of Griffon Manor faced many obstacles on their path to relocation. Racism and the perpetuation of stereotypical attitudes about blacks
proved to be one of the most formidable. This racism revealed itself in many
ways, including outright violence against blacks. For example, in November
1978, Frank Williams moved with his wife and two children into the white
community of Cayuga Falls. That same month, vandals threw firebombs at
the house and committed "other acts of violence" against the African American family. In March 1979, the terrorism continued when vandals threw a
"seven pound lead weight" through the window. Although no one was hurt,
Williams sent his children to live with relatives. Police continued to investigate, but they never found the perpetrators.[2] These types of incidents, reported in the press, certainly had an effect on blacks' attitudes toward whites
in the area.

Racism was also present in less obvious ways, including the pervasive
segregation in the community. At the time, racial and ethnic lines divided
Niagara Falls, with most of the city's black residents concentrated in the
downtown area along Highland Avenue. Whites feared this area and avoided
it at night. Donna Ogg and her husband frequently ventured onto Highland
Avenue, since he worked with people who lived there, but their comfort level
was atypical of white residents of Niagara Falls. Ogg explained, "I think it
was really understood that Caucasians did not move into the Highland Avenue area at night. My husband worked with a man who . . . was murdered,
a young man, who was white and was in the Highland Avenue area for no
good reason probably, and was killed. So . . . you stayed away from there after
dark for the most part."[3] Debbie Cerrillo summed up the feelings of many
white Love Canal residents when she stated that if a white person ventured to
Highland Avenue, "somebody would kill your ass."[4]

Observers traditionally perceive the tension between the renters and the
home owners as a class conflict, a struggle between the haves and the have-
nots. However, racial conflict lurked, barely concealed below the surface, at
Love Canal, just as it did throughout Niagara Falls.[5] For example, when asked
how the Love Canal situation had changed his outlook, one male member of
the LCHA admitted that he wanted to become more active in other group
activities, especially, he noted, the Ku Klux Klan.[6]

In addition to outright racism, the black renters faced the callous, stereo-typical attitudes of whites in the area, including other residents, politicians, and bureaucrats. The mere suggestion that blacks experienced Love Canal differently because of their race could bring heated denials from whites. Af-ter *The Killing Ground* aired on ABC, Joyce Sanders took issue with the por-trayal of the crisis. A Griffon Manor resident, Sanders wrote to the *Niagara Gazette,* "We blacks and minorities have always been discriminated against. Proof is in the Love Canal itself. Not once did you see a black on the program 'Killing Ground,' not even a black child and we do have children." Sanders ar-ticulated what other blacks in the area felt: the white home owners received preferential treatment. She also criticized Lois Gibbs for "acting outrageous," with "big dramatic speeches," and she demanded that the black community begin to work for its rights.[7]

Sanders's letter brought a heated response from one of the white activists, Laurie Nowak. Nowak reacted viscerally to the negative portrayal of Gibbs as a publicity seeker. "How dare you attack the integrity of Mrs. Gibbs and her neighbors," she wrote. "You are putting forth a great effort at seeing that the issue of Love Canal becomes a racial issue, and for one I think it stinks." Nowak believed that Sanders and others who brought up racial discrimi-nation were "a curse to not only whites, but blacks and other minorities as well."[8]

Renters also constantly fought the perception of black welfare recipi-ents as being less deserving of assistance, since they were not a "permanent" community and included "common criminals." In her response to Sanders, Nowak minimalized Sanders's understanding of the home owners' situation. "Of course," she wrote angrily, "you don't own your home do you? You don't know what it's like to have a home that you've worked so very hard for and then in one quick moment it's gone. Worth nothing. What do you think? That we can afford to buy a home, that it automatically means that we're wealthy and can turn around and buy another one[?] . . . Smarten up!"[9] Ac-cording to Nowak, Sanders had a limited view of the situation because of her status as a renter; she could not possibly understand the problems faced by the home owners or claim an equal stake in the neighborhood.

Other statements reflected the seemingly prevalent attitude among whites that the renters at Griffon Manor were a less permanent group. In an article ironically intended to prove that the situation at Love Canal brought all races and classes together, Mike Billington of the *Buffalo Courier-Express* noted, "Except for Griffon Manor, it's a generally stable area."[10] Nicholas Vianna, leader of the New York State Health Department's Love Canal Health Studies Team, expressed similar sentiments when explaining his exclusion of past Griffon Manor residents from health testing. Although his staff had used various means to track down former home owners across the country (some of whom had been in the neighborhood for only a short time), Vianna noted that "it would be 'impossible' to locate former tenants . . . [because] most of them were 'transients, [and] they didn't stay there long.'"[11]

Other bureaucrats echoed Vianna's sentiments. Lois Gibbs recalled that Mike Cuddy tried to persuade her to stay away from the Griffon Manor residents:

He was trying to be helpful. But he pulled all the files on the African Americans, histories of crimes that they committed and were found guilty of. And he has this readout that he hands to me, and he's like, "You know, those people over there are very dangerous . . . you shouldn't be going over there alone. You shouldn't be messing with them." And we never experienced any of that in our work. . . . I think that the state really feared if you got the African American people together with the white people, and you talked about this, that power base would be just be incredible. Politically, it would be incredible. And they didn't want that to happen.[12]

Gibbs may have seen Cuddy's actions as part of a government conspiracy to split the residents' power, but his comments revealed more about whites' ongoing attitudes toward poor blacks in the neighborhood.

Other problems emerged because the white home owners had little or no knowledge of or experience with the black community. Lois Gibbs and Debbie Cerrillo had both grown up on Grand Island, an area with a dearth of African Americans. In addition to a lack of exposure to blacks as friends or neighbors, several of the women of the LCHA had been exposed to racism through their families. Cerrillo's father, fondly remembered for his portrayal of Santa Claus every Christmas, passed on to his daughter common views among the white working class at the time. "I never even talked to a black person [before Love Canal]," Cerrillo recalled. "I mean, my father was Archie Bunker. [He said] they rape and pillage. That's all they're good for. . . . And I'm sorry to say that."[13] Youth also played a role in their naivete. Patti Grenzy said, "At that time, I was so young, I didn't realize how poorly they [blacks] were still being treated. . . . I wasn't aware there was so much prejudice."[14] None of the white women had even considered the African Americans' problems until they became involved with the renters, and Sarah Herbert, who became a leader of the renters, played a big role in educating them about the plight of the blacks in Griffon Manor.

Whites' ignorance of black issues frequently led to callousness and misunderstanding. Most home owners, for example, seemed to be under the impression that since the renters did not own property, they were free to leave at any time and therefore should not be included in any monetary settlement. Others believed that welfare automatically provided money for moving expenses. When interviewed about the possibility of compensation for the renters, one couple, prominent in the LCHA, stated:

[Wife]: But you know why they're [people outside the first ring] not going to get it [their homes paid for]? Because of Griffon Manor. There's no way they can establish 3, 4, 5 rings . . . they'll have to evacuate all of Griffon Manor.

[Husband]: All the people who should be taken care of is homeowners. Those [rental units] have been vacant and occupied, in and out. We're owners, and we came first, we invested our money in real estate and we should come first.

[Wife]: If they want to move, why don't they? Welfare pays to move them.

[Husband]: They haven't invested in real estate, so they don't understand. It's your minorities, and if we allow . . . I am not a prejudiced person, but if they allow the minorities to . . . if we continuously do this, then we'll do anything. If they want to move, damn, let 'em move!

[Wife]: There is other state housing, 3 or 4 other places in the city.[15]

An older housewife in the LCHA agreed. She stated, "Those people over there [tenants], I can't understand them. They are raising the roof about being compensated, . . . but there is nothing in the world keeping those people in their project. If they don't like it, why don't they move? I would."[16]

Realistically, very few of the tenants at Griffon Manor had the option to just pick up and move. By definition, the residents of housing projects had very little income and often depended on government assistance to obtain the basic necessities for their families. They had few resources to move to another housing project or to rent an apartment on their own.[17] The availability of housing was also problematic. At the time, welfare recipients filled public housing in the area nearly to capacity. In addition, single women headed many of the families, often a mother or grandmother looking after a large number of children or other relatives under one roof. These families had been located at Griffon Manor specifically because it was the only housing development in the Buffalo–Niagara Falls area that contained larger units to accommodate these extended families.[18] The development also housed an on-site Head Start program for the younger children. Griffon Manor was widely regarded as a nice, well-kept, trouble-free place to live. And, contrary to the home owners' views, renters felt that they had a significant financial stake in the neighborhood. One woman stated, "If you come right down to it the majority in the development is paying more rent to the Housing Authority than the home owners are paying in mortgages. And we don't have a deed."[19]

Certainly, factors other than racism might have figured into whites' attempts to exclude the renters from benefits. Some home owners simply wanted to ensure that their families' needs were given priority. However, the overriding atmosphere of racism and the general lack of knowledge of racial issues weighed heavily on African Americans' attempts to be relocated.

Marginalization by the LCHA

Racism may have initiated the tension between blacks and whites at Love Canal, but the formation and naming of the Love Canal Homeowners Association exacerbated it. With "homeowners" in the name of the organization, many of the renters, both black and white, felt that the association failed to represent them or take their interests to heart. The certificate of incorporation for the LCHA, filed and written primarily by attorney Richard Lippes, reflected an exclusionary attitude against the renters, stating that the LCHA's purpose was, among other things, to "provide and maintain suitable means of access between *properties* of its members and suitable sanitary arrangement for their comfort and health . . . to cultivate the spirit of brotherhood and human understanding . . . to promote friendship among the *property owners* of the Love Canal area . . . [and to] help promote the maintanance [*sic*] of *property values* within the Love Canal area."[20] The document neglected to mention renters, or any non–property owner, as members, although it included Griffon Manor in its definition of the "Love Canal neighborhood."

Lois Gibbs, looking back on the naming of the organization, stated emphatically, "We were stupid . . . we had to call ourselves something, and somebody said, 'Well, let's call it the Homeowners Association because that's a common name and you hear [it] in lots of different places.' So, it was really that simple. And then we were stuck with it."[21] Debbie Cerrillo, in contrast, remembered the name selection as being part accident and part a sense of entitlement by the property owners. Cerrillo stated that, when choosing the name, "they never used the word *renters* because we never thought about it at that particular time. . . . It was people who had a financial stake in the area. And we figured if you're on welfare, and you're living in the Griffon Manor, get a life."[22]

Some of the residents quickly realized their mistake in naming the organization and attempted to change its effect on non–home owners. Gibbs, especially, believed that including everyone involved was important to their struggle and to the power of the organization.[23] A formal name change proved more difficult than expected, however; it would have required changing the certificate of incorporation through legal means in Albany. Therefore, the group decided to establish greater inclusiveness through its bylaws. An early draft defined members as "all residents of the Love Canal area, and all non-residents in agreement with the purposes of this organization." It also specifically included non–property owners in the organization's purpose, stating that the LCHA would work to secure the "evacuation of all residents (who so desire) from the Love Canal area whose dwellings (houses or apartments) and immediate environs have been made unlivable by the chemicals." In addition, the organization set as its goal "the purchase of all private homes . . . at the full market value as of July 31, 1978," as well as "relocation for all apartment residents in comparable housing [and] payment . . . for all other past or present costs associated with, but not limited to, mortgage payments, insurance payments, property taxes, moving, etc."[24] Perhaps because Lippes deemed this language too specific, the final form of the bylaws more closely resembled the general, vague document adopted by most corporations. The group retained a more expansive definition of membership, however: "members of the corporation shall consist of all individuals[,] corporations, associations, or other organizations, who have paid their dues as designated."[25]

Despite these efforts to include the renters and be sensitive to their demands and needs, the LCHA found the early resentment hard to overcome.

Initially, the association's focus minimized the renters' participation. Before Gibbs established herself as spokesperson, the loudest rhetoric emerged from the men in the neighborhood, including Heisner. As discussed earlier, Heisner demanded property-tax relief and emphasized mortgage boycotts, actions and solutions that marginalized the renters, since they owned no property.

Marginalization by Task Force II

With their initial lockout, the renters emerged as a counterforce to the LCHA rather than a support group. The first time the state attempted to involve the Griffon Manor residents in planning for the remedial construction and evacuation in August 1978, the meeting degenerated into an emotional shouting match. Vera Starks burst onto the scene as a vocal leader at this meeting, demanding to know why the project residents had to stay in their apartments while the state moved others from their nearby homes. Agnes Jones, chairperson of the tenants' association at Griffon Manor, expressed anger over the renters' lack of representation in the process. Others expressed considerable concern for the Head Start program headquartered in the Griffon Manor recreation center, which included fifty children and a dozen staff members.[26]

This anger and resentment on the part of the African American renters became clearer at another meeting a few days later. Marilyn Dolson claimed that the home owners were receiving higher-priority treatment than the renters. One reporter quoted her as saying, "They're [home owners] going to scat, but we'll be here while you're digging." According to that reporter, the African American clergy had also become interested in the problem, and at least one minister acted as an advocate for her congregation. Margaret Wilson, pastor of the House of God Church in Niagara Falls, lamented the lack of people of color on Task Force II (the predecessor to LCARA) and expressed the hope that the blacks in the projects would not be ignored.[27]

Task Force II officials addressed the concerns of the Griffon Manor residents, holding another meeting specifically for them a week later, on 5 September 1978. But, according to the *Niagara Gazette*, the residents "were not easily convinced that the state is giving their safety as much consideration as the homeowners living nearer the chemical landfill." In addition, although the Health Department had released preliminary blood test results for some second-ring home owners, Griffon Manor residents complained that they had "not received their blood test results; they have been unable to learn the results of the air tests made in their apartments, and they were wondering why they will not be relocated along with families living in the first two rings of houses circling the canal."[28]

Jones's tenants' association, like Gibbs and the LCHA, had circulated a petition of demands and presented it to Task Force II. Jones and 180 signers requested that, before the actual remedial construction began, there be "development of a satisfactory evacuation plan, extensive testing and presentation of the results, and improvement in communication between the task force and Griffon Manor residents." Although these goals mirrored those of the home owners, an us-versus-them mentality began to be expressed by the renters. Jones angrily interrupted LCHA officer Debbie Cerrillo at the meeting and stated forcefully, "This meeting was not called for homeowners. It was called for us people as you people call us. . . . You're not going to be here. You're going to be relocated. I asked for this meeting, so let our people speak."[29] Jones's statements reflected the prior tension and the feelings of inferiority projected on the renters by the neighboring home owners.

Empowerment from the NAACP and Formation of the Concerned Love Canal Renters Association

Griffon Manor residents realized that they needed more than simple complaints to force action. As evidenced by their charges at various meetings, many of the black residents believed that the state had neglected them because of their race and their economic status. The Griffon Manor residents thus enlisted the support of various members of the black community, including clergy, politicians, and civil rights organizations such as the NAACP.

In mid-1978, William Abrams Sr. served as president of the NAACP chapter in Niagara Falls. As word of the Love Canal crisis spread through the city, Abrams quickly mobilized his organization to assist the black residents of the area. Abrams also had personal reasons for his concern. He and his family had lived in Griffon Manor from 1960 to 1968. He remembered planting gardens with his wife and neighbors and eating the vegetables grown there. His memories included more unpleasant aspects of Griffon Manor as well, including constant odors and children with birth defects. Abrams's wife had recently died of a liver illness that first manifested shortly before they left the project. The NAACP activist now believed that the presence of chemicals near their former home explained much about her illness and death.[30]

Abrams did not mince words when spelling out the renters' racial allegations. He alleged that the white home owners received free "health services as well as being relocated by government officials . . . [while] black citizens who live in the adjacent areas are being told they are in no danger from the chemicals that are buried in the Love Canal." Abrams also contacted the regional NAACP director, and both officers called for equal treatment of blacks in Griffon Manor regarding testing and investigation. Abrams went one step further, threatening legal action if the NAACP felt that the state neglected or discriminated against blacks at Love Canal.[31] Not long after, the state NAACP convention added its support, passing a resolution asking the governor to complete "adequate soil testing and to relocate tenants with known respiratory problems." The NAACP asserted that the renters did not want preferential treatment; they merely wanted equal treatment to the home owners.[32]

Griffon Manor residents, empowered by the assistance and support of the NAACP, decided to form a new group, separate from both the tenants' association and the LCHA, to press for their goals. In late September 1978, led by Griffon Manor resident Elene Thornton, the renters formed the Concerned Love Canal Renters Association (CLCRA). Thornton made some strident demands on Cuddy, including more blood testing, since many renters had been unaware of the previous testing, and financial assistance for anyone who wanted to leave the project. Cuddy quickly accepted the first demand but rejected the second, stating that "no medical justification" existed for such action. Fully backed by Abrams and the NAACP, Thornton also joined with Gibbs in threatening a lawsuit to stop remedial construction on the canal unless the state met their demands for safety and evacuation plans.[33]

Testing and relocation remained at the top of the CLCRA's list of demands. Spokesperson Vera Starks stated, "We have people with asthma, rheumatic fever, bronchitis, and pregnant women and we want them relocated." She also demanded additional air tests in the apartments before her group would allow construction to continue, and Thornton pressed for additional blood testing for residents. With regard to the latter demand, Nicholas Vianna, who directed the health studies, countered that there had been a dismal lack of

participation on the part of the renters. Of 1,000 health questionnaires distributed at Griffon Manor, only 16 had been returned; in contrast, nearly 100
percent of the home owners had returned their forms. He also noted that
twelve blood-testing events had already been held in the area, some specifically for Griffon Manor.[34]

Despite their numerous attempts to gain attention, the renters still faced
many problems. Sarah Rich, a leader of the CLCRA, noted that the blood centers tended to prioritize those coming in for tests, favoring those in the inner
rings and forcing outer-ring residents, including those at Griffon Manor, to
return some other time. Many said that they had never been contacted about
their health problems. Several others found the test results for their homes
unsatisfactory. In one case, results showed the presence of chemicals found
in paint thinner and gasoline, and the state promptly instructed the resident
to remove those items from her basement, even though she did not possess
any of the offending materials.[35]

During the investigation, other problems at Griffon Manor came to light.
As part of its study of the Love Canal area, the task force sent representatives
door to door to look into conditions at the housing project. Some of the residents had complained about "strange odors and sludge" in their basements,
similar to the concerns voiced by the home owners. The task force failed to
find any contamination but identified "severe sewer defects" as the cause of
the odors. In addition, residents reported broken windows, peeling wallpa-
per, and even widespread rat infestations. The problems were so pervasive
that the task force considered telling the renters to withhold their rent if the
housing authority refused to resolve the problems in a timely manner.[36]

In response to the government's apparent lack of concern and the tenants'
anger, Thornton moved on her own to begin health testing. She enlisted the
support of Dr. Beverly Paigen, who had been assisting the LCHA with its
health studies. Using a similar list of questions, Thornton intended to prove
that the renters at Griffon Manor suffered from the same types of serious
health problems as the home owners.[37]

Although Gibbs and her group obtained their demand for a safety plan
and decided to allow the construction to proceed, the CLCRA continued
to feel removed from the decision-making process and refused to stand
with the home owners on the matter.[38] In early October 1978, approximately a week before the remedial construction was scheduled to begin,

the renters—assisted by Barbara J. Smith, chair of the Love Canal Action Committee for the NAACP, and Donald Lane, a local politician running for state senate—threatened a lawsuit to halt construction.[39] The renters quickly made good on that threat when their demands continued to be ignored. The CLCRA hired local attorney Lester Sconiers, who filed a motion shortly before work crews began construction. The motion, filed in state supreme court, sought an injunction to stop construction until the state took adequate steps to remove renters with health problems in the same manner it had removed home owners. Judge Roger Cook refused to stop the work immediately, but he scheduled a hearing to listen to arguments about whether the renters were in jeopardy.[40] Judge Frank R. Bayger, believing that the remedial construction was necessary to stop the further migration of chemicals and therefore protect the remaining residents, later dismissed the injunction request altogether. Bayger also dismissed the black residents' charges of racial discrimination against the state.[41]

After the initial fights over remedial construction died down, the renters worked more closely with the home owners, although some tension persisted. Many factors played a part in this alteration in the working relationship, including changes in the home owners' attitudes and the emergence of a new "outsider" group. The arrival of the ETF in March 1979 as an advocate for the residents of Love Canal proved to be especially beneficial to those who lived at Griffon Manor. In addition, new leadership of the CLCRA likely affected the group dynamics. In early 1979, Sarah Herbert replaced Thornton as president of the CLCRA, with Sarah Rich becoming vice president.[42] Herbert proved to be more willing to let the LCHA speak for her group and take a leadership role. At the same time, Gibbs and other LCHA members became more aware of the separate problems of the renters and made a greater attempt to include them in solutions to the problems.[43]

Marginalization by LCARA

Even with the ETF supporting the renters' cause, solutions for this group remained elusive. Just as they had during the initial phase of activism, whites' attitudes continued to be problematic for the African Americans. Many solutions to the troubles at Love Canal initially ignored or marginalized the renters. In mid-October 1979, Governor Hugh Carey announced that the state would pay for the buyout of residents who wanted to leave. His announcement came on the heels of a plan developed by two New York legislators, republican senator John Daly of Lewiston and assemblyman Matthew Murphy. The Daly-Murphy plan provided that the state "would purchase the homes of the remaining residents at fair market value."[44] The LCHA reacted to the state's intention to purchase their homes with undisguised glee. They claimed "total victory and vindication," according to one paper. "We won, we won," a reporter quoted Gibbs as saying.[45] The LCHA held a party in late October at Lewis's Restaurant, and Gibbs remarked, "We've been in a party mood since yesterday."[46] Obviously, the home owners saw the announcement as a major victory, a turning point in their struggle.

The Griffon Manor residents, however, had a completely different view of events. Neither the governor's announcement nor the Daly-Murphy plan provided anything for them. Officials initially justified the renters' omission from the plan by citing the federal government's funding of the housing project; they reasoned that the federal government would therefore have to be involved in any solution for the renters.[47] The NAACP, taking the initiative over CLCRA president Herbert, stepped forward to denounce the plan strongly. Barbara Smith bluntly described the Daly-Murphy plan as one that "discriminates against the poor and is racist." She continued to argue that the renters had been affected by the chemicals in the same way as the home owners. She added that, similar to the home owners' logic, the renters were entitled to action because of their status as citizens. "The tenants are not excluded from the negative effects of chemical contamination," she told a reporter. "They are residents of the state of New York and as such are entitled to the same considerations as other citizens. If Daly and Murphy want to provide a 'spark of optimism' for the Love Canal residents, let it be for all residents."[48] Smith took her case to the NAACP state conference in mid-October, where the group promised to oppose any legislation that failed to include the tenants.[49] Publicity from the NAACP eventually forced the state to include Griffon Manor in its relocation plan.

Tension continued between the CLCRA and the LCHA, notably over the selection of LCARA members. In mid-July 1980, LCARA finally named its three resident representatives: Leotis Belk, John Lynch, and William Waggoner. Many residents of Love Canal were outraged by the selection, since only Waggoner actually lived in the area. The LCHA also expressed disappointment that the resident group included no women. Herbert, in contrast, told reporter Bob Dearing of the *Buffalo Courier-Express* that she felt "very happy about all of the appointments. I know they'll do a very fine job for all of us."[50] Herbert had good reason to be satisfied with the selection of Belk, a black pastor from Niagara Falls, and Lynch, who served as an ETF board member.

Despite Herbert's optimism, LCARA prioritized aid to the home owners, marginalizing the renters and frequently demonstrating an adherence to the prevalent stereotypical views of blacks in Niagara Falls. When the federal government agreed to assist New York State in purchasing the homes and relocating Love Canal residents in October 1980, LCARA allocated $500,000 for the renters and $17.5 million for the home owners. LCARA began to purchase Love Canal homes well before the issue of how to deal with Griffon Manor, or even what benefits the renters would receive, had been settled. Only a couple of weeks after Congress passed Superfund legislation, shortly before Christmas 1980, LCARA finally approved a plan to pay for "relocation expenses and the purchase of appliances" for renters who wished to leave Griffon Manor permanently. By this time, LCARA director Richard Morris had already completed the purchase of 120 homes. But even these minimal benefits for renters generated controversy, and in response to an outcry by the home owners, LCARA agreed to enforce "stringent criteria [for] the purchase of new stoves and refrigerators" for the tenants.[51]

Conflicts also arose over the type of relocation housing that would be provided for Griffon Manor residents. Because of the typically large families in Griffon Manor and the lack of available public housing, the Department of Housing and Urban Development (HUD) allocated twenty-seven "Section 8" certificates for "new or substantially rehabilitated HUD" homes to accommodate those families needing four or five bedrooms. This meant that the federal government would provide subsidized housing for the renters, who would pay 15 to 25 percent of their income for housing under the voluntary program and live in private homes located throughout the area.[52] HUD made the certificates available in October 1980, but it had to wait for the city to formally request them. In April 1981, however, the city "voted to delay acceptance of HUD certificates for . . . 'scattered site housing.'" Without the certificates, large black families could not afford to move, and they remained mired at Love Canal.[53]

Empowerment from the ETF

On the relocation issue, the ETF worked tirelessly with the renters, serving as a mediator with LCARA. The ETF contacted local politicians, LCARA representatives, and others on behalf of the renters.[54] Mayor O'Laughlin and councilman Joseph Smith repeatedly expressed their objections to placing black families in "27 homes scattered throughout the city." When HUD threatened to hold up $8 million for housing improvements unless the city approved the relocations, Smith stated, "I don't see where a local HUD office can blackmail us into a project we don't want. . . . Blackmail is blackmail whether it comes from a government or an individual." O'Laughlin went so far as to say that "the city already had the housing it needs" at Griffon Manor, which he termed, "the best housing units in town for large families."[55]

Officially, the city council disapproved of the measure because it reduced the number of homes contributing taxes to the city, but ETF members uncovered other reasons during talks with the mayor. O'Laughlin revealed strong concerns about blacks moving into white neighborhoods, and he referred to the scattered-site housing as "block busting." ETF leader Jim Brewster reported that O'Laughlin "fears Niagara Falls could become a vacuum cleaner that would draw more dependent people into the city."[56] Unfortunately, the racial composition of the large, poor families played a significant part in the city's decision to limit their housing options. O'Laughlin, for one, feared the forceful integration of Niagara Falls neighborhoods. ETF members maintained contact with the affected families, many of whom, they noted, were "feeling trapped [and] discriminated against, by not being able to move," until the ETF finally secured their relocation.[57]

Relocation proved to be a far more drawn-out process for the renters than for the home owners. Some of the tenants stayed at Griffon Manor because they were unable to find suitable housing elsewhere. Many left the housing project, however, and LCARA eventually consolidated the remaining residents into two groups of apartments. Approximately seventy residents, including Sarah Rich, remained in the project in 1986, when LCARA decided to tear down Griffon Manor entirely.[58] Many of the houses in the area had already been destroyed by this time, and the project sat in a desolate area. Griffon Manor's lot remained empty for only a short time. In 2000, the city completed a subsidized senior citizens' home on the site.

Thus, when the LCHA failed to represent their interests, and when governmental solutions and racism marginalized them, the ETF stepped in to assist the renters and fill a perceived organizational void. In many cases, the ETF also mediated between stereotypical white views and the needs of the black renters. Sister Margeen Hoffmann, executive director of the ETF, even contacted activist Jesse Jackson to see what solutions he could offer. Jackson, in turn, contacted Arthur Eves, a longtime New York State assemblyman from the Buffalo area.[59] Eves met with the renters on several occasions to discuss their problems and advise them of their rights and possible actions. One of his aides, Dan Workman, attended meetings with the CLCRA and LCARA and reported back to Eves. Finally, the ETF served as a sounding board for the renters, helping them to organize and delineating their goals.[60]

Marginalization by the African American Press

In addition to the difficulty of making themselves heard among the white population, the residents of Griffon Manor failed to attract the attention of the black press. At the time, Buffalo had two active black newspapers, yet neither covered Love Canal to any great degree. From the summer of 1978 through 1980, the height of Love Canal activism and news, the *Criterion*, the smaller of the two, carried only one story about Love Canal in general and completely neglected the black community there.[61] The *Buffalo Challenger*, touting itself as the "most progressive black weekly in Western New York,"[62] carried only two stories about Love Canal between the summer of 1978 and the end of 1980. The first appeared in the paper's Niagara Falls supplement on 22 May 1980, the day after President Carter declared an emergency in the area. It amounted to little more than an editorial but did raise some racial and class issues. The author asked pointedly, "Why haven't the residents of the Public Housing Complex on the 'Other Side' of the Love Canal been included in all of the efforts to ease health hazards[?] . . . Are federal officials remaining low-key because this is federal assisted housing? Are state and county officials quiet because the majority of Griffon Manor are minority, or on public assistance?" After insinuating the prevalence of class and racial discrimination in politics, the author resorted to victim blaming, stating, "Citizens cannot stand idly by & let their lives be blatantly ruined by insensitive officials. Some[thing] can, should and will be done."[63] According to the author, black residents' laziness and apathy were responsible for their current situation.

Two months later, the paper ran a short cover story in the main section of the newspaper entitled "The Other Love Canal." The article briefly detailed some of the problems facing the tenants, including the fact that about half the Griffon Manor residents still lived in the projects. They remained, according to the *Challenger,* because they could not find adequate housing of the appropriate size and cost. The newspaper had several solutions for the renters, including filing complaints with the Human Rights Commission, moving to Buffalo to take advantage of more abundant housing, or even pushing for a program to decontaminate, move, and buy the abandoned Love Canal houses for the tenants.[64] Overall, the *Challenger* provided very little insight into Love Canal and only a superficial reading of the situation for the black community.

The lack of coverage of Love Canal certainly did not indicate a lack of interest in urban environmental issues. Both African American papers covered these issues in some detail. Over the Love Canal period, the *Criterion* carried frequent stories about various environmental concerns, especially health and pollution issues. One article described the dangers of Dumpsters, which "are nesting grounds for rats, blow flies, diseases and plagues. In fact, any collection of trash quickly become breeding grounds for rats, man's worse [*sic*] enemy in the animal kingdom." The article went on to describe the relationship between rats and fleas and the spread of plagues.[65] The paper also carried articles on antinuclear efforts, the transportation of radioactive waste, plans to improve "blighted" areas, local cleanup campaigns, and pollution and housing problems.[66]

The *Buffalo Challenger* published similar stories about environmental issues. Rodent control was a frequent topic, with articles discussing the origins of rodents, the problems associated with them, and ways to eliminate them. The *Challenger* also dealt with more urban problems, such as lead poisoning. Articles warned parents to "be sure not to let your children chew on woodwork or eat flaking chips of paint, because they may be eating lead." The paper cautioned that lead poisoning can cause "brain damage . . . blindness, cerebral palsy, kidney damage, learning disabilities and even death." Barbara Banks, editor of the newspaper, also advocated antinuclear activism, stating, "In the name of billions of dollars in profit, the dollar-worshipping powers that control this

country are constructing new nuclear plants as fast as they can, with no regard to the fact that many of those already in existence are unsafe. The threat
of potentially disastrous accidents which could wipe out millions of people,
is very real." The *Challenger*, like the *Criterion*, also published articles about
neighborhood cleanups and the improvement of African American areas.[67]

Both black newspapers exhibited an ongoing concern with environmental issues, but not with the problems of Love Canal. Either they thought the
major Buffalo and Niagara Falls papers adequately reported on Love Canal,
even from the black perspective, or they simply failed to see it as an African
American issue. This lack of coverage and attention from the black community certainly contributed to the difficulties faced by the Griffon Manor
residents, enhancing their invisibility.

Avenues for Conciliation

Racism and stereotyping stood as two salient characteristics of life at Love
Canal for African Americans. Despite this, whites' attitudes toward blacks
spanned a wide range and certainly encompassed more tolerant and concil-
iatory approaches.

Common Language

Tensions lessened between blacks and whites after the first few months of
the struggle, stemming from the realization that they shared similar goals
and needs. Both groups of women entered the conflict out of concern for
the health and safety of their children, and they used maternalistic language
to focus their efforts. Vera Starks, for example, had four children at Griffon Manor, each of whom suffered from various ailments, including asthma,
skin problems, rheumatoid arthritis, and migraine headaches.[68] Like many
of the white women, her activism centered around protecting her children
and identifying the cause of their illnesses.

One black leader of the CLCRA lived in Griffon Manor with her elderly
mother and five children. Dependent on welfare for material support, all
members of the household earned only about $3,000 a year combined. Like
Lois Gibbs, this woman initially learned of the Love Canal situation through
television and newspaper accounts and then quickly connected her children's
frequent illnesses with the chemical contamination. "Then all of a sudden it

hit me that I'm right in it so to speak," she noted. Her children's health had been a continual source of worry and distraction. Her oldest son returned to the Love Canal area after serving in the military and became seriously ill. The next child, a daughter, suffered from "headaches [and] fits," and the middle boy complained of a runny nose and rashes. Another child had "trouble with [his] urine," as well as nightmares and headaches, for which he was seeing a psychiatrist. The mother worried most about her youngest child, a five-year-old girl who had chronic kidney and bladder infections. Concerns about her children's health and anger over her unsafe home prodded her to action. She stated, "I'm not as concerned about myself, but my kids and my mother I am. . . . [That's] the only thing that would make me real angry because it didn't have to happen. It could have been avoided if somebody had been truthful with somebody else. Because I moved here in good faith. I was finding me a decent place for my kids to live and if somebody had told me when I signed the lease there were more chemicals out here I wouldn't sign the lease."[69] Her language replicated the thoughts and feelings expressed repeatedly by women such as Gibbs, Cerrillo, and others and provided a common theme for the women involved in activism.

Examples of Tolerance

Several women in the neighborhood proved to be crucial bridges between the white and black communities. Such tolerance generally emerged among those who had a firsthand understanding of racial discrimination. For instance, Joann Hale's mother grew up picking cotton in Alabama, and Joann witnessed discrimination and segregation when visiting her relatives in the South. Watching a Ku Klux Klan parade as a child had made an indelible impression on Hale, and she hoped to educate her friends in the North about discrimination. She removed a poster publicizing Klan activities in Alabama and decided "to take this to my [grade school] class . . . because people in the North didn't realize what was really going on." Hale's mother also influenced her daughter's tolerant attitude, raising her so that she "didn't understand what the difference [between the races] was." During Love Canal, Hale made a special effort to talk to Griffon Manor residents and try to understand and convey their problems to the LCHA.[70]

One summer when she was about eighteen, Luella Kenny accompanied her parents to visit her older brother in Florida. She recalled being "completely shocked" at the pervasiveness of segregation, "never having seen, in those days, the separate bathrooms and all of this. And I can remember my father going into the wrong bathroom. He didn't know." That summer left a lasting impression on Kenny, who later became involved in the implementation of affirmative action programs.[71] Like Hale, Kenny went out of her way to communicate with the black residents of Love Canal, understand their issues, and serve as a voice for their concerns. However, these two women were the exceptions among many of the working-class whites at Love Canal.

As the Love Canal situation developed, the African American women reacted to many of the problems with declarations of both racial and class discrimination on the part of whites. They also consistently stressed a more inclusive solution to Love Canal relocation. Shortly after the formation of the CLCRA, president Elene Thornton asserted that the housing project had been "singled out for neglect by state researchers."[72] Another woman stated, "They [the LCHA] forgot us low income people, they think we're trash. We're people too. We've got kids and we worry."[73] Another black woman perceived elements of both racism and class conflict in her interpretation of events. She expressed skepticism about the intentions of politicians from the area and their efforts on behalf of the tenants, stating, "I haven't seen them [politicians], and I'm home all the time. They don't care. Mostly black people live in these projects, what do they care? Kill them all [laugh]." She also doubted the sincerity and goodwill of the white state officials. She had "heard rumors that they're gonna fix them [the Love Canal houses] up, and this is from a white person, and they gonna sell them to the blacks. And I said this is one black, I wouldn't buy if I could." Her criticism also included class elements. "To me," she stated succinctly, "who cares about poor people? I bet if these were rich people, they would've got out of here."[74]

A female African American leader of the CLCRA also linked the neglect of the tenants' concerns with class and race issues. She noted that some of the prominent politicians, including Governor Carey, Congressman LaFalce, and Senator Javits, lacked the time to visit the renters' groups. "You get the feeling that the reason you were overlooked is because you really . . . weren't looked at as a human being," she began. "You figure well the people in the development isn't really people anyway, they're just survivors. But we don't feel that way . . . because as we stated to them we're just not home owners but we got the same feelings and we love our kids just like the home owners over there and we feel like if we're in any danger we should have the same protection that the home owners have."[75]

Although these black women expressed maternalistic reasons for their activism and desire for change, their rhetoric involved a more radical critique of society. Instead of simply emphasizing the protection of their children, many black women saw the pollution of their homes as a product of prejudice toward their race and class. In addition, their focus on class and race indicated a far more inclusive attitude of entitlement to governmental help than that of many of the white women and men. This more inclusive attitude clashed with the racism and stereotypes common in the area to lead, ultimately, to the marginalization of the black community.

The snapshots presented in this chapter point to several lessons regarding the influence of race and ethnicity on environmental activism at Love Canal. First, perhaps not surprisingly, the African American women demonstrated a widespread commitment to, and acceptance of, the values of the civil rights movement. They certainly accepted their status as full citizens with political rights and status and their entitlement to healthy and safe living conditions. They saw their activism as part of an ongoing struggle against racism and classism in Niagara Falls in particular and the United States in general. Many whites, in contrast, rejected the ideals of the civil rights movement and continued to exhibit streaks of racism. Whites used these attitudes to justify fewer rights and marginalization for certain groups. Yet the marginalization of African Americans led them to embrace a more inclusive definition of those entitled to help. Rather than seeking to exclude people from relocation or aid, the renters argued for the inclusion of non–property owners, people of color, and the poor on an equal basis with white, working-class home owners. Their marginalization also forced them to accept assistance from outside groups, such as the NAACP and the ETF, in their struggle.

4

Class at Love Canal

Lois Gibbs and the LCHA grabbed the attention of the nation and, arguably, the world with their captivating rhetoric and tactics. The publicity surrounding Love Canal led to legislative changes as well as alterations in how ordinary people conceived of and handled hazardous waste problems. With such a media frenzy, it is not surprising that outsiders empathized with the affected residents and wanted to help. Supporters funneled much of this external support directly into the LCHA as financial contributions, but distinct groups also formed, adding their own brand of activism to achieve justice in dealing with hazardous waste problems. The ETF became one of these outside groups beginning in March 1979.

The ETF deserves significant attention because it embodied an alternative rationale for environmental activism. In addition, the group had several distinct demographic characteristics. It was fairly balanced genderwise, though largely white and middle class. ETF members were also highly educated. Because of these distinct differences in class and education compared with other groups at Love Canal, the ETF's experiences shed light on the influence of economic status on environmental activism. This middle-class, well-educated group was involved in Love Canal voluntarily, as self-styled activists. In contrast, the unlucky circumstances of their place of residence forced the neighborhood groups to deal with the issue. Of all the groups involved at Love Canal, the ETF exhibited the greatest acceptance of the values of the three main social movements—the environmental, civil rights, and women's movements. It worked toward equity in rights and entitlement to benefits across gender, class, and racial lines. Certainly, this can be explained, in part, by class. The middle-class activists had more time and resources to devote

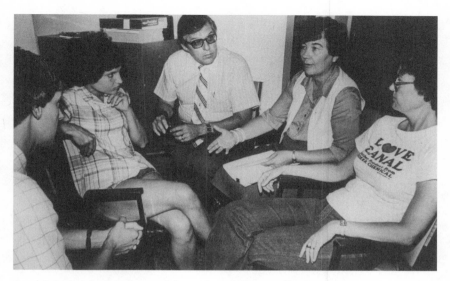

From left to right: Marie Pozniak, unidentified EPA official, Sister Margeen Hoffmann, and Luella Kenny. As executive director of the ETF, Sister Margeen was a forceful advocate for the Love Canal residents, particularly the African American residents of Griffon Manor. (Courtesy of Buffalo State College Archives, *Courier-Express* Collection)

to these issues. Yet many of the ETF members had full-time jobs, and they hardly led lives of leisure. In addition, many of the working-class women were not employed outside the home and lived comfortable, if not luxurious, lives. They too had time to devote to outside issues. The real difference lay in the ETF members' long-term middle-class status, which allowed them the luxury of a higher education. Access to a college education gave them the opportunity to learn, reflect on, and absorb the values of the various social movements outside of their specific circumstances.

Several snapshots follow to demonstrate the class differences—and the parallel differences in education—between the middle-class ETF and the working-class LCHA. First, the demographics of the primary members of each group reveal the differences in class, education, and exposure to social justice issues. Second, snapshots explore the groups' justifications for activism. The ETF developed a sophisticated, complicated rationale centered around a Christian theory of stewardship, but incorporating elements of environmentalism; organismic, gendered views of nature; Native American philosophy; science; and literature. In contrast, the LCHA developed a maternalistic rationale centered on the health of their families, particularly their children. Third, the two groups differed in their tactics and methods of achieving their goals. The ETF, firmly rooted in the middle class, worked within the political system, using lawsuits and developing solutions to problems within the power structure. The LCHA, however, broke the law to bring attention to its concerns. Finally, the groups' goals in terms of issues peripheral to Love Canal varied widely. The ETF saw Love Canal as only one environmental problem among many and later broadened its focus to include other environmental crises, demonstrating an acceptance of wider environmental values. The LCHA, in contrast, basically disappeared with the "solution" to Love Canal.[1] Only a few members, Gibbs being the most notable, continued any type of environmental activism after relocation.

Demographics

ETF Membership

The ETF and the LCHA shared a common concern about the health effects of hazardous waste in the Love Canal area. Beyond that, a vast chasm separated the two groups in numerous ways. One of the more obvious differences involved the demographic characteristics of their members. As a nonresident group,[2] the ETF was composed of people who had made a voluntary choice to become involved, rather than being forced into activism by their circumstances. The group contained many thoughtful people who had been active in various issues throughout their adult lives. Much more solidly middle class and professional than their counterparts in the LCHA, many of the ETF activists had college degrees, and some had graduate degrees. In addition, the ETF gender ratio was far more balanced, although women dominated the day-to-day activities of the organization. An examination of some of the major players follows.

Each of the main ETF members had obtained a bachelor's degree or higher. The Reverend Paul Moore, founding member of the ETF, had a doctorate and had taught English for a time at Buffalo State College.[3] Donna Ogg, a mother and an English major from the University of Pittsburgh, served as director of outreach ministry at the Lewiston Presbyterian Church at the time Love Canal exploded.[4] The Reverend Jim Brewster, a Methodist minister, obtained his doctorate in divinity from Drew University in New Jersey.[5] Terri Mudd, a longtime board member and driving force behind many of the direct aid activities for the Love Canal residents, held a bachelor's degree in political science from Immaculate Heart College in Los Angeles and a master's degree in English from Niagara University.[6] Roger Cook held a master's degree in sociology and had come to the Buffalo–Niagara Falls area in 1967 to begin work on a PhD at the University of Buffalo.[7] Sister Margeen Hoffmann, executive director of the ETF, continued her education after becoming a nun; she obtained a bachelor's degree from St. Teresa's College in Minnesota and then a masters' degree in social planning from Boston College Graduate School of Social Work in 1974.[8]

Most of the ETF members had previous experience in environmental and social justice issues; some had devoted their lives to such causes. Moore, for example, demonstrated for peace and backed the ordination of homosexual priests in the Presbyterian Church prior to Love Canal. Ogg's environmental concern and activism had been fostered by childhood camping and hunting trips with her parents. Although she never thought of herself as an environmentalist, Ogg regularly attended hearings concerning the Lake Ontario Ordinance Works, another waste site near her home, and the Chemical Waste Management site, the only active hazardous waste disposal facility operating in New York State.[9] As campus minister at the University of Buffalo, Brewster worked in the antiwar movement, counseling and assisting students who protested the war in Vietnam. Deeply interested in politics, Mudd and her husband, who worked for Hooker Chemical, became the organizing force behind the development of the Democratic Party in their Republican-dominated area.[10] Cook had been involved in antiwar demonstrations and activities in Michigan, participated in prison reform efforts in Albany, and protested at the West Valley Nuclear Plant.[11] Hoffmann pressed for change within the Catholic Church after Vatican II,[12] although she always chose to "subvert the system from within," as she was fond of saying. She assisted antiwar protesters in Washington, D.C., and did civil rights organizing in South Carolina and Chicago, where she became acquainted with Jesse Jackson and Operation Breadbasket. She later accepted an assignment to direct the Rochester Area Churches Emergency Response (RACER), an ecumenical relief effort for the victims of a Minnesota flood in July 1978.[13] Each of these dominant personalities in the ETF possessed a solid background in voluntary social activism, as well as a high level of education.

LCHA Membership

The demographics of the LCHA activists contrast strikingly with those of the ETF. Almost all the Love Canal women had grown up in the Buffalo–Niagara Falls area, and quite a few were lifelong residents of the Love Canal neighborhood. Many of their fathers, and later their husbands, were employed by or otherwise connected to Hooker Chemical or the Niagara Falls chemical industry. Most of the women had finished high school, but few continued their education beyond that. Of the main group, only Luella Kenny possessed more than a high school diploma, and, interestingly, she crossed over to work with the ETF as well as the LCHA. Most of the women married soon after high school and quickly began to have children. They saw motherhood as a noble, uplifting profession, something to which they aspired and at which they worked hard. These working-class families generally adhered to strict gender roles within marriage, with the husband going out to earn a living and the wife staying home. As full-time mothers, the women of Love Canal were rarely employed outside the home. When they were, they held temporary, low-level, part-time positions to earn pin money, to provide extra income when their husbands were out of work or on strike, or to supplement the family income around the holidays. Most of the adult family members voted and considered such political participation important, but they were generally not politically active in any other way or knowledgeable about the American political process or specific issues.

A few LCHA members had demonstrated an interest in wider social issues but failed to become involved to any great degree. Joann Hale, for example, distributed antiwar flyers during high school and even asserted a latent feminism. Typically, girls took home economics and boys took wood shop during high school. Hale, however, demanded the right to take wood shop and became the first female at her school to do so. Later, her husband, Gary, took a position with Rollins Leasing, a trucking company that hauled chemicals for Hooker. The Hales settled into family life, with Joann concentrating on her role as mother and wife.[14] As discussed earlier, both Hale and Kenny also had some understanding of the injustice of racism through their family contacts in the South.

Thus, compared with the ETF members, the LCHA women had less education and no experience with social justice–type activism prior to Love Canal. Some, such as Hale and Kenny, demonstrated a commitment to the values of the civil rights movement and the women's movement, but the majority of the women focused mainly on the insulated world of the working-class housewife. They considered political participation important, but voting was the extent of their involvement. These demographic differences between the main players in each group led to a striking difference in their justifications for involvement, their perceptions of Love Canal's environmental problems, and their understanding of the wider environmental meaning of the crisis at Love Canal.

Justification for Involvement

ETF: Stewardship and Environmentalism

The Reverend Dr. Paul Moore, pastor at the First Presbyterian Church in Lewiston, a community near the beleaguered Love Canal neighborhood, followed the news stories of the summer of 1978 with some interest. According to friends and colleagues who came to know him well over the next two years, Moore had a "keen sense of injustice" and a strong desire to use his position as pastor to redress wrongs.[15] In mid-August 1978, before the fencing around the canal had been completed, Moore took a tour of the small neighborhood to gauge the situation for himself.

In a letter to his congregation entitled "The Land Is Cursed," Moore related his thoughts and feelings after his visit. It had been raining as he toured the homes, and "an ominous chill in the air dampened my spirits. The sky was glowering and forbidding." He drew a comparison between Love Canal and the plague-ridden city of Thebes in Sophocles' *Oedipus the King*. Moore reminded his readers of the play's story line:

The action of the play takes place in the ancient city of Thebes languishing under the withering blast of the deadly plague. The crops are blighted, the herds diseased. Women moan and cry. Pestilence sweeps the city, emptying the houses of the living and filling up the homes of the dead. All the people are sick to death. The fruits of mighty Mother Earth increase not. Women gripped with the travail-pangs struggle in vain . . . no birth-joy follows. A city crying! None has pity. On the ground lie the myriad dead, unwept, spreading contagious death. The city lies under a curse because Oedipus has defied the laws of the gods: he has murdered his father and married his mother.[16]

Oedipus, Moore believed, represented humankind of the late twentieth century. "In Niagara County," he stated firmly, "God's law has been broken, his eternal covenant violated, and we are reaping the bitter consequences: ecological disaster and human tragedy."[17]

On 8 February 1979, in response to ongoing testing results and the cries of the LCHA, the state ordered the temporary relocation of pregnant women and children younger than two from the outer rings, mimicking the decision made six months earlier with regard to the inner-ring homes. Perhaps because of the renewed media interest and outcry, Moore and Ogg decided to organize an interfaith effort to assist the residents of Love Canal. On 22 February 1979, they sent a letter to churches in the Buffalo–Niagara Falls area requesting a meeting on 13 March at the Wesley United Methodist Church on Colvin Boulevard, across from the canal. The pair hoped to organize a collective response to the health, financial, and psychological strains at Love Canal.[18]

The Moore-Ogg letter spawned an enthusiastic response among many of the churches. More than 200 people, including academics, scientists, Love Canal residents, church leaders, and laypersons, attended the meeting, which Ogg and Moore designed to be "deliberately dramatic." Several residents testified to their ongoing health problems and financial concerns. Ogg recalled that speakers focused on "what had happened, what was anticipated would happen, [and] what the health effects could possibly be from the chemicals that were pretty well known to be in there at that point."[19]

A week after the informational meeting, on 20 March 1979, members from more than twenty churches representing Catholics, Protestants, and Jews formed the Ecumenical Task Force to Address the Love Canal Disaster.[20] The new organization, which elected Moore chairman pro tem and Ogg as secretary pro tem, decided to restrict membership to "representatives of the religious community." The ETF established five main goals: "providing direct aid to residents, assuming the advocate role in applying political pressure, gathering and interpreting appropriate data, seeking reconciliation through justice, [and] advocating the complete neutralization of toxic wastes."[21] The enormous tasks of the organization soon overwhelmed Moore and Ogg, so the ETF hired Sister Margeen Hoffmann as executive director to oversee the group's day-to-day activities.

Moore and Brewster developed the majority of the biblical rationale for the ETF's involvement at Love Canal. A generalized Christian theology formed the common link for members of the ETF,[22] so the group needed a strong biblical basis to justify its actions to other congregations and gain support from church-funding organizations. Most of this rationale centered around the concept of stewardship. Moore, the first to articulate and develop this concept, described the "apt, but sobering words of Isaiah: 'The earth lies polluted under its inhabitants, for they have transgressed the laws, violated the statutes. Therefore a curse devours the earth and its inhabitants suffer for their guilt. There is an outcry in the streets . . . desolation is left in the city. The earth staggers like a drunken man, its transgression lies heavy upon it, and it falls, and will not rise again.'" He added that in Niagara Falls, "God's law has been broken, his eternal covenant violated, and we are reaping the bitter consequences: ecological disaster and human tragedy. . . . This is God's good earth; not ours. We do not own the earth; we are but stewards of the earth. God has established an eternal covenant with the dwellers on the earth: 'Take care of my earth, and you will live; exploit it, and you shall surely die.'"[23]

A more complete version appeared in the ETF's first annual progress report, which documented its first eighteen months of existence. Elaborating on his earlier work on stewardship, Moore wrote, "I speak as a Christian charged by God in the Scriptures with a cultural mandate to be a careful, meek, and responsible steward of this good earth which in the beginning came from the hand of the Creator pure and fresh and clean—a lovely, living thing of exquisite beauty, a magnificent habitat fitted by ingenious design for God's highest creation—the human family—to live, move, have their being, and—in cooperation with their Creator—fashion a social order grounded in justice." He also repeated the earlier warnings of doom and destruction should humankind not obey God's command to care for the earth.[24] Moore placed humans at the center of God's creation, describing them as caretakers of the earth and its other inhabitants. Moore's work on stewardship, as well as more secular efforts, became the cornerstone of the ETF's justification for involvement at Love Canal.

Brewster later reaffirmed that belief in stewardship, stressing the "uniqueness of humankind" in the universe, a God-given trait, and the fact that this uniqueness gave rise to special responsibilities and freedoms. Brewster added to Moore's biblical foundation in early 1981 in a speech entitled "Theological Reflections—Eden and the Love Canal," in which he compared Love Canal to "the garden poisoned." The inspiration for this effort, he stated, came from the works of transcendentalist philosopher Henry David Thoreau. Brewster used Thoreau's work as "part of a teaching ministry." Thoreau, he said, "was dealing with an American Eden, as well as other writers in those days, suggesting that America could be the kind of Eden which was not apparent in Europe.... Also, of course, one of the emphases [is] that when you move to a place like Love Canal, you move there because it is your Eden. And there was that very strong feeling in newspaper advertisements in the 1950s, around this being an ideal suburban place where you could raise children without the city problems, etcetera. As a result, though, that Eden changed."[25] In equating Love Canal to a destroyed or poisoned Eden, Brewster added elements to the ETF's biblical rationale.

Hoffmann also added to the ETF's religious justification for involvement, although she stressed a more general concept of the need for leadership and vision. In her reading of Proverbs 29:18, one phrase—"Where there is no vision, the people perish"—caught her attention. The saying seemed to apply to Love Canal and other communities plagued by hazardous waste, where the "major task is to have the insight and foresight of how to respond." As time went on, Hoffmann also found the analogy of "the Flood, Noah, and the rainbow" important as a way to provide hope for the future. Hoffmann saw the ETF as leading the Love Canalers, and the wider community, out of the "flood" of the hazardous waste problem.[26]

In addition to a biblical rationale, the ETF justified its participation at Love Canal through the church's traditional role of helping the oppressed and less fortunate in society. Closely aligned with this rationale was the Christian church's tradition of assisting victims of natural disasters. Early justification for ETF involvement centered on these themes, which many accepted as appropriate reasons for church intervention. The ETF consistently referred to the Love Canal residents as "victims" or "unfortunate dwellers," "rejected ones," and even "unwanted citizens."[27] The initial attempt to get people involved relied on images of pity and helplessness to demonstrate the

need for charitable action. The ETF continued this type of rhetoric throughout its existence. For instance, in 1980, Hoffmann justified the ETF's presence
by stating, "churches have a mandate: they *must* be concerned with the welfare of individuals. They must address the concerns of the poor, the needy,
and the victimized. They, as *institutional* representatives of God, must be active and responding to the needs of the people."[28]

In addition to these religious justifications, the group used a specifically
ecological or environmental rhetoric that was occasionally tied to religious
or biblical language but was sometimes secular in nature. This ecological
language incorporated a wide variety of influences, including an almost pa-
ganistic touch, with mixtures of ecofeminism and Native American–type
philosophies.

Moore also incorporated a preindustrial, organismic philosophy into his
justification for environmental activism. In pressing for ecological change,
he stated, "I speak for the Earth—our loving mother who gave us birth and
faithfully sustains us. I speak for her, because she cannot speak for herself.
When, as a vulnerable woman, she is ravaged and raped by brutal exploit-
ers and hear[t]less profit-takers, and then discarded as a worthless, spent
thing—wounded and sore—it is my duty to stoop to her weakness, bind her
wounds, and heal her hurt."[29] Moore's words stressed a gendered interpretation of nature, seeing the earth as a weak, helpless female who has been sexu-
ally victimized by men yet needs the assistance of brave, strong men to keep
her alive.[30] Along with the passage from Isaiah, this rhetoric became the most
quoted justification of the ETF.

Ogg added to the secular justifications for involvement. Rachel Carson's
groundbreaking *Silent Spring* had a profound effect on many members of
the ETF. After reading its opening passage about the ideal community struck
silent by a "strange blight" accompanied by the illness and death of wildlife, fish, and vegetation, Ogg drew a direct comparison between Carson's
fictional community and Love Canal. Ogg stated, "The community in Carson's fable *does* exist. This community *has* experienced all the misfortunes
she describes. The imagined tragedy *has* become a stark reality."[31] Implicitly,
Ogg also followed Brewster's explicit comparison of Eden and Love Canal—
a perfect community before the knowledge of chemical contamination.

Native American philosophy also played a part in ETF rhetoric. The organization subscribed to the popular belief that Native Americans exemplified

"proto-environmentalists." *Earthcare,* the ETF's resource guide published in 1987, contained a lengthy excerpt from a statement purportedly made by Chief Seattle in 1854 entitled "The Earth Is Our Mother." The Native American leader made the speech as his tribe contemplated giving land to the encroaching whites. Chief Seattle warned the whites to take care of the land and to remember that "every part of this earth is sacred to my people. Every shining pine needle, every sand shore, every mist in the dark woods, every clearing and humming insect is holy in the memory and experience of my people. . . . The shining water that moves in the streams and rivers is not just water, but the blood of our ancestors." He also understood the white men's motives for coming into his territory and their attitudes about the environment. He noted that the "earth is not his [the white man's] brother, but his enemy, and when he has conquered it, he moves on. . . . He kidnaps the earth from his children. . . . He treats his mother, the earth, and his brother, the sky, as things to be bought, plundered, sold like sheep or bright beads."[32]

Chief Seattle and his people believed that their environment was a vital part of their history and culture and should be treated with reverence. In a way, the incorporation of this Native American philosophy demonstrated the complexity of and perhaps the contradictions in ETF thought. Native American philosophy generally links all living things and other elements of the world with souls and assigns them an equal place on earth; Christian theology, in contrast, clearly places humans at the top of the hierarchy on earth. Many elements of Chief Seattle's speech, however, verified the ETF's basic philosophy of treating the earth with care. Seattle also reiterated the theme from Isaiah that Moore adopted. The chief noted, "Our God is the same God [as the white man's]. . . . This earth is precious to Him, and to harm the earth is to heap contempt on its Creator. . . . Contaminate your bed, and you will one night suffocate in your own waste."[33]

Maternalism, the dominant language of the LCHA, played a far more muted role in the ETF. In the middle of a speech to the Niagara County legislature, Hoffmann asked the lawmakers to take a chance and help the victims of Love Canal, stating, "it is for this generation of children and the children yet to be born that we ask you to take a risk."[34] Looking back on her involvement with the ETF, Mudd, the mother of six, stated that her Love Canal activism "was a very natural outgrowth of my sense of parenthood."[35] Concern for the residents was integral to the ETF's involvement, yet language that stressed the children never played a dominant part in its rationale. This lack of maternalistic language may have been a nod to the LCHA's ownership of the issue. It also indicated that gendered language was fluid at Love Canal: not all women adopted maternalism as their most pressing justification.

LCHA: Maternalism

In contrast to the sophisticated interpretation of the ETF's activism, the LCHA stuck with a justification centered on maternalism—with considerable success. The LCHA women repeatedly and consistently cited concern for their children's and families' health as their prime motivator. This rhetoric proved more appealing to the media than the ETF's multilayered justification. Whereas the ETF received almost no notice, newspapers filled their pages with pictures of Gibbs and others marching and claiming a right to defend the health of their children. Other chapters noted the prevalence of maternalistic rhetoric within the LCHA. In the examples that follow, the LCHA's maternalistic language centered on children spilled over into activism through the tactics they used.

Gibbs gained confidence in her leadership abilities once Heisner left the LCHA. Attorney Richard Lippes and Gibbs's brother-in-law, Wayne Hadley, instructed the young woman in media tactics, although Gibbs soon outpaced her tutors in political and media savvy. She also escalated her tactics, adeptly moving from working within the legal system to resorting to direct action. As she did this, she chose to focus on health- and child-centered concerns almost exclusively, creating and responding to more and more dramatic events to gain front-page headlines.

The women of the LCHA believed that they needed constant media coverage to gain the attention of politicians and the public, and they worked hard to stay in the headlines. They planned each activity with the media in mind, looking for quotable material and events that provided photographic opportunities. "Everything was done deliberately," Luella Kenny noted, "and in many cases, trying to play to the political scene of the time [and] the press."[36] This focus had a maternalistic edge: Gibbs recalled that the group deliberately planned activities that included their children, such as kids holding signs that read, "I want to be a mommy someday." "Because it was really about our kids," she noted, "and our kids' future."[37] When other news stories threatened to grab the headlines, the home owners devised new tactics or tales to refocus the media's attention on their efforts. Debbie Cerrillo recalled that when "Mt. St. Helens [erupted] that wrecked our front-page work. We worked hard to stay on that front page. We needed to do some serious head banging, continually."[38] Barbara Quimby admitted, "it was a terrible thing to say, but, a volcano would erupt, the pope got shot at, and it was like, 'Oh, no. This is the first time we've been off the front page. And we've got to get back on the front page.'"[39] Getting back on the front page also involved the children. Joann Hale remembered the "horror story of the day" as being particularly effective. "When the children started being born, you know, the ones that were born, say, in 1978. If there was something wrong, then you would automatically have the media put something on it."[40]

Marches and 1960s-style protests especially intrigued the group, since the press covered such events, and the resulting photographs vividly demonstrated their concerns. The women noticed that maternalistic tactics captured the media's attention more than others, and they used those tactics more prominently. Children parading with signs became one of their favorite strategies at marches and other protests, although critics often accused them of using their children as pawns. The women, however, saw things differently. Many viewed their children's participation as empowering, allowing the children to speak for themselves. Gibbs stated that when the LCHA used children in parades, "we got shit for it a lot of the time, too. . . . But I think it was a good move, and I think it worked. . . . And it wasn't about exploiting them. It was really about protecting them, and if that's what we needed to do . . . to put a sign in their hand to get them to safety, then that was a small price to pay."[41] Patti Grenzy echoed that sentiment, observing, "It may not look appropriate to the rest of the world, but what's more appropriate than this kid standing up for himself? I mean, they're the ones that are being affected the most."[42]

One of their most well-publicized marches took place on Mother's Day 1979. Planned as a "March for Mother Earth," the event drew about 200 people from numerous groups, including unions, local environmental clubs, the NAACP, the ETF, renters, and outsiders, who marched from the affected neighborhood directly through the Hooker Chemical complex down the street. Gibbs saw the march as a way for people to express the fear caused by the "environmental dangers to their families, and [for] the Love Canal women who are afraid to become mothers because of it, and [for] Mother

LCHA protest march, April 1979. Debbie Cerrillo and Lois Gibbs are carrying the effigy in the center of the picture. (Courtesy of Buffalo State College Archives, *Courier-Express* Collection)

Earth."[43] Children carried signs stating, "Lindane Makes Poor Sandboxes," "C-56 makes me sick," and "God gave me the right to live—let him be the one to take it away." The adults sang folk songs as they marched, such as Woody Guthrie's "This Land Is Your Land," and they carried signs that stated, "No More Corporate Murder! We demand a safe, healthy future."[44]

Although the working-class women incorporated their children into some protests, they considered other activities inappropriate for younger family members. For instance, during a particularly tense time when the LCHA took two EPA officials hostage, Grenzy noticed that one woman with a child remained on the streets. Believing that the FBI had "sharpshooters" in various positions, Grenzy approached the woman and told her adamantly, "You can take your baby home, because it's not safe here. . . . Get the hell out of here!"[45] Concern for their children's safety also took precedence over staged displays for the benefit of the media during the picketing at the construction site. In the frigid weather, several of the women brought baby strollers stocked only with dolls, just in case they were unsuccessful in blocking the trucks that were coming and going.[46]

Protests over the remedial construction project also demonstrated a visible link between the maternalistic language and tactics of the LCHA women. After the initial emergency declaration by Robert Whalen, families in the inner rings with pregnant women and children younger than two left the area. As health department officials discovered that the chemical contamination had spread, the number of residents evacuated expanded, first temporarily and then permanently. At first, this included only the first ring; then it encompassed those on both sides of 97th and 99th streets abutting the canal, known together as the inner rings. Although it took some time to go into effect, Governor Carey arranged to have the state purchase these inner-ring homes in 1978. In addition, the state began efforts to "clean up" the area, once all the first-ring residents had been evacuated.

This cleanup effort generated considerable concern from the residents, both because of the lack of an adequate evacuation plan and because of concerns over the nature of the waste to be removed. Frustrations in the LCHA grew exponentially as Gibbs's demands to have all pregnant women and several families with severe health problems in the outer rings relocated fell on deaf ears. In response, resident Charles Bryan, supported by Gibbs, organized a picket of the remedial construction site.

The peaceful picketing began on the morning of 8 December 1978, a cold, wet Friday. Gibbs quickly realized the value of picketing as a media tool. On the second day of the demonstration, in frigid, twelve-degree weather, police arrested several of the residents, including Marie Pozniak, Charles Bryan, and Pat Pino. The picketers hoped to stop the trucks, laden with dirt from the area, from leaving and transporting the contaminated soil elsewhere.

The picketing tactic reflected and incorporated maternalistic concerns in a variety of ways. For example, Gibbs tried to impress on the workers the threat to their own personal safety and the implications for their families. As workers entered the area, she yelled into their cars, "You'll be carrying it home to your children." One of the women came armed with an empty baby stroller, which she pushed in front of cars trying to enter or leave the area. The next day, Gibbs and seven other residents forced police to arrest them, and more arrests followed.[47]

Even Patti Grenzy's advanced pregnancy became a vehicle for the expression of maternalism. As the picketing began, Grenzy yearned to join her friends, but she hesitated. Eight months' pregnant, and looking like she "was ready to drop any minute," Grenzy "didn't think it was respectful for a pregnant woman to be out [picketing]." She settled for bringing coffee, tea, and hot cocoa to the freezing picketers, until a discussion with Gibbs, Cerrillo, and Pozniak changed her mind. The three women encouraged her to picket and even to get arrested, asking, "What's more right than a pregnant mother trying to protect her unborn child?" After discussing the matter with her husband, Grenzy decided to participate in the demonstration and try to get arrested. The police, however, were less than cooperative. According to Grenzy, they realized "that it would look bad for a policeman to arrest a pregnant woman." The police argued with the women over the propriety of their actions. One police officer cautioned the group, "Ladies, think about what your children are going to think." The women responded, "Our children are going to know exactly what happened, and we know what they're going to think. They're going to be proud of us." Eventually, the police arrested Grenzy, booked her at the station, and placed her in a jail cell with several other activists.[48]

The picketers garnered significant publicity and sympathy among nonresidents as their images appeared on television and in newspapers. Several students from Buffalo-area universities joined the picketing, as did representatives from the New York Public Interest Research Group (NYPIRG).[49] In addition, the ETF's Roger Cook, an instructor at the State University of New York (SUNY) College at Buffalo, decided to join forces with the residents and get arrested for the first time. Cook, who lived directly across the Niagara River from Love Canal on Grand Island, told a reporter on the scene, "The cause seemed just. We're all affected by [it]. It's a much bigger issue than the Love Canal."[50] The story was even carried by New York City papers, reaching a far wider audience than ever before.[51] Letters to the editors of local newspapers generally supported the residents. One writer, another SUNY professor, described the arrests as "pornographic . . . and represent[ing] a strategy of blaming the victim." He mentioned one man who "was apparently arrested for protesting his and his son's poisoning and the lack of treatment they received from New York State officials." The professor then cited the basic American right to protest, observing, "After all, we are supposed to have a government of, for and by the people, not a government of, for and by the monopoly corporations and some narrow-minded state officials."[52] The LCHA's focus on health- and child-centered concerns had already leaked into public opinion.

The picketing dwindled over the next month as the extreme cold and the winter weather took their toll on the protesters. In addition, although a local judge had dismissed the charges against the picketers who had been arrested, he warned them to stay away from the work site.[53] Thus, the LCHA shifted its attention to other actions.

In summary, the rhetoric and justifications of the LCHA and the ETF revealed striking differences between the two groups. The well-educated, middle-class group's esoteric justification revealed an understanding of the deeper concerns and wider meanings expressed within the environmental movement by the late 1970s. In contrast, the focused, unified, maternalistic language employed by Gibbs captured the attention of the press and the public and proved far more effective at achieving the group's goals, but it showed little comprehension of environmental values beyond the health issues at Love Canal. really?

Tactics

Although women handled the day-to-day operations in both the ETF and the LCHA, class, not gender, determined which tactics and methods the groups pursued. The middle-class group, more firmly embedded in and benefited by the power structure of American society, stuck closely to legalistic and peaceful strategies. The ETF worked closely with the residents to keep roofs over their heads during some of the darkest hours of relocation, demonstrating a commitment to work within the system to effect change. In addition, one of the ETF's foremost goals was to maintain relationships with some parties that the LCHA considered the "enemy." The working-class group, more marginalized and increasingly desperate as time wore on, began resorting to extralegal tactics. Frustrated and angry with the government, the LCHA abandoned its legal protests and took two EPA officials hostage in May 1980 to gain the attention of President Carter.

ETF: Working within the System

As part of its direct aid initiative, the ETF helped the African American renters at Love Canal find other homes. In August 1979, with the temperature rising and more residents complaining of illness from the ongoing remedial construction, the state housed several families at Niagara University. It moved them and others to motels when the students returned in September, and the number of families in motels grew to 150 over the next month.[54] The ETF assisted these "motel people" in several ways. For instance, the state had agreed to pay the motel bills and minimal meal costs for residents who obtained certification from a doctor stating that conditions in the neighborhood provoked illness in at least one member of their family. The ETF brought in Dr. Kenneth Barney to examine the residents and provide the necessary certification, in accordance with the state's specifications.[55] Barney, a psychiatrist, evaluated the residents using standard psychiatric methodology and found that continuing to live in the area would damage their mental health. The state initially balked at these evaluations. Michael Cuddy, the relocation director, "said the 'simultaneous certification' by a single physician 'challenges our credulity.' He informed the relevant motels that "the state will bear no further expense in providing their shelter."[56]

Once the state rejected the medical evaluations, the LCHA's attorney, at the urging of the ETF, filed a lawsuit to force the state to abide by its original decree, which had not limited the certifications to a certain type of doctor or methodology. The courthouse victory hardly made circumstances any easier for the residents, however. Each family had to be recertified weekly in order to continue staying in the motels. Tensions grew, and Hoffmann and several other ETF members counseled the residents, allowing them to vent their fear and anger.[57] They also provided additional assistance when new problems cropped up during the relocation process.

Problems increased as Labor Day approached, since the area hotels were booked to capacity for the holiday, displacing the residents in favor of paying tourists. Hoffmann arranged for them to move into the basement of Stella Niagara, a local retirement home for nuns. Although residents preferred this to returning to their contaminated homes, the stay at the convent was less than ideal. Tensions ran high, especially when the state delayed the decision to return residents to the motels. Ann Hillis, expressing her frustration with the situation, threw a knife at Cuddy when he visited the convent.[58] Despite the tension, the nuns tried to make the stay as pleasant as possible, socializing with the residents and organizing a Labor Day picnic for them.[59]

By early October, with the remedial construction nearly completed, the state announced that it would no longer pay the residents' motel bills; they would have to move back into their homes or make other living arrangements at their own expense. Several families returned to Stella Niagara, having nowhere else to go and unwilling to move back into their homes. Sam and Eleanor Torcasio and their daughter Lauren, Janet Ecker and her daughter Lisa, and Ralph and Ann Hillis and their son Ralph Jr. shared the second floor of an educational building at the convent through the Christmas holidays. Even with little space or privacy, the families appreciated the nuns' help tremendously.[60]

While maintaining its commitment to helping the residents, the ETF also tried to establish lines of communication with local corporations and LCARA, the agency charged with purchasing the contaminated homes and revitalizing the neighborhood. Although its advocacy for the residents of Love Canal made it impossible to have any meaningful relationship with Hooker Chemical, Hoffmann felt strongly that the ETF should not shut out any entities that might help solve the problems of hazardous waste at Love Canal and elsewhere. Corporations remained an important focal point for her, especially as the ETF's concerns extended beyond Love Canal. Hoffmann related with pride that she attempted to "walk between" the two "worlds" of the corporations and the working-class people of the falls. That philosophy stemmed directly from her "subvert from within" attitude toward activism. She said that her approach to the corporations "came from sort of my background and manner of working. Some things are not negotiable and we always said health there was not negotiable. And the things that the people wanted and needed. But I think that you have to communicate. That's the only way you can do it is try to sit down at the table."[61]

She developed a close relationship with Richard Knowles, manager at the DuPont plant in Niagara Falls. In fact, Hoffmann's advice and assistance with neighborhood groups found a receptive audience at DuPont. At one point, she noted, DuPont wanted to pass out "leaflets about . . . one of their plants leaking. . . . It was the day before Halloween. And I said, 'You're going to go out on Halloween and you are going to distribute these flyers? That is about the worst idea I have ever heard in my whole life. . . . Don't do it.' And they didn't do it." Knowles also listened to Hoffmann's advice about talking to affected residents directly. He personally walked the streets of a neighborhood, knocking on doors to inform residents of a potential hazard from the plant. DuPont also helped the ETF arrange a conference entitled "Blueprint for Action," which brought together industry leaders and activists to search for solutions to environmental problems.[62]

In addition to developing and maintaining relationships with corporations, the ETF was one of the only groups at Love Canal to attempt to establish a positive relationship with LCARA. The ETF remained cautiously optimistic about LCARA and the revitalization of the area in 1980. Its executive board noted that revitalization "is indeed the religious principle. Out of helplessness to bring strength . . . out of death, resurrection and immortality." It commended the creation of LCARA, stating that it "provides an important potential for affected residents and government to work together in resolving the difficult issues at hand." Yet the ETF expressed considerable concern that the agency failed to address whether the neighborhood was actually safe for human habitation.[63] Although the ETF tried to maintain a working relationship with LCARA, this soon became a thorny issue.

In an effort to make itself useful, gain some much-needed funding, and exert an influence on LCARA, the ETF offered the use of its scientific advisory group in October 1980. Decisions about the safety of the neighborhood, Hoffmann noted, must include "objective analysis of data," something the advisory group could provide. She urged LCARA not to wait for an upcoming EPA report on the habitability of the area but to undertake its own study.[64]

LCARA accepted the ETF's offer, signing a $35,000 contract for the provision of scientific services and advice as needed. Worries abounded on both sides about the soundness of the scientific advice. LCARA member Angelo Massaro noted, "I am looking for an objective approach. I want the ability to terminate services if we feel it is not objective."[65] John Lynch, an ETF board member as well as one of LCARA's resident representatives, wanted to resign his LCARA position in 1981 because he did "not feel that the Agency will respond critically to the EPA report should it turn out positive."[66]

Lynch's voice proved prophetic when the EPA finally issued its report in May 1982 and declared Love Canal habitable. Although the ETF scientists criticized the report, which the EPA itself eventually described as inaccurate, LCARA quickly accepted the results and pressed for revitalization of the area.[67] The ETF demanded that LCARA conduct its own review of the report and threatened to "advise church members in Western New York" to avoid the neighborhood if its conditions were not met.[68] The relationship never recovered from the double blows of LCARA's unqualified acceptance of the EPA report and Morris's decision to move into the neighborhood (see chapter 2). The ETF tried to speak out against LCARA and in favor of environmental causes, but with no money and support dwindling, the organization faded into obscurity by the late 1980s.

LCHA: Breaking the Law to Gain Attention

As the Love Canal crisis dragged on, Gibbs faced various challenges to her leadership and proved adept at utilizing new strategies and tactics. Frustration mounted, however, within the group as the first year stretched into the second. As noted earlier, the LCHA picketed the remedial construction site and held numerous other marches and demonstrations, but the state withheld a final solution for the outer-ring residents. Health had always been the group's focus, and anger over conflicting health information often prompted more radical tactics. This was the case when the EPA released the results of its chromosome study in May 1980.

As discussed earlier, the chromosome study revealed a startlingly high rate of chromosome damage among some of the residents. Faced with growing confusion, fear, and anger among the residents, the EPA sent public-relations officer Frank Nepal to the neighborhood on 18 May 1980, the day after it released the results. Nepal had the unenviable task of meeting with the various residents' groups to try to defuse the situation. At about three o'clock the following afternoon, Nepal met with the ETF and then proceeded to the LCHA office, where Gibbs pressed him for answers about the chromosome study and its significance. Not being a doctor or a scientist, Nepal was unable to answer her questions, but he volunteered that Dr. James Lucas, another EPA official, might be able to help her. At Gibbs's request, Nepal called Lucas and asked him to come to the LCHA office.[69]

As Nepal dealt with the residents inside the office, Barbara Quimby became more and more alarmed at the crowd gathering outside. As one of the "genetically damaged" residents, Quimby feared for her daughters' health and had reacted angrily when the EPA told her that there would be no further chromosome tests on any of the children. As had been her routine for the past two years, she drifted over to the LCHA office. On the way, however, she noted some unusual behavior: Marie Pozniak was setting fire to a lawn with gasoline, and several other people were rocking parked cars. Convinced that the crowd, which seemed to be on the verge of a riot, posed a danger, Quimby entered the building, where Gibbs informed her that the LCHA had decided to take the two EPA officials hostage.[70]

Both Gibbs and Quimby fervently maintained that the LCHA held the two men hostage to "protect" them from the crowd. Yet Gibbs called the White House to inform President Carter that the men would not be released until Carter declared Love Canal a disaster area. Meanwhile, Quimby set about informing the hostages of the Love Canal residents' plight, producing file after file and telling the two men about the various health problems experienced in the area. Others brought cookies and brownies for the men to eat. Reporters filtered in and out, interviewing Gibbs and the hostages extensively.[71]

Although the LCHA women tried to make the situation seem light and humorous, and although neither Lucas nor Nepal felt physically threatened or feared for their lives, they never felt that they were free to leave, either. Several of the male residents blockaded the doorways, and other men watched the bathroom window when they allowed Nepal to relieve himself. Nepal tried to leave at one point, stating that he had no fear of the crowd, but several of the women refused to permit it. Lucas made a similarly ineffectual attempt to escape. Gibbs warned both men that the crowd would be unfriendly and advised them not to go outside. Quimby was so concerned that when they released the men several hours later, she accompanied them through the crowd to the police car, hoping that her presence would dissuade the residents from violence. She apparently stuck too close, because the police threw her into the car along with Nepal and Lucas.[72]

Others present had differing views of the situation. Joann Hale, also inside the office at the time, recalled that the people outside were "upset," "mad," "disgusted," and "stressed," but she did not perceive the same threat level that Gibbs and Quimby did.[73] Sources also reported conflicting estimates of the size of the crowd. Nepal made no mention of a crowd outside the building when he arrived.[74] When Lucas arrived shortly after four o'clock, he "observed approximately a dozen children and about six adults congregated outside" the building.[75] Sometime into the ordeal, when Nepal attempted to leave, he estimated the crowd at 75 people. At about six o'clock, when Gibbs spoke for the first time to attorney Lippes, she guessed the crowd's size to be 50 to 100 people. The FBI (which became involved only after Gibbs made her call to the White House) estimated that shortly after five o'clock, the crowd consisted of 100 to 150 "individuals of all ages, most of whom were milling about outside an eight-foot chain link fence surrounding the residence." Although they saw some people inside the fence "agitating the crowd and jeering at law enforcement officials," the FBI agents reported no physical damage to property. Indeed, the use of the phrase "milling about" hardly indicates a great concern that the crowd would turn violent.[76]

The LCHA, and especially Gibbs, worried the FBI more than the crowd outside did. Agents' reports repeatedly stated that "someone inside the residence declared that if the hostages left, they would be killed." Although the FBI interpreted this to mean that the hostages were in physical danger from those inside the house, the statement could have been referring to the threat from those outside. The LCHA finally released the two men at around eight o'clock, after being persuaded by negotiations with Lippes and the realization that FBI "sharpshooters" occupied several adjacent buildings.[77] Gibbs's remarks to the crowd as she freed the hostages figured prominently in the FBI's reports, and numerous media representatives at the scene quoted her comments. She asserted, "If we don't get something Wednesday the White House better look the hell out. If there isn't a disaster declaration, then today's action will look like a Sesame Street picnic."[78]

With the deadline approaching, Gibbs anxiously awaited word from the EPA regarding Love Canal's fate. At noon on Wednesday, Gibbs finally called the EPA press office herself, and the receptionist read the news release to her. As the champagne flowed liberally, Gibbs announced that the Federal Disaster Assistance Administration had agreed to pay for the temporary relocation of the rest of the Love Canal community. Gibbs felt that this was the final victory. She stated, "Although it was only to be a temporary move, we knew that if they moved us temporarily, we would eventually be moved permanently. . . . We celebrated by taking the red carnations we had been wearing since the taking of the hostages and throwing them into the air, saying we are now free! Our babies would be safe from further exposure to Love Canal poisons."[79]

Despite Gibbs's optimism, the EPA failed to provide immediate relief and offered no concessions on permanent relocation. As she had before, Gibbs marshaled her forces for one last media blitz. She and other residents appeared on the *Phil Donahue Show* and *Good Morning America* and protested at the Democratic National Convention in New York City over the summer of 1980. Finally, in late September, the White House informed Gibbs that the federal government would assist New York in coming up with the additional $15 million required to purchase the rest of the Love Canal homes.[80] Gibbs and the LCHA—willing to step outside the boundaries of the law in the name of protecting their children—won their long struggle for relocation.

Goals

ETF: Expanding Its Environmental Focus

As the ETF delved more deeply into the Love Canal problem, it experienced an organizational crisis. It had originally been formed with a single-purpose mission, and many members thought that once the Love Canal crisis had dissipated, the organization should disband. Others, prompted by a growing awareness of the widespread nature of the problem of hazardous waste, envisioned a permanent role for the church, using the knowledge gained at Love Canal in other communities. After much soul-searching and debate, the ETF decided to continue and broaden its work, formalizing the change with the adoption of a new name. In November 1979, the Ecumenical Task Force to Address the Love Canal Disaster became the Ecumenical Task Force of the Niagara Frontier. The bylaws of the new organization stated, "It is the primary purpose of the Task Force to provide relief from the physical, psycho/ social, and economic distress of persons living in areas affected by the ecological tragedy of chemical and radioactive contamination."[81] Although the work at Love Canal continued over the ETF's lifetime, by 1982 the emphasis had shifted from direct aid in that specific area to a more overtly political and legal advocacy role in western New York State. This trend sharply distinguished the ETF from the LCHA and other residents' groups, which rarely addressed any dimension of the problem outside the borders of the neighborhood.

This broad focus stemmed at least partially from ETF members' personal knowledge of and involvement in other environmental problems prior to

Love Canal. Ogg, for example, had followed the trials and tribulations of hazardous waste issues near her own home in Lewiston, attending hearings on these matters. That experience was one reason she sought to help the Love Canal residents. Cook and Moore had both been involved in antinuclear issues and had gained an understanding of the hazards of radiation. Generally, the ETF began with a wider understanding of the problems of hazardous waste than did the home owners' groups, and it considered Love Canal only part of the problem rather than its reason for being.

Because of their greater activism prior to Love Canal and their interest in social justice issues, ETF members quickly connected environmental problems with other social ills. Hoffmann, having worked in low-income schools, noted the links between environmental problems and class issues. One of the lessons learned through her work at Love Canal, she noted, was that "the people of poverty and the people of pollution are one people." Likewise, Love Canal was not just a New York problem, she asserted, "Equally damning is a growing movement of countries and corporations from the 'developed' world relocating their plants and shipping their toxic wastes to 'underdeveloped' countries where labor can be bought cheaply and strict regulations can be more easily avoided." "Love Canal," Hoffmann noted, "is not only a local problem, but a global problem."[82] In contrast to the white women of Love Canal, Hoffmann's wider experience and education allowed her to connect the larger issues of class and environmental hazards.

Although Hoffmann eagerly used class as a method of analysis, neither she nor the ETF proved willing to ignite the racial issues surrounding Love Canal. The controversy over the delayed Section 8 housing requests for the mostly black renters of Griffon Manor was one example. The ETF met with Mayor O'Laughlin and tried to convince him that relocating the renters was "more complex than a simple black/white image." ETF board members, perhaps realizing that racism in the area might be too difficult to overcome, suggested that the organization "should not directly confront the issue of 'permanent underclass' and 'overt racism' in City Government and the Falls in general, but rather attempt to factually indicate what is occurring and all[ow] others to interpret [it]." They decided on a cautious plan of action, allowing ETF staff to collect information and then have the board examine issues of race before proceeding.[83]

As a result of its enlarged mission, the language flowing from the ETF became more strictly "environmental" or "ecological." In a draft of a brochure prepared in 1982, for example, the ETF stated, "Above ground storage and 'secure' landfills MUST BE ENDED!" The brochure elaborated on ways to accomplish this, including "recycling and waste exchange . . . incineration . . . raw material and energy recovery . . . disassemblage."[84] In a paper prepared for the Diocese of Buffalo, the ETF stated that "alternative methods [to deal with hazardous waste] . . . would include: Chemical treatment (neutralization, precipitation of solids, ion exchange, etc.); Biological treatment to break down organic compounds; Physical treatment to reduce, solidify, or separate (evaporation, carbon absorption, filtration, membrane osmosis, etc.); [and] Thermal treatment (incineration, wet oxidation, pyrolysis, plasma arc, etc.)."[85] Generally, the ETF perceived the solution of the hazardous waste problem as a technological one: build better technology to eliminate it.

From time to time, the ETF acknowledged individuals' responsibility for hazardous waste. This rhetoric, however, remained vague and underdeveloped, eclipsed by the constant pounding of technology as a solution. Roberta Grimm, an ETF member, stated, "We need to be alert to the life styles we perpetuate, to question waste and extravagance."[86] Likewise, the ETF noted that Love Canal, as well as other hazardous waste disposal sites, "challenges us to examine our way of life, . . . and our responsibility for human generations to come."[87] Lynch echoed this wider critique when he spoke against the revitalization of the area in 1983. "We are riding a techno-toxic high," he noted, "attempting to transcend life's boundaries. In reality, we are now under threat from what we produce."[88] The ETF had begun to realize that Americans' patterns of consumption and their need for convenience contributed to the production of hazardous waste—going a step beyond LCHA members' environmental understanding.

The ETF's adoption of environmental values had limits, however. The organization considered itself distinct, and members went out of their way to separate the ETF's image from that of other environmental groups. As an attachment to the minutes of the 24 March 1981 board meeting, Roger Cook, serving as secretary, included some cartoon drawings for the board's entertainment. The cartoons highlighted the differences between ETF workers

and "typical" Sierra Club members. For instance, the typical Sierra Club net-
worker was portrayed as a caveman with a large club in one hand, the Sierra
Club scientist was a madman pounding at things on a table, the Sierra Club
legal adviser had money flowing out of his pockets, and the Sierrra Club
environmental director was portrayed as a godlike figure holding puppet
strings. The cartoon characters representing their ETF counterparts were angels with halos, carrying Bibles in their pockets. Cook portrayed Sister Margeen Hoffmann as an angel holding several small people in her arms.[89] This
desire to distinguish itself from the "regular" environmental groups became
especially pronounced when the ETF sought funds from the outside community. In a 1981 letter to church congregations in Niagara and Erie counties
pleading for donations and prayers, the ETF noted forcefully, "We are *not*
another 'environmental group.' *We are the religious community* helping and
reaching out to those who are victims of environmental disaster."[90]

Board members and staff heard numerous horror stories from Niagara
Falls residents and other contacts. Hazardous waste issues became so complicated and time-consuming that individual board members kept up-to-
date on specific sites and reported back to the general body. Jim Brewster
drew the straw for the situation at Hyde Park, also known as Bloody Run. He
recalled that the landfill in northern Niagara Falls "had an extraordinarily
high concentration of dioxin. Probably the most dioxin anywhere in this
part of the world, I guess. And it was leaching out of a fairly large dump site
directly through bedrock directly to the gorge face of the Niagara River, and
you could see discoloration of the shale in the rock face, and eventually this
would filter down into the Niagara River, affecting water quality, even, for
example, especially Canadian cities that would be downstream."[91] In fact, the
dioxin levels at Hyde Park exceeded the total amount of dioxin used during
the Vietnam War.[92] More than 80,400 tons of waste had been dumped at the
site over the years, making Love Canal seem small by comparison.[93]

Brewster and the ETF became aware of the Hyde Park landfill issue
through the reporting of Ray Tyson in the *Niagara Gazette* and communi-
cations with several Hyde Park residents, including Fred Armagast. A small
creek named Bloody Run received the runoff from the landfill and ran directly past Armagast's home.[94] Compared with Love Canal, there were few
residents in the low-income area along the creek, so they were grateful for
the ETF's interest and asked for help in filing a lawsuit. The Hyde Park site

also interested the ETF because it sat a short distance from the Niagara River and threatened both American and Canadian water supplies.[95]

The ETF, through attorney Barbara Morrison, appealed to Judge John Curtin to grant the organization amicus curiae, or "friend of the court," status in May 1981. The ETF also began coordinating the various citizens' groups, keeping them informed and up-to-date. By getting involved in the lawsuit, the ETF hoped to benefit the public at large, as well as to "present to the public and the court, the flaws contained in the EPA-Hooker plans on clean-up and containment of the chemicals."[96] The ultimate goals included pressuring "the court to specify [the] duration of time [the] company must monitor the site . . . then we will already have more than what the EPA now requires."[97] The ETF saw its amicus curiae status as "the beginning of bringing issues of liability, responsibility, and justice to bear for the first time through the courts, on the issue of hazardous waste."[98]

Fourteen months after the clerk filed the original settlement plan, and after lengthy hearings, Curtin finally approved the settlement in April 1982. The ultimate agreement contained many elements the ETF had pressed for; it included plans for remedial construction of the site, and it required Occidental Chemical Corporation (Hooker Chemical's successor) to "identify the extent of contamination" and do anything necessary "to protect the public health and environment."[99] This success at Hyde Park encouraged the ETF's other activities, including numerous events in New York and around the country.

LCHA: Focusing on Local Issues

Despite all the problems in the general Niagara Falls area, the LCHA rarely showed any concern about issues outside the immediate Love Canal area, even after it achieved relocation of the residents. Lois Gibbs noted:

[The LCHA] did a couple of things. The West Valley Nuclear Waste Depository thing that was happening not too far from us, those folks came out and helped us on a couple of occasions. Some of their scientists [helped]. So, in return, we went and we testified at hearings, and we, I think, one time did a picket line with them. There were some folks in the Lewiston-Porter area where they wanted to expand a landfill there and an incinerator. They had come up and given us support in different ways, so we, in turn, went to a couple of their public hearings and provided support. So, we got involved in other things, but it really . . . was because they did something for us, we wanted to repay them. It wasn't because

direct
Solidarity   *not*
environmentalism

we really were getting into the larger environmental movement and issues. It was more, you did this nice thing for us, so we're going to do this nice, supportive thing for you.[100]

In the summer of 1980, after the agreement to relocate the outer-ring families, Gibbs packed her belongings and her children and drove to Virginia. Her marriage to Harry had disintegrated during the crisis, and Gibbs felt an overriding desire to continue her work in some capacity. She founded the Citizens Clearinghouse for Hazardous Waste—later renamed the Center for Health, Environment, and Justice (CHEJ)—in Falls Church, not far from where her future husband, Stephen Lester (who had assisted in a scientific capacity at Love Canal), worked in Georgetown. Today, Gibbs finds her activism highly satisfying. She enjoys assisting other grassroots groups in their struggles against environmental health hazards, and she believes that the LCHA provides an interesting model for activism. In her words, the LCHA was "an incredibly democratic civic organization that grabbed the attention of not just the White House, but the world. And [it] changed the public's perspective on a particular thing, meaning chemical exposure."[101]

Luella Kenny, a board member of the CHEJ, continues to be active in environmental causes as well, although she stayed closer to Love Canal. When Occidental settled the legal case, the judge required the company to donate $1 million toward a health fund to assist 1,328 former residents with ongoing health problems. Kenny serves as chair of that health fund. She notes, "I couldn't let go of it [the issue of Love Canal]. I couldn't in good conscience . . . see other people in similar situations . . . and not be able to help them. . . . I've gone around the country quite a bit, speaking to different groups." The fund has been extremely successful and, if fact, has doubled in size even after paying claims. Kenny remains frustrated by the high level of illness among health fund beneficiaries, including "a lot of cancer." In addition, she constantly hears about "second-generation problems" from children of the residents.[102]

Gibbs and Kenny, however, are exceptions among the working-class women of the LCHA. Most of the activists were more than happy to leave the protesting behind when they moved away from the neighborhood. Barbara Quimby echoes the sentiments of other residents when she says, "I don't get more involved. No, in fact, I'm the other way. For the longest time, I just

why not continued?

wanted to close my drapes. . . . I just want to be a homemaker. I want to bake cookies and I just want to be home"[103] Debbie Cerrillo notes, "I give Lois all the credit in the world to continue like she has. She made a career out of it. I could not. . . . For about . . . 10 or 12 years, I so withdrew from all of that because I not only lost my home, got a new home, lost my marriage, lost my kids, had to start all over again. Lost everything and started 65 miles away from home."[104]

Many of the residents moved to Grand Island to escape Love Canal. They chose the island because it lacked the huge number of waste sites and dumps proliferating all over the Niagara Falls area. Quimby moved to Grand Island because "they said it was one of the safest places in the area. We had a map. . . . So every time I'd find a house and come back, Lois would have the map and say, 'My God, you can't live there.' And it was like, I guess I'm going to Grand Island, because there was no where else to go." Even there, however, environmental problems plagued them. Quimby and Kenny both became involved when local officials proposed to spread toxic "sludge" from the surrounding area over the island. Quimby stormed into a local meeting and said, "Are you crazy? You spread that? This is the safest place in this area to live and you're going to put that sludge [down]?" Quimby and others succeeded in stopping the dumping of waste on the island.[105]

Some of the other activists have been sporadically involved in local environmental issues. Cerrillo remarried and moved to Holley, New York, about an hour east of Niagara Falls. Despite the desire to "withdraw," she has become involved in an issue in nearby Brockport. She notes, "It's GM and Black and Decker. . . and General Electric. There's a big environmental mess, and . . . under the Erie Canal there's a pipe that goes into a neighborhood, looks just like Love Canal. The same kind of homes. It's so eerie. It's such a draw to me to go over and help."[106] Patti Grenzy, who moved to Lockport, stays informed about local environmental issues. She was particularly incensed over the location of the new high school in Niagara Falls very close to an old dump site.[107] These few women, however, represent a distinct minority of the 900 families evacuated from Love Canal.

One of the pervading outcomes of Love Canal was extreme disillusionment with the government. The government bureaucracy's failure to act as they expected shattered the residents' illusions, prompting anger and, in some cases, additional activism. Gibbs stated:

The kids' health [was] number one. But the number two thing that really motivated me was this idea that I grew up with a sense of government cares about the people. That's just the culture of the blue-collar community. . . . And the idea that the government made a decision, at the local and state level, and to a certain extent the federal level, that they did a cost-benefit analysis, and [decided] that it was okay to sacrifice us. That we weren't worth twenty million dollars really pissed me off. And it goes back to the kids and the value of my children. But it's one of those values that just made me so angry . . . because I didn't have an income outside the household [the government believed] I was worth nothing by their calculations. And because Melissa was going to follow in my footsteps, likely, she had no value. And that Michael's value was a value equivalent, with an inflation factor to his father, which was ten, twenty, thirty thousand dollars or whatever. I just found that morally so appalling and so wrong, that . . . really bothered me.[108]

Quimby also became severely disillusioned with the government. She noted, " I found out dollars come before people. . . . I thought . . . when you're in danger they [the government] could come on the white horse and the knight will come and save you. Well, I thought, when my government finds out there's dioxin here, they're going to come and get me. And when they didn't, I got *scared*."[109] Grenzy observed, "We've always been taught that our government will protect us. You're an American. You're protected by your country." For her, Love Canal sorely tested that belief.[110]

Certainly, for working-class women who had been brought up to have faith in their government, criticism did not come easily, and, in contrast to the extended critique by ETF members, LCHA members generally ended their analysis of the problem with a critique of the government. They also failed to recognize Americans' consumption habits as contributing to environmental problems. Gibbs and the CHEJ currently focus on many of these problems, but at the time, the LCHA did not address deeper environmental issues "because it's a chemical city where we lived and worked and played. Even if we decided we would never use PVC plastic again, because that was a really bad thing, we're making PVC plastic. So, you can't say we're not going to buy something that our husbands are producing."[111] In contrast, the ETF members, with their middle-class status, education, and distance from blue-collar chemical jobs, saw the deeper roots of ecological problems as espoused by the environmental movement.

The Result: Tension between the ETF and the LCHA

With their differences in membership, goals, tactics, and rhetoric, tension sometimes ran high between the LCHA and the ETF. This tension stemmed in part from personality conflicts between the two dominant women, Gibbs and Hoffmann. Brewster noted wryly, "It's awfully hard to have two Mother Teresas in the same disaster."[112] Ogg believed that much of the discord arose because the residents thought the ETF was condescending and considered them incapable of achieving their goals on their own. Gibbs confirmed this feeling, describing the relationship between the LCHA and the ETF as "very poisonous." Gibbs resented the ETF's presence, especially after the arrival of Hoffmann, who seemed to think that the "victims" should turn the fight over to the "professionals." Gibbs recalled, "Sister Margeen started off on the wrong foot. She came in one day [to the LCHA office] . . . and she said, 'Okay, this is who I am. This is my experience with flood and disasters. You guys can all go home. I'll take over now.'"[113] Having already made significant progress in achieving their goals through their own initiative, the residents deeply resented being made to feel like helpless victims.

The tension between the two groups went both ways, however. ETF leaders sometimes resented taking a backseat to the LCHA and definitely had strong opinions about the appropriateness of some of the home owners' tactics. In August 1979, the LCHA asked the ETF to assist with a candlelight vigil to be held at the Love Canal fence "in memory of those who died, and for the safety and well being of those who still live near the Love Canal."[114] Hoffmann recalled, "When Lois said, 'We're going to have this vigil. Can you bring the candles?' . . . We thought we were going to say a little prayer, be part of the vigil. . . . And I said, 'I have never been an altar boy. I don't carry candles.'"[115]

Hoffmann also expressed concern about the potential for violence at various times during the crisis. For example, in 1979, when the state threatened to remove residents from their motels over Labor Day weekend, rumors swirled about using guns to keep their rooms. After bureaucrats repeatedly minimized her concerns about the "motel people," Gibbs stated, "I have 150 residents who are willing to be arrested, who may be carrying shotguns, who are going to sit there and not leave the motel even if the state cuts off the funds."[116] When Gibbs and others took two EPA officials hostage in 1980 to get President Carter's attention, the ETF described this behavior as "inappropriate" and renounced "even the threat of violence."[117]

The ETF also took issue with some of the very visible, confrontational tactics used by the LCHA. Hoffmann found marching with coffins in front of the state capitol to be in poor taste. Ogg disapproved of the LCHA's use of children in marches. During the hostage situation, she said, the home owners had "gathered their kids together . . . handed them placards, and created a parade down the street, because all the news media was there. And so, this was a real attempt to attract attention and even sympathy by parading the kids there. We didn't think that was appropriate. We thought the kids were suffering enough. . . . We didn't think these kids needed to have placards stuck in their hands and parading up and down the street, just to have their pictures on TV."[118] Used to working within the church to achieve change, Hoffmann noted, "I don't believe in confrontation. You have to be able to manage a crisis, because so rarely is a crisis resolved to everyone's satisfaction."[119] She expressed public disapproval of the very tactics that gained Gibbs and the home owners so much attention and media coverage and worked so well for them.

Although the ETF disagreed with many of the tactics employed by the LCHA women, it did not hesitate to use similar tactics when it believed that doing so might be effective. For example, the ETF used Mayor O'Laughlin's Catholic upbringing to its advantage. Hoffmann and the mayor "were friendly. He was friendly to me," she said, "because he was a good Catholic, and had gone to Catholic school. . . . I was always 'Sister Margeen.' It was never anything that I was not. That's who I was, what I represented."[120] Ogg remembered that when the state refused to accept the psychiatrist's certifications regarding the ongoing danger to residents' mental health, "the ministers and priests arrived. I think every single one of them was wearing a clerical collar, and some of these guys I had never seen in clerical collars before. They were dealing with a guy who had been raised in the Catholic church. And they knew what impact this clerical collar was going to have on him."[121] The ETF used the authority vested in the clergy to gain the upper hand, yet it disapproved when the women of Love Canal manipulated their status as mothers to accomplish the same goal.

Many of the differences between the ETF and the residents' groups (both black and white) stem from dichotomies in their vision of and relation to the problem, as well as differences in class and education. First and foremost, the ETF's status as a nonresident group forced members to articulate a justification for involvement that moved beyond concern for their own homes or families. Composed of an interfaith group of self-selected, middle-class, highly educated men and women, the ETF developed a more complex, logic-driven, and diverse rationale. With a more equal gender balance among its vocal leadership, the ETF focused far less on maternalism and more on biblical stewardship for the earth and the church's traditional role of providing charity.

ETF members' long histories of outside activism provided them with past successes and experiences to draw on, as well as a personal sense of their own agency. Their educational opportunities allowed them to learn about the environmental movement's values and to work toward implementing them. In addition, the ETF connected the environmental problems at Love Canal with deeper societal conflicts—namely, race and class issues. The ETF promoted racial equity and accepted the values of the civil rights movement. The organization spent a good deal of its time assisting the black renters to obtain relocation. Overall, the ETF proved more willing than the LCHA to fight for the most marginalized Love Canal residents. Its role as part of the church and as a representative of more diverse populations pressed the ETF into a more conservative activism, resisting the tactics of violence and lawlessness employed by the LCHA and choosing instead to work within the legal system to effect change. For example, the ETF filed legal briefs to hold the state accountable, searched frantically for housing solutions, and tried to maintain working relationships with industry and LCARA. Rather than holding hostages, the ETF made references to Sophocles, Rachel Carson, and biblical prophets to make its point. Thus, to the average citizen, the ETF seemed to be an esoteric, intellectual group more concerned about elegant phrasing than children's health. This chasm between the two groups led to a high level of tension. The LCHA felt patronized, and the ETF disapproved of the tactics used by the working-class women. Overall, however, Gibbs and the LCHA controlled the situation and the media image more successfully and influentially than the ETF did.

5

Historical Implications of Gender, Race, and Class at Love Canal

Scholars and activists often refer to the events of Love Canal as important "firsts": women were vocal and influential participants in the struggle, the nation became aware of the danger of toxic waste and the immediacy of the problem, and the federal government reacted by passing legislation. Yet, a historical examination of gender, race, and class at Love Canal illuminates important sources of continuity. Following the format of earlier chapters, this chapter examines several historical snapshots of activism and follows the trails of gender, race, and class to understand how activism at Love Canal fits into the bigger picture of the environmental movement as a whole.

Historical Comparisons: Gender

Gendered language was fluid at Love Canal, although certain patterns emerged among the different groups. The most prominent language among the women at Love Canal was certainly maternalism. Concern for the health and safety of their families, especially their children, crossed both racial and class lines. Men involved at Love Canal emphasized economic concerns most visibly, but this economic response varied somewhat with the men's class and status. The elite men who dominated LCARA focused almost exclusively on the adverse effects on tourism and tax dollars. The working-class men in the neighborhood used economic concerns as a basis for their activism, pressing for a freeze on mortgage payments or taxes.

Yet this dichotomy was hardly set in stone. Economic worries motivated several women in the neighborhood, especially businesswomen and single mothers responsible for the financial well-being of their families. Conversely, the male resident representatives of LCARA focused on health issues. In addition, groups enlarged the frame of the debate by introducing and emphasizing different aspects. Working-class whites cited citizenship rights as a basis for activism. The African American renters believed that race and class bias perpetuated their situation, and their activism explicitly emphasized a more inclusive solution at Love Canal. The ETF saw its activism as part of the broader environmental movement and incorporated language stressing the widespread nature of the problem and the idea of stewardship as a way to work toward change and prevent future problems.

The gendered language at Love Canal provided a way for different groups to comment on what they considered men's and women's appropriate roles in society. The working-class women, for example, certainly accepted the idea of a public, political voice for women; they also stressed their rights as citizens, voters, and taxpayers—all main goals of the first-wave women's movement. Yet they defined their activism as antifeminist. They saw their activism as a way to defend and enhance a woman's right to be a stay-at-home mother and wife. The working-class women at Love Canal felt that the women's movement had excluded them and even denigrated their life choices, and they used their environmental activism to counter those perceived ideas. For the women of the LCHA, the maternalistic language they used in the 1970s had a complicated meaning; it simultaneously pressed for an expanded societal role for women and emphasized their importance in the home.

Among the men at Love Canal, ideas about gender roles were no less contradictory. Although, again, male views were hardly monolithic, men generally took a less positive view of women's gains and their entry into public life. The working-class men, notably Harry Gibbs and Norman Cerrillo, repeatedly asked their activist wives when their families would return to "normal," by which they meant their wives staying at home, raising the children. Other working-class men gladly supported their wives and encouraged their activism as part of their roles within the family. Middle-class men, especially those in the ETF, accepted women in leadership roles; the ETF hired a female leader and staff and included a significant number of women on its board of directors.

In contrast, the men of LCARA consistently marginalized women as they attempted to participate in political solutions to the neighborhood's problems. Mayor O'Laughlin and other members frequently described the women as "hysterical" or "emotional," labeling them as unfit to be part of the decision-making process. LCARA specifically excluded women from its membership, even though several women volunteered to serve and possessed knowledge of the area and the issues. O'Laughlin and others referred to the male resident representatives who opposed the economic arguments of the majority and insisted on raising health concerns as obstructionist, antidemocratic, and too individualistic. O'Laughlin justified his reorganization of LCARA in January 1983 (intended to usurp the opposition) as follows: "This agency was brought to its knees by two people—so much so that we could not even pass an insurance program to protect the homes which we have bought, which in turn would protect the taxpayers. Where in your vast store of legislative memory can you show that two members out of nine is a democratic way of operating when the two can veto any legislative action?"[1] O'Laughlin's public pronouncements denigrated the men who refused to be team players or submit to authority figures—veiled insults to their masculine participation in the political process. Thus , men in leadership positions, whether within the family or in the community, tended to resist an increased role for women. In addition, they marginalized men who adopted the health-centered language of the women.

Other historical examples prove useful in assessing the implications of these attitudes in the late 1970s. Several periods in U.S. history advanced important ideas about gender roles. For example, in the later stages of the first-wave women's movement during the Progressive Era, women pressed for political equality, and their presence in public life increased dramatically through various reforms. The second-wave women's movement enlarged those goals to include equity in the workplace; it later challenged ideas about the gendered division of work in the home and took a stand against domestic violence. In both times, women reacted in varying ways. During the Progressive Era, some women refused to fight for the right to vote or even actively opposed it; others pressed for suffrage through racism and ideas of exclusion. In the 1970s, when some women championed the sharing of domestic duties, others became part of the reactionary New Right that propelled Ronald Reagan to power, stressed woman's ultimate role as homemaker, and attempted to reverse the ideology of equality and the legal concepts benefiting women. Both periods not only affected women's roles but also produced significant reaction among men. Many men resisted the desired changes with reluctance or outright hostility, as women seemed to intrude into previously masculine territory; others accepted the ideas of the women's movement and questioned traditional gender roles.[2]

Maternalism pervaded both eras of the reevaluation of gender roles in environmental reform in the twentieth century. An examination of maternalism, however, must be taken in historical context to determine its meaning and impact.

Women's Environmental Activism during the Progressive Era

During the Progressive Era, elite white women became involved in an array of environmental interests at the local and national levels. Like the working-class women at Love Canal, white women's rhetoric during the Progressive Era explicitly linked their status as mothers and housewives with their increased activism. Three examples from this era—conservation and preservation activities, urban improvement through settlement houses and sanitation reform, and the reduction of smoke pollution—illustrate these trends.

Upper- and middle-class women played a pivotal role in many of the early issues surrounding conservation and preservation.[3] Many of these women justified their involvement using maternalistic rhetoric. Some women noted that their conservation efforts complemented their role in the home. Mrs. Overton Ellis stated, "Conservation in the material and ethical sense is the basic principle in the life of woman."[4] In 1908, Lydia Adams-Williams criticized male tendencies to exploit and overuse resources, stating, "It [will] fall to woman in her power to educate public sentiment to save from rapacious waste and complete exhaustion the resources upon which depend the welfare of the home, the children, and the children's children."[5] Adams-Williams felt that it was her duty as a woman to prevent the loss of resources to future generations. Using this "conservative" language, women frequently stretched gender roles, entering the male-dominated public sphere. Women's tactics included political lobbying, drafting legislation, petition writing, and face-to-face meetings with politicians. Even before they could vote, women impressed on male politicians their influence over male voting habits.[6]

The settlement house movement also provided fertile ground for urban environmental reforms during the Progressive Era, and again, women used maternalism to justify their activism.[7] Jane Addams (1860–1935) became one of the pioneers of the settlement house movement, incorporating many environmental reforms into her agenda. After founding Hull House in 1889, she initiated programs to establish city playgrounds as well as summer camps in the country. Although Addams fervently denied that the settlement house programs were exclusively for children, the women directed many of their efforts toward the young residents of the tenements. One of the first programs was a kindergarten, followed by the establishment of a boys' club.[8]

Addams also campaigned vigorously for garbage pickup and sanitation reforms in the neighborhood. In addition to lobbying local politicians, she educated the immigrant neighborhood women about the importance of proper garbage disposal. Sweeping their doorways was insufficient, and leaving refuse in the streets, Addams warned, could cause sickness and death, especially among children. Addams admonished the already overworked immigrant women that they must "not only keep their own houses clean, but must also help the authorities to keep the city clean."[9]

The Women's Club at Hull House later took a prominent role. After expressing concern over the high infant death rate in the area, Addams directed the club's energies into the garbage issue. Twelve of the Irish immigrant women, along with several Hull House workers, investigated alley conditions in the neighborhood. Addams acknowledged the sacrifice required of these women. After finishing a hard day's work and then preparing a meal for the family, "it would have been much easier [for each woman] to sit on her doorstep . . . than to go up and down ill-kept alleys and get into trouble with her neighbors over the conditions of their garbage boxes. It required both civic enterprise and moral conviction to be willing to do this three evenings a week during the hottest and most uncomfortable months of the year." During that first summer, the Women's Club members reported 1,037 violations to the health department.[10]

Addams's philosophy that such activism fit in with established gender roles encountered skepticism among the immigrant women. Addams remembered that some of them were "much shocked by this abrupt departure into the ways of men." Addams and others attempted to explain the situation logically: because garbage caused disease, they reasoned, activism in this area could be equated with nursing the sick, a traditional feminine duty. Still, workers encountered some resistance among the immigrant population.

Some "saw that their housewifely duties logically extended to the adjacent alleyways and streets," but others were not convinced.[11] Addams relied heavily, in the early stages, on the support and participation of the neighborhood's working-class women for success.

Her advocacy of women's involvement in civic affairs in general included maternalistic justifications. Women, according to Addams, had a historic role in keeping the city clean. "From the beginning of tribal life," she wrote, women "have been responsible for the health of the community. . . . From the days of the cave dwellers, so far as the home was clean and wholesome, it was due to their efforts. . . . From the period of the primitive village, the only public sweeping which was performed was what they undertook in their divers dooryards." Therefore, "may we not say that city housekeeping has failed partly because women, the traditional housekeepers, have not been consulted as to its multiform activities?"[12] More specifically, she cited maternalistic reasons to explain her concern over the unemptied garbage boxes. Children, she noted, constantly played around the boxes, climbing on them as toddlers or using them as barricades for games when older.[13] Another settlement house worker, Lillian Wald, explicitly linked the garbage crusade with the ongoing conservation movement and saw her activism as "child conservation," along the same lines as "the conservation of material wealth, mines, and forests, hogs and lobsters."[14]

Similarly, bourgeois women's clubs played an integral role in the early battle against smoke pollution in the late nineteenth and early twentieth centuries,[15] and they too justified their activism through maternalism. These women noted the adverse effects of smoke on the health of nearby families, and they pointed out that smoke increased women's already heavy domestic workload: laundry hung outside to dry often became covered with soot, forcing frequent rewashings. Women in St. Louis stated, "The present condition of our city . . . endangers the health of our families . . . and adds infinitely to our labors and expenses as housekeepers."[16]

From the 1890s to the 1910s, women actually controlled the definition of the smoke problem through their efforts and rhetoric.[17] In cities such as Pittsburgh, St. Louis, Cincinnati, New York, and Chicago, organized women stressed the issues of health, aesthetics, and morality in combating the perceived threats of smoke pollution.[18] In Pittsburgh and St. Louis, under the

Women's Health Protective Association of Allegheny County and the Citizen's Smoke Abatement Association, respectively, women organized in 1892 to fight the thick smoke over their cities. Both groups emphasized health issues, especially among children, in their justifications. In St. Louis, for example, the women stated, "We feel that the present condition of our city, enveloped in a continual cloud of smoke, endangers the health of our families, especially those of weak lungs and delicate throats, impairs the eyesight of our school children, and adds infinitely to our labors and our expenses as housekeepers, and is a nuisance no longer to be borne with submission." Presented with this reasoning, city councils responded quickly. In early 1892, Pittsburgh passed a smoke control ordinance "prohibiting any chimney or smokestack associated with a stationary boiler to emit bituminous coal smoke." St. Louis's 1893 nuisance law was more comprehensive, forbidding "the emission into the open air of dense black or thick gray smoke" and creating a commission to aid in enforcement.[19]

Women's roles as wives and mothers also influenced their tactics during the smoke pollution movement. For example, in 1908, women in Chicago organized the Anti-Smoke League under Annie Sergel to combat smoke pollution, supporting the electrification of the city's railroad lines as a solution. These women took the novel approach of initiating a housework strike to protest the pollution, allowing them to work full-time on the reform issue. In addition to refusing to do housework, the women implemented economic boycotts of certain products, promising to "spend no money in the acquirement of furniture or of objects of art with which to decorate our homes, nor of gowns to beautify our persons; that we even pack away all unnecessary ornaments which we now have in use, thus preserving them from the hands of the destroyer; all this with the hope of emerging next year most beautiful butterfly fashion from the smoky chrysalis of soot and cinders to which a money-loving corporation might forever have doomed us." Despite their efforts, effective opposition by railroad companies and their employees delayed the issue of electrification until the mid-1910s.[20]

Implications of Progressive Era Maternalism

Although they often used conservative language, women's rhetoric allowed them to encroach into male-dominated areas with little opposition. For instance, by becoming involved in smoke pollution reform, women organized, lobbied for change, and influenced legislation and even the terms of the debate. None of these activities constituted part of women's traditional role, yet these women developed a rhetoric to support the extension of their activism outside the home.

Although middle-class and elite women involved in conservation, settlement house work, and smoke pollution control consistently employed a maternalistic rhetoric, as did the working-class women at Love Canal, the implications of this language are markedly different. During the Progressive Era, suffragists actively fought for the franchise and a greater public role for women. However, the Progressive Era women's movement did not stress equality for women; rather, it focused on the continuation of separate spheres for men and women while it promoted women's increased political participation. Environmental activism mimicked these goals. Women adopted a language stressing their traditional roles as wives and mothers, or keepers of the home; they moved into the public sphere through environmental activism and fell into step, unconsciously or not, with the goals of the women's movement.

At Love Canal, in contrast, the context of the times and the motives of the women themselves led to a very different conclusion, despite the similarity of language. Although the second-wave women's movement stressed equality in the workplace and public and private equality between men and women, some women found it too radical and even antifamily. Many women perceived the women's movement as being openly hostile to those who chose to stay home and raise their children. The women of Love Canal reacted strongly against this negative image. As a result, their maternalistic language, rather than being a vehicle to press for the goals of the movement, became a way to protest these perceived negative messages. Rather than using their activism to assert the goals of equality or access to outside employment, the women of Love Canal saw their efforts as a way to revalue their roles as mothers. Yet their activism also wove reluctantly into the women's movement: women assumed public leadership roles, expressed expertise in science and public policy issues, and lobbied for legislation. Although the language at Love Canal mirrored that of the Progressive Era, the implications were very different.

Men's Environmental Activism during the Progressive Era

Like maternalism for the women, economic arguments pervaded male environmental activism during the twentieth century. For example, in the Progressive Era, the female activists involved in smoke pollution reform came face-to-face with concerns about economic fortunes—their main enemy. The dominant attitude, especially among city planners and leaders in the early 1880s, equated smoke with economic progress and prosperity. If a city had smoke, it had productive industry and therefore wealth. This attitude transcended regional lines. In Houston, the *Post* triumphantly declared, "Smoke stacks are a splendid sign of a city's prosperity. Smoke stacks are multiplying in Houston. Ergo: the signs of prosperity are multiplying in Houston."[21] Pittsburgh city leaders equated smoke with manly virtue and a strong work ethic, and they demeaned criticisms of smoke with accusations of "sentimentality and frivolity."[22] In Chicago, one man pronounced that the "Creator who made coal knew that there would be smoke, and knew that smoke would be a good thing for the world."[23] In addition, some people continued to believe that smoke acted as a disinfectant, purifying the air of disease.[24]

In the area of smoke pollution, early efforts by women generally resulted in a response by city lawmakers and the adoption of some type of regulation or legislation. However, beginning in the 1910s, women began to lose control over how reformers defined the problem. Cities found the initial laws difficult to enforce, and the courts encountered significant opposition to them. When the courts struck down these first laws, cities clarified the legislation, making smoke pollution control more technical. These amended laws usually included "the creation of a separate smoke inspection department, the requirement that chief inspectors be professional engineers, and the empowerment of smoke inspectors to access any offending equipment."[25] With these components, cities stressed not only the discovery of violators, which could involve the public, but also the need to identify causes and solutions, which required (male) experts.[26] Despite the fact that men controlled the final outcome, women exerted a strong influence over the smoke pollution reform effort; thanks to women's groups and other civic organizations, some type of smoke reform legislation had been passed in every major metropolitan area by 1912. Strikingly, women exercised political power eight years before passage of the Nineteenth Amendment.

The reliance on so-called experts also played a part in the conservation movement. Efficiency in the guise of federal control and expert management of natural resources was a key theme in this reform effort, led by powerful personalities such as Theodore Roosevelt and Gifford Pinchot. The "gospel of efficiency" in environmentalism, as described by Sam Hays, materialized because of Roosevelt's dissatisfaction with the use of western resources, including water, forests, and mineral rights. In the president's view, states and localities tended to pursue selfish, haphazard, and short-term solutions. Roosevelt thus worked diligently and successfully to promote a more "rational" approach guided by experts, including scientists and professional bureaucrats.

In forest management, for example, Pinchot developed the concept of "sustained yield" forests in the 1890s—that is, the philosophy that annual use should not exceed annual growth. Roosevelt articulated this rationale succinctly in 1901, stating, "The fundamental idea of forestry is the perpetuation of forests by use. Forest protection is not an end in itself; it is a means to increase and sustain the resources of our country and the industries which depend upon them."[27] Pinchot echoed Roosevelt's ideas in his *Primer of Forestry,* published in 1905. Seeing the forest as a "most useful servant of man," Pinchot explained that forests serve when they "sustain and regulate streams, moderate the winds, and beautify the land, but it also supplies wood, the most widely used of all materials."[28] He spent considerable time attempting to train new forestry experts to carry out his ideas. Pinchot's flock of experts, hoping to stabilize the forest industry, studied fire control, use of waste materials, and more efficient ways to utilize wood.[29]

In contrast to conservationists such as Roosevelt and Pinchot, who focused on how natural resources could be used to human beings' best economic advantage, preservationists, led by John Muir, focused on the inherent value of natural resources. Muir and his preservationists saw nature as not only pleasing to the eye but also healing to the human spirit, which had been battered by the increasingly bustling industrial world. They advocated the development of national parks as an antidote to urban evils. Muir stated, "Garden- and park-making goes on everywhere with civilization, for everybody needs beauty as well as bread, places to play in and pray in, where Nature may heal and cheer and give strength to the body and soul. It is impossible to overestimate the value of wild mountains and mountain temples.

They are the greatest of our natural resources."[30] He also noted that "thousands of tired, nerve-shaken, over-civilized people are beginning to find out that going to the mountains is going home; that wildness is a necessity; and that mountain parks and reservations are useful not only as fountains of timber and irrigating rivers, but as fountains of life."[31]

The conservationist versus preservationist argument reached a head during the Hetch Hetchy dam controversy in the early twentieth century. After the disastrous earthquake that hit San Francisco in 1906, the growing city searched desperately for a reliable water source and settled on Hetch Hetchy Valley, which was part of Yosemite National Park. Conservationists such as Pinchot argued that Hetch Hetchy's best or highest purpose would be as a reservoir for San Francisco. Co-opting one of the preservationists' arguments, the conservationists also argued that the dam would provide recreational opportunities for people in the area. Muir and his followers (many of whom were women who had previously sided with Pinchot) opposed the idea, and Muir announced dramatically, "Dam Hetch Hetchy! As well dam for water-tanks the people's cathedrals and churches, for no holier temple has ever been consecrated by the heart of man!"[32] Despite Muir's determined opposition, the conservationists won, and water soon rushed from Hetch Hetchy to San Francisco. The Hetch Hetchy controversy thus demonstrated two early and powerful types of rhetoric: that stressing the value of nature as a commodity or resource to be used by humans, and that stressing the spiritual and aesthetic uses of nature.

As women became increasingly visible in environmental campaigns during the Progressive Era, many men reacted by attempting to merge their activities with contemporary definitions of masculinity. To avoid being labeled "sentimental" in an era filled with insecurities over manliness, men linked their involvement in environmental issues to the male worlds of science and business. Conserving forests, for example, was necessary because it was efficient or would preserve resources or would lead to more productive workers. Birds should be protected not because they were beautiful or sang pretty songs but because they safeguarded the economic interests of farmers by destroying certain insects.[33] Men who adopted so-called sentimental rhetoric were often the object of derision. For instance, cartoons that appeared during the Hetch Hetchy controversy depicted Muir, who advocated preservation of the valley for aesthetic reasons, as a woman with a broom, bonnet, and skirt. The American Forestry Association (AFA) went a step further and attempted to marginalize women directly. After initially incorporating women into the organization as "a kind of grassroots auxiliary to the professional conservation movement," the AFA began to exclude women as it sought to professionalize and become more "scientific."[34]

Implications of Economic Arguments

Elite white men at Love Canal later mimicked Pinchot's economic priorities in the skirmish over revitalization of the neighborhood. Mayor O'Laughlin's primary concerns were his city's dwindling tax base and the adverse effect of the hazardous waste issue on tourism. As they had been during the Progressive Era, men who stood with women in terms of environmental goals tended to be marginalized. O'Laughlin reshuffled the members of LCARA, diluting the voting power and voices of the male resident representatives who argued for increased attention to the health and safety of the residents. After heading off that opposition, O'Laughlin and his allies acted to move people back into the Love Canal area, "revitalizing" its image for tourism and tax purposes.

The working-class men's concern with economic issues also came through clearly. Thomas Heisner's first reaction to the crisis included a call for a mortgage payment strike. Other men expressed considerable anger over falling property values rather than the danger to their families' health. Economic concerns also restrained men from taking action: afraid for their jobs, they refused to speak or act openly at Love Canal.

As another point of comparison, the working-class men faced tremendous amounts of gender-based criticism during Love Canal, as did Muir during the Progressive Era. Harry Gibbs grew increasingly angry over being labeled "Mr. Lois Gibbs." Coworkers chided other men for not being able to keep their wives "in line." Allegations of sexual misconduct aimed at some of the LCHA men abounded. When Ed Pozniak began to spend a lot of time at the LCHA office, several of the women's husbands made veiled allegations of sexual improprieties by Pozniak. Lois Gibbs noted, "It's almost like male jealousy against other males. 'Why is Ed Pozniak always at the office? And what is he doing there?'" other husbands queried.[35]

Both periods—the Progressive Era and the 1970s—demonstrated male language and activism during a time of growing female activism and prominence. Many men of both eras reacted with an environmental activism that emphasized economics, rationality, or efficiency, relying on and reinforcing their roles as breadwinners in the family and leaders in the political world.

Historical Comparisons: Race

Just as the gendered language at Love Canal had important historical precedents, so did the activism of the African American women.[36] Throughout the twentieth century, black women struggled with environmental issues, and they linked those concerns to ongoing efforts to achieve equality and justice for African Americans in general, just as the Griffon Manor women did. One powerful snapshot, illustrating the activism of the National Association of Colored Women (NACW) during the 1950s, demonstrates these precedents.[37]

The NACW's Environmental Activism

The NACW's environmental activism began shortly after the formation of the group in the 1890s. Concerned about pervasive racism directed against African Americans, and particularly African American women, the NACW saw its mission as breaking common stereotypes and empowering women through the motto of "lifting as we climb." Early on, the women of the NACW developed a maternalistic philosophy to justify their activism and move toward the group's overall goals of redeveloping the image of blacks. Emphasizing the importance of the home, the NACW's rhetoric stressed women's duty to create a good home environment and thereby raise moral, honest, thoughtful black men. M. S. Pearson, a contributor to the NACW's newsletter, wrote effervescently that home was "where associations cluster sweet with beautiful memories, where the ills and sorrows of life are borne by mutual effort, and its pleasures equally divided. Where the whole year round is a scene of cheerful and unwearied effort to swell the tide of domestic happiness. Where sweetness breathes as naturally as a wild flower, There, there is home."[38] Beginning in the Progressive Era, the image promoted by the NACW stressed women as "queens" of the home, highly expert in producing a moral, stable environment.[39]

African American women consistently used this concept of the home as a safe place and woman's role as educator to justify their activism in a variety of fields. Believing in the great moral power of the home, the NACW made its reformation a primary goal, especially in the early years. Mary Church Terrell, the first president of the organization, stated, "Believing that it is only through the homes that a people may become really and truly good, the National Association of [C]olored [W]omen has entered this sacred domain, [and] we want better homes."[40] This goal justified higher education for black women, so that they could educate their children effectively and ameliorate the conditions of the city.

The NACW's philosophy of racial uplift and maternalism guided it into many different areas, including environmental activism. Generally, however, these environmental reforms were not considered ends unto themselves. At least partially, the women of the NACW believed that by improving the environment of African Americans, they would alter the image presented to whites, thereby improving their position. Most frequently, they organized cleanup campaigns in African American neighborhoods to spread knowledge of germ theory and eliminate flies, rats, and waste. They also worked toward the humane treatment of animals, planted trees, and established parks in African American areas. Many of the urban struggles revealed the desperately poor situation of many blacks, even those considered more middle class. Entire African American neighborhoods suffered from a lack of sanitation and other city services.

This environmental activism continued during the 1950s when the NACW initiated a nationwide cleanup campaign known as the Community Project Contest (CPC).[41] In 1955, in the midst of the Montgomery bus boycott and the eruption of the national civil rights movement, NACW women launched a nationwide campaign to improve black neighborhoods. Financed through a $50,000 grant from the Sears-Roebuck Foundation, the CPC involved a competition among clubs in the NACW's five regions for the best improvement of an urban neighborhood. Interestingly, this campaign revealed much about the condition of African American neighborhoods long after the NACW made cleanup a priority.

NACW president Irene Gaines was a guiding force in the overall development of the CPC. In justifying the organization's involvement in the project,

Gaines and the NACW expressed considerable concern "about the problems of children." This included worries about "the general health and well being of underprivileged citizens caused very often by poor living standards involving bad housing, ill health, malnutrition, . . . [and a lack of basic] education, employment and recreation."[42] In encouraging local clubs to enter the contest, Gaines wrote, "We see all about us the ugly spread of housing decay and erosion. Houses are weather beaten, dilapidated, and decadent. Clusters of such houses are breeding grounds for crime, delinquency, and demoralized lives." In addition to this moral reasoning, Gaines again emphasized a maternalistic justification for neighborhood improvement: "The greatest prize of all in this contest—a prize that every participating Club can win—is the better neighborhood you can develop for yourselves and your children."[43]

Gaines's background included activism aimed at housing problems. In 1932, President Herbert Hoover appointed her to sit as a member of his Conference on Housing. A social worker by training and education, she also served as a caseworker for the Cook County (Chicago) Bureau of Public Welfare. Gaines visited and gathered information from more than 2,000 homes during her tenure, later testifying before both the city and state legislatures to push for passage of a slum clearance bill and funding. In addition, Gaines participated in numerous housing groups, including the Southside Housing and Planning Council of Chicago and the Chicago Women's Joint Committee on Adequate Housing.[44]

Many common threads acted to pull Gaines and the NACW into the CPC during the mid-1950s, but the successful completion of the project was far from easy. The initial concept of a national neighborhood improvement project began in May 1953 under Gaines's auspices in Los Angeles; this included discussions with the Bryant and Ford foundations.[45] The origins of the project also drew from Gaines's experiences during a 1954 tour of the Southwest, where she visited local and regional clubs along the way. Although she had certainly encountered poor living conditions in Chicago, her view from the window of the train during this trip reinforced the widespread problem of substandard living conditions among African Americans. In addition, she began to recognize the national character of housing problems to a larger and more personal degree.[46]

The Sears-Roebuck Foundation intended the first year of the contest to be a pilot program. In each of the five regions of the NACW, the club chose a representative area: Washington, D.C., from the northeast region, California from the southwest region, Alabama from the southeast region, Washington from the northwest region, and Illinois from the central region. If these pilot programs were successful, Sears would "extend [the project] to include the participation of our club women in every state" where the NACW existed.[47]

A brochure sent to the various regional offices described the prizes, numerous examples of the types of projects that could be undertaken (all with environmental overtones), and the judging criteria. The prize money offered a significant incentive to clubs: the winner in each region would receive $1,500, down to a fourth prize of $250. In addition, the overall grand-prize winner, to be selected from the regional winners, would receive $5,000.[48]

Projects could include the renovation of homes—either outside or inside. The local women's clubs could form committees to organize the residents and plan for "major and minor repairs; for replacement of windows, doors, porch railings, roofs, floors, ceilings and all outside renovations." They could also "organize and work with the housewives of selected areas in interior paint-up, clean-up, and home decorations" or hold neighborhood how-to clinics on various topics, including do-it-yourself household renovations or improvements, zoning requirements, or the best types of plants to use in landscaping projects. Backyards could be cleaned "on a block basis to remove trash, and accumulations of discarded furniture, ashes, and old paper." Women might involve youth groups in antilitter campaigns, clearing vacant lots for a playground or providing garbage cans to residents.[49]

Owing to a lack of leadership and financial improprieties by the first project director, the CPC foundered severely and accomplished little during the original grant period. Gaines saw this as a source of tremendous embarrassment to the NACW. The NACW's failure to take advantage of the opportunity provided by Sears, which had bestowed the largest grant ever given to a black women's organization, would certainly not reflect positively on either black women or African Americans in general.[50] Gaines forced the resignation of the first project director, and Sears eventually agreed to extend the project for an extra two months to 31 March 1957, but it refused to grant additional funding.[51] Gaines hired Ora Brown Stokes Perry to lead the faltering program in mid-November 1956. Perry had a long history of pioneering activism, including being the first black lawyer appointed as a probation officer in Richmond, Virginia, and being a field-worker for the Women's Christian Temperance Union.[52]

After attempting to rebuild the Sears Foundation's faith, Perry revitalized the program with personal visits to each of the project states. During these visits, she noted that black women were not only actively engaged in valuable renewal and cleanup activities but also involved in improving interracial relations in some areas. In Los Angeles, for example, under the energetic leadership of Gertrude Reece Hicks, the local NACW club enlisted the assistance of many governmental officials. "Here the Mayor, the City Council, civic, religious, educational and welfare agencies . . . [joined Hicks] in the all-out effort to free their city of dirt and smog and make it really 'A city of the Angels,' as the name Los Angeles implies." Los Angeles women planned a community center to serve all races and nationalities in the area, which, Perry stated, "when completed, will be one of the most imposing community centers in the United States."[53]

Many of the projects, especially those involving city services, vividly illustrated the discrepancies between white and minority neighborhoods. In Longview, Washington, Perry described a triracial alliance of blacks, Hispanics, and Native Americans "united for the one central purpose of building a better community. They have joined with the Association women in laying the sidewalks and having the streets paved." In Birmingham, Alabama, Perry witnessed racial tensions "beyond all human belief" between blacks and whites. However, she also saw African Americans willing to work for themselves and develop "a new sense of personal dignity and pride in their own accomplishments." The Birmingham project also illustrated the unequal distribution of city services across the South. Inadequate city laws pertaining to garbage removal forced club women to take action. "On a certain date," Perry described, "they turned out enmasse and removed all of the old, battered, dirty garbage cans from their premises, thus pointing up the need for better sanitary laws. This seemed like a simple project, but when one realizes that these dirty garbage cans are the gathering places of millions of flies and mosquitoes which are the carriers of malaria, typhoid and tuberculosis; one can readily see how important this project was to the people of that Southern City, and to any neighborhood so infected with pests and pollution."[54] The Birmingham project demonstrated the continuing importance of basic public health issues to black women.

Final judging of the project took place at national headquarters in New York between 6 and 12 May 1957, with the winner announced by Sears representative Harry Osgood at a dinner held on 1 June 1957. Each of the winning projects revealed middle- and lower-class black women's deep concern for local environmental issues. Tuscaloosa, Alabama, took that state's first prize. Club women there began the process of improving the sanitary conditions in their city through both cleanup projects and additional city services. They removed "unsanitary and disease-breeding hog pens" from their neighborhood, replacing them with "attractive vegetable and flower gardens." At the individual level, efforts at "home improvement and general community beautification" included the repair of walks and driveways, landscaping, and tree planting projects. The project also included cooperation with city officials to install sewers to replace the open drainage ditches still in use and to make the streets more usable.[55]

The Los Angeles first-prize winner brought the plight of one black neighborhood to the attention of the entire city. After developing heavy grassroots support for improvements in the Naomi Street area, the women's project intrigued the City Health Department, the City Planning Commission, the Parks and Recreation Department, the Building and Safety Division, the Fire Department, the city relocation manager, state assemblymen, and the mayor's office. The city government eventually decided to use the African American neighborhood as a test project for urban renewal efforts in the entire city.[56] Gertrude Hicks received a special plaque from the national organization, commending her role in "the emergence of Negro Clubwomen as major factors in improving neighborhoods on a very wide scale, and for her intensified efforts to change for the better certain sections of the city of Los Angeles, bringing to the attention of the Mayor and city officials the plight of persons living in blight infected neighborhoods."[57]

Chicago women earned a prize with a Progressive-style neighborhood cleanup in which children and others assisted in a "transformation campaign from the alley through the house to the front yard." In addition, women encouraged action from both landlords and tenants. As did some of the other projects, the level of improvement in Chicago shed light on the poor living conditions and lack of basic services that many minorities had to accept. Part of the problem, the activists felt, stemmed from "absentee landlords [who] refused to provide decent housing for tenants—no stairways in the rear, no lights at times, no water at times, panes of glass broken out of windows, apartments and kitchenettes infected with vermin. . . . Landlords were asked to clean up—paint up—and fix up. Porches and windows were repaired and tenants were encouraged to keep their windows spic and span." In addition, club women encouraged the tenants "to keep yards planted in grass and flowers and to make the landscape around their dwellings more beautiful."[58]

The winner in Washington, D.C., focused on renovations to a local house. In addition, it participated in the "Clean Up—Good Behavior Campaign" from April to November 1956. Participants emphasized the removal of litter and went door-to-door to deliver 4,500 pamphlets describing how to beautify one's house and neighborhood. The women enlisted community support and participation, asking residents for "written complaints of any bad health, housing, street and other conditions which were dragging their neighborhood down from high standards of living." In addition, "community blight was attacked through neighborhood workshops. Residents were asked to keep the slum from their doors."[59]

The Longview, Washington, group won both the northwestern regional prize and the national grand prize. Victoria Freeman, president of the Longview Woman's Study Club, initiated, organized, and energized the widespread campaign in her neighborhood. Longview had long suffered from neglected or nonexistent services from the white urban government, including "dusty, muddy streets, trash-filled alleys, overgrown vacant lots and other eyesores and inconveniences." The women initially began an intensive cleanup campaign to remove garbage from the neighborhood alleys, but control of the street dust quickly rose to the top of their list of necessary improvements. One woman lamented, "It is so dusty here you can't even sit out on your porch in the evening." Freeman led the study club before the city council to petition for "local improvement district" status for road and sidewalk paving. Mayor H. R. Nichols refused the request for concrete streets because of the low tax value of the homes in the area, but he and the city engineer suggested that a "light bituminous surface (two shot oil) could be applied to the streets for $16 a lot if the City Council would approve" it. When residents requested the improvements for Seventh, Eighth, Ninth, Delaware, and Douglas streets, the city set the price tag at $1,845. Undaunted, the women raised the money by holding turkey and ham dinners. Although most of these events took place at private residences, including Freeman's, restaurants also began to order from the women, who eventually served more than 1,000 meals. The Longview project spurred other improvements, such as the addition of concrete sidewalks and funding to begin work on the "installation of drainage facilities" in the area.[60]

Although Sears failed to renew the project, the NACW proudly touted the accomplishments of the club women in each of the five regions. National publications especially recognized the Longview club for its contributions. The 1959 national brochure presented Longview as an example of what a small number of women could do with drive and determination. "A single club of 10 women in Longview, Washington changed the complexion of a whole town, winning prizes totaling $6,500.00."[61]

These examples demonstrate that environmental reforms remained a vital component of black women's activism during the early civil rights movement. In addition, the NACW's activism during the 1950s achieved some significant results. Members brought issues to the attention of local governments and obtained some hard-fought concessions and benefits through the increased activity and prominence of the concurrent civil rights movement.

Implications of 1950s Activism

The NACW's activism exhibited several similarities with that of African American women at Love Canal. Both groups, marginalized by pervasive racism, used environmental activism to promote racial equality. Of course, in the 1950s, overt racism and segregation existed in both the North and the South and was either legal or at least socially accepted. In the 1950s, segregation also meant that blacks continued to live in deeply degraded areas that lacked even the most basic city services provided to whites.

The NACW members encountered racism on a daily basis through the administration of the CPC, just as the Griffon Manor women did in their attempts to obtain relief. The attitudes of Sears representative Harry Osgood, who oversaw the NACW program, reflected the racist realities of 1950s America. He noted, "Everybody gains from participation in the project," which included improvements in "civic outlook, personal living, [and] acceptance of responsibility." Project secretary Marion Jackson observed that, according to Osgood, "one thing that the Negro needs is development of responsibility. Many have reached greater economic levels but have not reached the point that they take pride in [things] other than pride in expensive automobiles

[and] flashy clothes." Black people, Osgood told the women, needed the project to develop a sense of responsibility and improve their poor living conditions.[62] Despite completely ignoring racism and the systemic marginalization of blacks as causes of their predicament, Osgood's diatribe may have appealed to the NACW's rhetoric of self-help and image making.[63]

In the Progressive Era and the 1950s, the women of the NACW saw their environmental work as part of an effort to change the image of blacks in general and African American women in particular in the minds of many Americans. For example, during the Progressive Era, NACW women squared their activities neatly within the context of Booker T. Washington's plan for racial uplift and within their own interpretation of the value of the mother's role in the home. The NACW never explicitly criticized the U.S. government or overtly blamed whites for blacks' environmental woes. Instead, they chose to frame their activism, which clearly fit into a civil rights mold, in a safer way. Legitimately concerned for their physical safety and the integrity of their organization, members of the NACW framed their activism as African American women's empowerment and improvement. But, as with white women's activism during the Progressive Era, the NACW's activism in the 1950s must be evaluated in the context of the period. Despite the seemingly "conservative" language on both race and gender issues, black women forced the issue of racial equality and a public role for women when American society harbored no such illusions.

The women of Griffon Manor clearly and explicitly linked their struggle (and the lack of progress) to racism as well. As quoted earlier, one African American woman succinctly stated, "They [politicians] don't care. Mostly black people live in these projects, what do they care? Kill them all (laugh)."[64] Women at Griffon Manor pressed for inclusion regardless of race, and they certainly accepted notions of equality and the criticism of American society espoused by the civil rights movement of the 1950s and 1960s. This more overt and explicit critique of whites, politicians, and society in general indicated a shift for African Americans to a more accepted place in society by the 1970s. The addition of this type of critique can be seen as a major accomplishment of the civil rights movement: the black women of Griffon Manor felt secure in their critique, whereas the NACW women did not. Although the language of the groups differed, the overall result was the same: the groups used environmental activism as a way to combat their subordinate status in society. They both accepted and promoted an inclusive view of who should receive environmental benefits.

Because of their marginalization in society, success in their respective endeavors required outside support. The NACW relied on a grant from Sears-Roebuck to promote and implement the Community Project Contest nationally among its member clubs. Without the funding and incentives from the grant, the NACW lacked the resources to support the scope of such a project. During Love Canal, with their voices on the verge of being silenced, the African American women of Griffon Manor reached out to the NAACP's local chapter and to the ETF for assistance in their efforts.

In contrast to this similarity in goals and support, the results of the activism of African American women in the two periods varied. Although the CPC was a nationwide effort on a larger scale than anything attempted during the Progressive Era, all the results remained local. The NACW's local groups at least gained the attention of some local politicians and bureaucrats, but no nationwide environmental law, regulation, or movement emerged from their activism. The concerns of the African American renters at Love Canal failed to be transmitted outside their own area by the African American press, and local elites largely ignored their concerns. However, on a wider scale, after the torrent of activism within the civil rights movement over the next two decades, results for African Americans became more national. Beginning in 1982, the issue of "environmental racism" burst onto the national scene. Activists openly linked the pervasiveness of poverty and racism with excess environmental harm, as had the Griffon Manor women a few years earlier. This new awareness culminated in an order by President Bill Clinton to include considerations of environmental justice in governmental decision making. Both the NACW and the Griffon Manor women reflected the ideas of environmental justice, yet national results, recognition, and solutions needed the foundation of the civil rights movement to gain wider support.

Historical Comparisons: Class

Within the ETF, the decidedly middle-class group at Love Canal, activists adopted a more encompassing view of the problem of hazardous waste. Rather than simply seeing the problem as "in their backyard," the ETF members connected their activism to an environmental and ecological outlook.

They also stressed a more inclusive view of the situation than did most of the working class, pressing for all elements of the neighborhood including the poor African Americans, to receive the same level of benefits. Other middle-class activism over the twentieth century serves as points of both comparison and contrast with the activism at Love Canal. Here, a snapshot from the early 1960s involving a middle-class women's group involved in the peace movement is useful.

Middle-Class Activism in the 1960s

While the NACW members worked for clean streets and garbage pickup, middle-class white women across the country began an environmental campaign of a different sort. In the late 1950s and early 1960s, a loosely organized group of women known as Women Strike for Peace (WSP) emerged. WSP's concerns centered around the health implications of the continued testing of hydrogen bombs, as well as the implications of the nuclear arms race raging between the Soviet Union and the United States. Women's groups were an important part of the wave of antinuclear activism during the late 1950s and early 1960s, especially at the grassroots level.[65] As they had in other periods, women developed rhetoric stressing their roles as mothers and housewives to move beyond the strict gender-defined confines of the 1950s into the public sphere.[66] WSP members proved to be adept at this tactic and helped prod the Kennedy administration into signing a ban on atmospheric testing of atomic and hydrogen bombs in 1963.

Although WSP lacked a formal leadership structure, Dagmar Wilson played an important role in the formation and leadership of the new group. Wilson and WSP also demonstrated a broad perspective on environmental problems, linking the environment to other issues, as the ETF would in the next decade. Concerned by the effects of nuclear weapons (starting with the first detonation of an atomic bomb in 1945), Wilson attended a lecture by psychiatrist Jerome Frank. In a talk that resonated deeply with the young woman, Frank noted that a society that had built the bomb should be able to construct a lasting peace. Wilson immediately joined a local chapter of the National Committee for a Sane Nuclear Policy (SANE) but quickly became disillusioned. She disliked the group's exclusionary policy toward communists, as well as its male-dominated hierarchy. She also became enraged when SANE failed to act against the jailing of Bertrand Russell for his antinuclear activities. SANE's inaction on issues affecting children, especially the contamination of milk by strontium 90, further incensed Wilson and drove her to additional efforts.[67]

In 1961, Wilson and a few friends had been "sitting in her garden" discussing events, including the atomic bomb, when they decided to send a chain letter across the country to initiate nationwide urban demonstrations.[68] Several days later, a small group gathered again at Wilson's home. She stated, "We were worried. We were indignant. We were angry. The Soviet Union and the U.S.A. were accusing each other of having broken a moratorium on nuclear testing. What matter who broke it when everyone's children would fall victim to radioactive Strontium 90? . . . Perhaps, we told ourselves that night, in the face of male 'logic,' which seemed to us utterly illogical, it was time for women to speak out."[69]

Lawrence Scott, a member of SANE who was present at the meeting, suggested that the women begin a peace strike.[70] Part of their impetus came from the civil rights movement, which had gained some successes by the early 1960s. But, Wilson said, "We had to do something that was different from any other gestures of this kind that had been made. . . . You know they had the sit-ins and the walks and the rides and everything else you could think of, and it took us quite a long time before this idea struck us."[71] They decided to hold a nationwide strike focused on the health effects of nuclear fallout.

On 1 November 1961, a collie named Candy carried a sign during a demonstration in Washington, D.C., that read, "No More Strontium 90." Candy walked patiently from the Washington Monument to the White House to the Soviet embassy behind her mistress, Mrs. John P. Hall, along with approximately 500 other women and children. Before beginning their march, the women gathered to listen to a speech by Methodist minister Henry Hitt Crane and to hear actress Faye Emerson read Tennyson's poem "Locksley Hall." At the White House, they presented a petition, signed by approximately 1,000 women, intended for first lady Jacqueline Kennedy. The group gave an identical petition to officials at the Soviet embassy to be forwarded to the wife of Soviet premier Nikita Khrushchev. A delegation of four women gained access to the Soviet embassy and spoke for almost an hour with first secretary Botislav Borisov as well as two women, a cultural attaché and a teacher at the Soviet embassy school.[72]

The Washington strike was not an isolated event. Across the country, in many major urban centers, women protested and presented petitions indicating their desire for peace and a halt to further nuclear testing. In New York, between 300 and 400 women protested at the building housing the Soviets' United Nations delegation and at the Atomic Energy Commission's office. As in Washington, the group delivered letters with their demands to both the Soviet and American sides. Six women, accompanied by two children, met with second secretary Vladimir Filatov, who listened to their requests and promised to relay their messages to Khrushchev. Chicago's protest included about 1,000 women: 600 in suburban Winnetka sent letters and telegrams to leaders of both the United States and the Soviet Union, as well as other public officials, and the rest participated in a march downtown. In Los Angeles, about 2,000 women journeyed from City Hall to the Federal Building. In Sacramento, women gained an audience with a supportive Governor Edmund Brown, who declared, "I hope your message rings round the world." In Cleveland, a small group of about 50 women gathered to protest and pass out information to passersby; this demonstration included an appearance by the wife of millionaire Cyrus Eaton. In Watertown, Massachusetts, about 500 people, including Harvard and Brandeis students, marched from Cambridge to Waltham. Several dozen women paid a visit to Colorado governor Steve McNichols's office in Denver, as well as to both senators from the state.[73]

The *New York Times* reported similar demonstrations in "twenty or more" cities, including "Newark and Elizabeth, N.J.; Albany, Syracuse, Ithaca and other New York cities; Detroit, Chicago, Los Angeles, San Francisco and elsewhere across the country." *Newsweek* included Cincinnati, St. Paul, Boston, Ann Arbor, and "many suburban communities."[74] Deep South cities were notably absent, perhaps because of racial preoccupations in the region. The day of the strike was also the deadline for the removal of all signs segregating bus terminals in the nation, by order of the Interstate Commerce Commission.[75]

Despite being labeled a peace march, the November 1961 demonstration and WSP's other activities to reduce the threat of nuclear annihilation included significant elements of environmental concern, particularly over the effects of strontium 90. Strontium 90, a radioactive element produced in thermonuclear explosions, rises high into the atmosphere after the detonation of an atomic device and then falls to earth through precipitation.

Because of its chemical similarities to calcium, once strontium 90 is in the soil, plants tend to absorb it like calcium; it then moves through the food chain into animal meat, milk, and vegetables. The radioactive isotope has been linked to various types of cancer.[76]

Candy the dog's "No More Strontium 90" sign joined numerous other placards in the November protest, emphasizing a concern for children and their health. One New York marcher "in a powder-blue suit" carried a sign reading "Children Need Milk Strontium-Free." Another woman's poster, in the shape of a milk bottle capped by a skull, linked contaminated milk to deformities with the simple message, "Milk Death Disease Deformity." In New York, signs read "All Children Are Threatened by Fallout" and "My Child Wants to Be a Parent Too."[77] A Watertown woman made a more dramatic appeal based on the same theme: she placed a sign around her daughter's neck that read, "I want to be a mommy someday."[78] One activist, Blanche Posner, explained that the strike was intimately connected to women's roles as mothers and concern for their children's health. "When they were putting their breakfast on the table," she stated, "they saw not only Wheaties and milk, but they also saw strontium 90 and iodine 131. . . . They feared for the health and life of their children."[79]

WSP proved effective at directing and organizing women's concerns about strontium 90. Milk contamination and children's health remained a high priority. Immediately after the November strike, participants in the main Washington group organized the Committee on Radiation Problems "to deal with the problem of milk that had been contaminated by nuclear fallout from the Russian tests."[80] This committee, led by Jeanne Bagby (one of the original founders of WSP, along with Wilson), gathered and disseminated information to be used across the country. Committee information also proved useful for lobbying. In early 1962, President Kennedy and Abraham Ribicoff, secretary of health, education, and welfare, received a memorandum from the committee "expressing profound concern about radiation hazards and demanding that radiological monitoring be improved."[81] The committee stuck to a maternalistic rationale for its activism and the measures it advocated. "As mothers whose children may become expendable through a statistical approach, we feel that current protective measures may not be adequate, especially in consideration of the overall cumulative effect," the report stated.[82]

In addition to lobbying, women resorted to threats of boycotts or other consumer tactics, effectively placing pure milk at the forefront of their campaign with the slogan "Pure Milk Not Poison." Some women chose to boycott milk during nuclear testing periods, while others stockpiled powdered milk in an attempt to avoid radiation dangers. Their efforts also included demands for dairies, milk processors, the Department of Agriculture, and Congress to develop counterradiation measures to purify milk and for the government to end atmospheric tests.[83]

WSP continued marching, demonstrating, and lobbying against nuclear weapons through 1962 and 1963. Along with numerous other groups across the nation and around the world, WSP applauded the ratification of the U.S.-Soviet Treaty Banning Nuclear Weapons Tests in the Atmosphere, in Outer Space, and Underwater.[84] Kennedy credited the women's rhetoric with influencing his thinking about nuclear issues; he accepted the women's activism and used their maternalistic definition of the problem publicly. Shortly before his assassination, he stated, "I have said that control of arms is a mission that we undertake for our children and our grandchildren, and that they have no lobby in Washington. No one is better qualified to represent their interests than the mothers and grandmothers of America."[85] Women realized that the treaty was only a partial success, as underground testing continued, but they recognized it as a step forward and continued to work toward a complete ban. By 1963, however, WSP turned from antinuclear issues to one that it considered more pressing: the war in Vietnam.[86]

Implications of 1960s Middle-Class Activism

This snapshot of middle-class white women's activism in the 1960s has some similarities with the ETF's activism at Love Canal. Both the ETF and WSP, for example, sought to include previously ignored or marginalized populations and recognized the wider scope of environmental issues. Class status explains these fundamental similarities, especially the benefits of higher education. For the ETF, racial and class issues registered prominently. Sister Margeen Hoffmann explicitly connected environmental problems with poverty, both nationally and internationally. The ETF focused on helping the African Americans affected by Love Canal and sharing their plight with lawmakers and white elites. In contrast, WSP failed to make race or class an integral part of its environmental activism.[87] Perhaps this neglect stemmed from a general belief that the problems of strontium 90 transcended racial and class lines, affecting populations randomly and universally. Perhaps, too, the civil rights movement still had a lot of work to do, and racial and class issues simply failed to register among these middle-class white women.

Despite a lack of explicit support for the poor or African Americans, WSP existed within a framework of social justice, as did the ETF. Wilson's entire motivation for the formation of WSP centered around her anger over SANE's exclusion of communists and its failure to act for children's health. She fervently believed that a reaction against nuclear weapons and fallout must be inclusive, regardless of political affiliation or age. In addition, WSP worked expressly for the inclusion of women as full participants in the political process at a time when society still emphasized women's role within the home. WSP dramatically challenged gender rules through a safe avenue, advocating a role for women as experts in the science of nuclear fallout and its health effects. Shortly after the November strike, women from the New York metropolitan area stated, "We know that we have no role if it is not to work unsparingly for the future of our children and we wish to be as competent, as resourceful and as equipped as possible in the pursuance of this work."[88]

WSP's refusal to deny communists membership led to suspicion and investigation by the House Un-American Activities Committee (HUAC) in December 1963.[89] Several participants in WSP testified at HUAC hearings "to determine whether Communists are exerting influence upon the so-called 'peace movement' in a manner and degree affecting the national security."[90] WSP participants refused to be intimidated by the committee members. Speaking over or interrupting the congressmen, several women provided insight into their rationale for participating in the movement. When asked whether she had participated in any WSP strikes, one woman set the congressmen back on their heels by stating emphatically, "I am sure I must have. Whenever I saw a crowd of women with signs saying, 'We don't want any more poison in our babies' milk,' I would drop whatever I was doing and go and walk with them."[91]

Others attempted to explain to HUAC members that their pacifist leanings had originated in nonthreatening sources. One woman stated firmly, "You don't quite understand the nature of this movement. This movement was inspired and motivated by mothers' love for their children. . . . They feared for the health and life of their children. That is the only possible motivation." The congressmen should be grateful for WSP's attempts to halt nuclear testing, the woman continued, since "every nuclear test has resulted in malformations, has resulted in stillbirths, has resulted in leukemia, has resulted in cancer, has resulted in the possibility of a nuclear holocaust."[92] As well as trying to persuade the legislators to join their cause, others attempted to portray the HUAC members as men who denigrated not only free speech but also healthy, safe children. One woman sparred verbally with the red-baiters, stating, "I think that this [hearing] is an attempt to prevent me and other people from exercising our rights to speak as women for peace and to protect our children."[93] WSP members saw their activism as part of their citizenship rights and pressed for their right to be heard in political society. Although they did not directly address racial issues, WSP members, using their status as wives and mothers, worked to bring women, children, and health concerns into the national debate over nuclear weapons.

Educational levels, tied to class status, certainly affected the extent to which these women incorporated inclusiveness into their activism. Armed with college educations, most of them readily grasped the basic level of science needed to promote their viewpoint, leading them to see a wider scope to the problem. WSP members became well versed, for example, in the life cycle of heavy radioactive metals. Similarly, the ETF sought to include the African American renters in the solution, and it connected the hazardous waste at Love Canal to similar problems in a much wider geographic area. In addition, the ETF saw the ecological and environmental implications at Love Canal more clearly and explicitly than did the working-class whites. The high educational levels of the women involved in these struggles gave them the necessary foundation to grasp and negotiate through these complex national issues.

Conclusions

Love Canal is one of the most discussed and influential case studies in environmental history. Yet with all the discussion, certain elements have been overlooked. First, the differences in gendered language and activism are more fluid than traditionally seen. The women at Love Canal certainly used a language that stressed the health of their children, but some also emphasized economic concerns. Far from being absent, male involvement included maintaining busy households and persuading unions to offer assistance. Men tended to be most concerned with economic issues, but some pushed for the same health-centered goals as the women. The gendered activism at Love Canal also revealed varying views on gender roles themselves: women tended to accept more goals of the women's movement than men did, but they explicitly rejected feminism through their activism. On this same theme, the women certainly pressed for privileges based on the rights of American citizenship and taxpayer status. The extent of working-class absorption of ideas about racial equality also differed by gender: men tended to accept far less expansion of roles for minorities than women did, and they pressed for less inclusion in solutions.

Race and class also played a role. Race proved to be a thorny issue at Love Canal. Distinctly marginalized from all sides, the African American women at Griffon Manor turned to the local NAACP chapter and the ETF for assistance. They directly connected their activism with the civil rights movement's goals of equality and citizenship and contested the racism present in the area. Class distinctions in activism also became apparent and were directly tied to educational level. The ETF, a middle-class group, absorbed more of the values of the environmental movement than did the working class. It articulated a well-thought-out, complex rationale for involvement, including elements of both theology and ecology. The ETF proved to have very inclusive ideas about solutions to the crisis; it assisted the poor African American renters as readily and enthusiastically as it did the working-class whites at Love Canal. ETF members refused to accept violence and continued to work within the system to benefit the residents. The more frustrated, marginalized working-class group, in contrast, commonly resorted to threats of violence and even kidnapped two EPA officials.

Finally, Love Canal's activism has a rich, storied history. Women espoused maternalistic language throughout the twentieth century, just as men used economic justifications for their activism. African American women's activism continued to be distinctly marginalized, and they required outside help from groups closer to the power elite to achieve wider success. Middle-class activism historically demonstrated an absorption of national-level issues regarding the environment. Middle-class and white environmental activism also tended to produce higher-level results, such as national legislation or attention rather than neighborhood solutions.

Significant details lurk beneath the surface of the standard story of Love
Canal. Environmental activism reveals much about the importance of race,
class, and gender in American society, and it is a lens by which to examine the absorption of larger social movements within the general population
and people's views about larger concepts.

NOTES

INTRODUCTION

1. Several sources provide detailed accounts of Love Canal. Lois Gibbs has published her own firsthand account of the struggle. See Lois Gibbs, *Love Canal: The Story Continues . . .* , 20th anniversary rev. ed. (Stony Creek, Conn.: New Society Publishers, 1998). Michael Brown, a reporter for the *Niagara Gazette* during the crisis, published his account in *Laying Waste: The Poisoning of America by Toxic Chemicals* (New York: Washington Square Press Publications, 1979). Adeline Levine tells the story from the perspective of an on-site sociologist in *Love Canal: Science, Politics, and People* (Lexington, Mass.: D. C. Heath, 1982). Allan Mazur examines the validity of several sides of the story in *A Hazardous Inquiry: The Rashomon Effect at Love Canal* (Cambridge, Mass.: Harvard University Press, 1998). In "Making Environmental Politics: Women and Love Canal Activism" (*Women's Studies Quarterly* 29 [Summer 2001]: 65–84), Rich Newman also examines differences from a "standard" or "textbook" story of Love Canal by placing women's activism at the center of change. Both Levine and Mazur also note the pivotal importance of women's activism in the crisis. For a description of hazardous waste science and disposal prior to Love Canal, see Craig E. Colten and Peter N. Skinner, *The Road to Love Canal: Managing Industrial Waste before EPA* (Austin: University of Texas Press, 1996).
2. Gibbs, *Love Canal*, 1.
3. Lois Gibbs, transcript of telephone interview by author, 19 April 2002, Falls Church, Va., 21–23, 34.
4. Ann Hillis, transcript of telephone interview by author, 29 May 2002, Florida, 2.
5. When I use the term *race*, I am referring to its cultural construction rather than suggesting some sort of innate biological difference. I use the terms *black* and *African American* interchangeably.
6. See, for example, Levine, *Love Canal*. Mazur, *Hazardous Inquiry*, also neglects gender issues. Many of the residents also saw the struggle in these terms. For example, see Gibbs interview, 17–18.
7. Sources spell Griffon (or Griffin) Manor inconsistently. I have chosen to use *Griffon*. Griffon Manor is also referred to as the LaSalle Development in some sources.
8. For some recent studies that deal with these issues in a more general sense, see Phil Brown and Lois Gibbs, *Toxic Exposures: Contested Illnesses and the Environmental Health Movement* (New York: Columbia University Press, 2007); Jason Corburn, *Street Science: Community Knowledge and Environmental Health Justice* (Cambridge, Mass.: MIT Press, 2005); Julie Sze, *Noxious New York: The Racial Politics of Urban Health and Environmental Justice* (Cambridge, Mass.: MIT Press, 2006).

CHAPTER 1: HISTORICAL SNAPSHOTS OF THE LOVE CANAL AREA

1. Susan Wattle, transcript of telephone interview by author, 5 June 2001, New York, 22–24.

2. Kathleen DeLaney, "Disaster at Niagara Falls: Love Canal: Neighborhood Crisis, Worldwide Legacy," *Mid-Atlantic Archivist* 31, no. 3 (summer 2002): 7; Josh Barbanel, "At Love Canal, Some Hope to Start Over," *New York Times,* 17 May 1982.; "Love Canal Education and Interpretive Center," AKRF Web site, http://www .akrf.com/Projects/Medical_Cultural_Ed/project_love_canal.html (accessed 13 November 2006).

3. Linda Schneekloth, "Love Canal Education and Interpretation Center," e-mail correspondence with author, 30 July 2006.

4. "Strong Opposition Voiced to Love Canal Museum Proposal," *Environmental News,* 15 July 2001, http://www.lockport-ny.com/enviro.htm (accessed 26 July 2006); S. K. Brown, "Seeing Red: Love among the Ruins? Forget about It and Move On," *Niagara Falls Reporter,* 29 January 2002, http://www.niagarafalls reporter.com/skbrown25.html (accessed 26 July 2006).

5. Wattle interview, 24.

6. Michael Vogel, *Echoes in the Mist: An Illustrated History of the Niagara Falls Area* (n.p.: Windsor Publications, 1991), 17. For additional histories of Niagara Falls, see Pierre Berton, *Niagara: A History of the Falls* (Toronto: McClelland and Stewart, 1992); Ralph Greenhill and Thomas Mahoney, *Niagara* (Toronto: University of Toronto Press, 1969); and Margaret Dunn, *Niagara Falls: A Pictorial Journey,* photography by Michael D. Romanowich (Niagara Falls, N.Y.: M. Dunn, 1998).

7. Louis Hennepin, *A New Discovery of a Vast Country in America* [1678], vol. 1, ed. Reuben Gold Thwaites (Chicago: AC McClung, 1903), 54, 55, http://www.ameri canjourneys.org/aj-124a (accessed 26 July 2006).

8. Ibid., 40–41.

9. Ibid., 46, 57.

10. Ibid., 44.

11. Ibid., 80–88; quotes from 80, 83.

12. Ibid., 89–95.

13. Ibid., 80, 89–95.

14. Vogel, *Echoes in the Mist,* 32–37, 61–79; Michael Brown, *Laying Waste: The Poisoning of America by Toxic Chemicals* (New York: Washington Square Press Publications, 1979), 14.

15. Vogel, *Echoes in the Mist,* 65–76.

16. Ibid., 148, 132, 162, 134–135.

17. Alfred Runte, *National Parks: The American Experience,* 3rd ed. (Lincoln: University of Nebraska Press, 1997), 7.

18. Olmsted quoted in ibid., 9; see also 5–9, 59.

19. Allan Mazur, *A Hazardous Inquiry: The Rashomon Effect at Love Canal* (Cambridge, Mass.: Harvard University Press, 1998), 8–9.

20. Martha Kendall, *The Erie Canal* (Washington, D.C.: National Geographic, 2005); George Svejda, *Irish Immigrant Participation and the Construction of the Erie Canal* (Washington, D.C.: U.S. Office of Archeology and Historic Preservation, 1969); Linda Thompson, *The Erie Canal* (Vero Beach, Fla.: Rourke, 2005).

21. Brown, *Laying Waste,* 8. Love's canal may have been doomed even without the depression of 1893. Nikola Tesla soon developed alternating current, which, as opposed to direct current, allowed the power source to be used much farther from its place of generation. In addition, Congress passed a law protecting the falls from water loss and thus from schemes like Love's that would have diverted the flow. See Adeline Levine, *Love Canal: Science, Politics, and People* (Lexington, Mass.: D. C. Heath, 1982), 9.

22. Brown, *Laying Waste,* 8; Mazur, *Hazardous Inquiry,* 19–20.

23. David Pollack, "Family Recalls Fires at Hooker Dump," *Niagara Gazette,* 5 June 1977, 1.

24. Ibid. Brown details the Schroeders' and their extended family's problems in *Laying Waste,* 4–7.

25. Brown, *Laying Waste,* 5; Levine, *Love Canal,* 10.

26. Deed filed in Niagara County, 6 July 1953, quoted in Levine, *Love Canal,* 11; Brown, *Laying Waste,* 8–10.

27. Levine, *Love Canal,* 12; Brown, *Laying Waste,* 10.

28. Brown, *Laying Waste,* 8; Mazur, *Hazardous Inquiry,* 9–14.

29. Edmund Pozniak, transcript of telephone interview by author, 4 June 2001, Grand Island, N.Y., 4; Barbara Quimby, transcript of telephone interview by author, 6 June 2001, Grand Island, N.Y., 9; Luella Kenny, transcript of telephone interview by author, 18 July 2001, Grand Island, N.Y., 6; Deborah Curry (formerly Cerrillo), transcript of telephone interview by author, 29 January 2002, Holley, N.Y., 12.

30. Pozniak interview, 4; Quimby interview, 7; Lois Gibbs, transcript of telephone interview by author, 19 April 2002, Falls Church, Va., 8.

31. In addition to the secondary sources cited here, the *Niagara Gazette* and the *Buffalo Courier-Express* provided almost daily coverage of and commentary on the Love Canal situation.

32. Brown, *Laying Waste,* 3–7, 10–14, 15–25; Levine, *Love Canal,* 14–21; Lois Gibbs, *Love Canal: The Story Continues . . . ,* 20th anniversary rev. ed. (Stony Creek, Conn.: New Society Publishers, 1998), 25–36.

33. Brown, *Laying Waste,* xiii, 5, 21, 31–32.

34. Ibid., *Laying Waste,* 4–34; Curry interview, 25.

35. Levine, *Love Canal,* 17, 18.

36. Ibid., 23; Brown, *Laying Waste,* 16–23.

37. Gibbs, *Love Canal,* 26–28; Brown, *Laying Waste,* 47.

38. Gibbs, *Love Canal,* 28–35.

39. Norman Cerrillo, transcript of telephone interview by author, 7 June 2001, Grand Island, N.Y., 5; Curry interview, 15, 18–19.

40. Levine, *Love Canal*, 28
41. Brown, *Laying Waste*, 25–28.
42. Gibbs, *Love Canal*, 49–51.
43. Ibid., 56–57.
44. Ibid., 49–55; Brown, *Laying Waste*, 33.
45. Paul Westmore, "Board Votes to Reopen Cleveland Ave. School," *Niagara Gazette*, 11 August 1978.
46. Nomenclature regarding the locations of homes in the Love Canal neighborhood can be confusing. Initially, homes that directly abutted the canal were designated ring one, and homes directly across the street from ring one were designated ring two. Rings one and two made up the "inner ring." Although some mention was made of a ring three and so on, after the relocation of the inner ring, the rest of the neighborhood was generally referred to as the "outer rings." The LCHA formally listed the boundaries of the neighborhood as "from 93rd and 103rd Streets [east and west boundaries] and Buffalo Avenue to Bergholtz Creek [north and south boundaries]." Gibbs, *Love Canal*, 59. (See the map.)
47. Levine, *Love Canal*, 43, 46; Brown, *Laying Waste*, 38–41; Francine Delmonte, "Disaster Agency Is 'Low-Key,'" *Niagara Gazette*, 11 August 1978.
48. Mike Brown, "Tons of Dioxin Agent in Canal," *Niagara Gazette*, 10 November 1978; Mike Brown, "Dioxin Found in Love Canal Trenching," *Niagara Gazette*, 9 December 1978.
49. Levine, *Love Canal*, 106–152, 213–215; Brown, *Laying Waste*, 41; Gibbs, *Love Canal*, 217. Gibbs reported that only 67 of the 900 families decided to stay.
50. Levine, *Love Canal*, 157–169.
51. Gibbs, *Love Canal*, 204–216.
52. *United States of America, et al. v. Hooker Chemicals and Plastics Corporation, et al.*, 680 F. Supp. 546 (W.D.N.Y. 1988); Levine, *Love Canal*, 106–152, 213–215. U.S. District Court Judge John Curtin ruled in 1994 that Hooker was not responsible for punitive damages. See Mazur, *Hazardous Inquiry*, 224.
53. Gibbs, *Love Canal*, 217–218.

CHAPTER 2: GENDER AT LOVE CANAL

1. Historian Lisa Brush presents a compelling definition of maternalism for purposes of examining women's environmental activism over time. In positing that "maternalism is feminism for hard times," Brush provides a logical rationale for the continuing use of maternalism, especially after the gains of the second-wave women's movement. Brush defines maternalism as "arguments that support women's personhood and claims to integrity, autonomy, dignity, security, and political voice on the basis of what Molly Ladd-Taylor calls mother-work. Maternalists claim entitlement to citizenship rights and benefits on the basis of mother-work as a source of women's political personhood. The argument is that mother-work involves meeting children's needs for protection, nurturance,

and moral training. To protect, nurture, and train children, mothers must have access to the conditions that will allow them to flourish as persons: bodily integrity, moral autonomy, material security, relational integrity, and political efficacy." Brush argues that when little support exists for women's rights, women may use maternalism to achieve gains for themselves in society. Lisa Brush, "Love, Toil, and Trouble: Motherhood and Feminist Politics," *Signs* 21 (winter 1996): 429–454.

Molly Ladd-Taylor argues for a more narrow definition of maternalism, stating that she does "not believe that maternalists can properly be called feminists. Maternalists were wedded to an ideology rooted in the nineteenth-century doctrine of separate spheres and to a presumption of women's economic and social dependence on men." Molly Ladd-Taylor, "Toward Defining Maternalism in U.S. History," in "Maternalism as a Paradigm," *Journal of Women's History* 5, no. 2 (fall 1993): 110. Eileen Boris, in contrast, presents a case for a more flexible definition, stating that the terms of discourse by maternalist women varied over time and should not be viewed as static. In her research on industrial homework, Boris found that women's emphases adapted in response to changing situations. She states that "the meaning of maternalism and its appropriateness depends on which women, on their standpoint, or position." Eileen Boris, "What about the Working Mothers?" in "Maternalism as a Paradigm," *Journal of Women's History* 5, no. 2 (fall 1993): 95–131.

Another ongoing debate within the maternalist field involves racial issues. Gwendolyn Mink argues for the racial exclusiveness of maternalism, stating that white women used the debate to the detriment of black women. Gwendolyn Mink, *The Wages of Motherhood: Inequality in the Welfare State, 1917–1942* (Ithaca, N.Y.: Cornell University Press, 1995). Several historians have argued instead that maternalism was used by black women as well as white women. For example, Elisabeth Lasch-Quinn traces the development of black women's activism from "mother power" to activism in civil rights areas by using the black church as an example of a settlement house. Elisabeth Lasch-Quinn, *Black Neighbors: Race and the Limits of Reform in the American Settlement House Movement, 1890–1945* (Chapel Hill: University of North Carolina Press, 1993). Around the turn of the century, with the disfranchisement of black men, black women switched their attention from maternalist rhetoric toward fighting racism and discrimination. Boris's research indicates that African American women used maternalistic rhetoric to demand better jobs during World War II. Boris, "What about the Working Mother?" 107.

The most well-known books discussing maternalism in women's activism include those by Robyn Muncy, Linda Gordon, and Theda Skocpol. In *Creating a Female Dominion in American Reform, 1890–1935* (New York: Oxford University Press, 1991), Muncy examines women's influence in the growth of social work during the Progressive Era, including the founding of the Children's Bureau. She finds that as social work gradually became professionalized, men took over, influencing welfare goals and achievements. Building on Muncy's work, Gordon presents a gendered analysis of the history of welfare reform in the United States in *Pitied but Not Entitled: Single Mothers and the History of the Welfare State* (Cambridge, Mass.: Harvard University Press, 1994). She demonstrates that programs such as the Social Security Act of 1935 emerged with stratified systems of benefits and included not only gender biases but also class and racial prejudices. Perhaps best known is Skocpol's *Protecting Mothers and Soldiers: The Political Origins of Social Policy in the U.S.* (Cambridge, Mass.: Belknap Press of Harvard University Press, 1992), which details the use of maternalism as a strategy for women's activism in the area of welfare reform.

2. Allan Mazur, *A Hazardous Inquiry: The Rashomon Effect at Love Canal* (Cambridge, Mass.: Harvard University Press, 1998), 59–63.

3. Michael Brown, *Laying Waste: The Poisoning of America by Toxic Chemicals* (New York: Washington Square Press Publications, 1979).

4. "2 Tots Headed for Grandmas," *Niagara Gazette,* 3 August 1978; Jerauld E. Brydges, "Canal Residents Vow a Tax Strike," *Niagara Gazette,* 3 August 1978.

5. Brydges, "Canal Residents Vow a Tax Strike."

6. "Angry Crowd Greets Officials," *Niagara Gazette,* 4 August 1978.

7. Thad Komorowski, "Love Canal Situation Turns Woman's Life Upside Down," *Niagara Gazette,* 22 August 1978.

8. Brydges, "Canal Residents Vow a Tax Strike."

9. Ed Safranek, "Canal Area Homeowners Split; Seek Quick Aid, " *Niagara Gazette,* 6 August 1978; David Shribman, "Love Residents to Withhold Tax, House Payments," *Buffalo Evening News,* 8 August 1978.

10. Ibid.

11. Shribman, "Love Residents to Withhold Tax, House Payments."

12. Jay Rosen, "Serenity of Area Belies Turmoil of Love Canal," *Buffalo Courier-Express,* 12 August 1978; Francine Delmonte, "2 Canal Group Officials Ousted," *Niagara Gazette,* 13 August 1978.

13. M. E. Lindberg, "Love Canal Emergency Evacuation Ready to Roll—Provided It's Needed," *Buffalo Courier-Express,* 10 October 1978; Gary Spencer, "20 Families with Medical Problems Denied Relocation Ad [*sic*] at Love Canal," *Buffalo Courier-Express,* 13 October 1978.

14. Gary Spencer, "Demands May Delay Canal Cleanup," *Buffalo Courier-Express,* 19 August 1978; Lois Gibbs, "Love Canal Priorities Set Straight by Leader," *Buffalo Courier-Express,* 20 August 1978.

15. Gary Spencer, "U.S. Aide Says Homes Might Be Made Safe," *Buffalo Courier-Express,* 11 August 1978.

16. "Health Top Worry as Canal Plight Tests Government," *Niagara Gazette,* 20 August 1978.

17. "Neighborhood Now 'Ghost Town,' Only 7 Canal Families to Remain," *Niagara Gazette*, 19 December 1978; "Task Force II to Eye Future of Love Canal," *Buffalo Courier-Express*, 19 December 1978.

18. Bob Dearing, "The Unlovely Love Canal," *Buffalo Courier-Express*, 26 January 1979.

19. Arch Lowery, "Falls Group to Weigh Future of Love Canal," *Buffalo Evening News*, 8 February 1979.

20. Jerauld Brydges, "Panel to Weigh Possible Uses of Love Canal," *Niagara Gazette*, 8 March 1979.

21. Lois Gibbs, "Incinerate Canal Waste," *Niagara Gazette*, 8 April 1979.

22. "Love Canal Unit to Send Suggestions to Albany," *Buffalo Courier-Express*, 19 May 1979.

23. "Undeserved Black Eye for Falls," 17 March 1979, Ecumenical Task Force (ETF) Collection, State University of New York–Buffalo Archives.

24. Mark Francis, "'Killing Ground' Is 'Brutal,'" *Niagara Gazette*, 26 March 1979.

25. Jim Baker, "ABC to Shatter Niagara Falls in Its 'Killing Ground,'" *Buffalo Courier-Express*, 27 March 1979.

26. Bob Kostoff, "Falls Mayor Accuses ABC of Bias on Canal," *Buffalo Courier-Express*, 30 March 1979. O'Laughlin later reiterated this view during an appearance on the *Phil Donahue Show* in June 1980. See Lois Gibbs, *Love Canal: The Story Continues . . .* , 20th anniversary rev. ed. (Stony Creek, Conn.: New Society Publishers, 1998), 188–189.

27. Thad Komorowski, "Canal Homes May Be Sold," *Niagara Gazette*, 24 April 1979.

28. "State Eyes Start of Razing at Canal," *Buffalo Courier-Express*, 30 July 1980.

29. Bob Dearing, "Handicapped, Some Retarded to Perform Love Canal Tasks," *Buffalo Courier-Express*, 10 May 1979; "Canal Work Rejected for Handicapped," *Buffalo News*, 11 May 1979; "Morris May Purchase Home in Love Canal," *Niagara Gazette*, 18 May 1981; Bob Dearing, "Handicapped Person to Work in Love Canal's Outer Rings," *Buffalo Courier-Express*, 20 May 1981.

30. Paul Maclendon, "Carey Proposes State Purchase All Canal Homes," *Buffalo Evening News*, 27 October 1979; "Gibbs Wants Seat on New Task Force," *Buffalo Courier-Express*, 30 October 1979.

31. Bob Dearing, "Carey Names New Canal Task Force," *Buffalo Courier-Express*, November 1979.

32. Ibid.

33. "State Seat on Canal Panel a Must," *Buffalo Courier-Express*, 30 April 1980.

34. "Niagara Stalls on Love Canal Plan," *Buffalo Courier-Express*, 28 March 1980.

35. "Niagara Panel Holds Ground on 'Authority,'" *Buffalo Courier-Express*, 1 April 1980.

36. G. M. Seal, "Board Asks Creation of Love Canal Body," *Buffalo Courier-Express*, 20 May 1980.

37. "Board Ready to Name 3 to Authority," *Buffalo Courier-Express,* 24 June 1980.

38. "Canal Agency Will Try to Complete Its Roster," *Buffalo Courier-Express,* 16 July 1980.

39. Bob Dearing, "Canalers Are Reassured by Revitalization Unit," *Buffalo Courier-Express,* 13 July 1980.

40. Bob Dearing, "Love Canal Agency Names Final 3 Panel Members," *Buffalo Courier-Express,* 17 July 1980.

41. Mike Billington, "Women Are Critical of All-Male Agency," *Buffalo Courier-Express,* 10 August 1980.

42. Ibid.

43. "Love Canal Revitalization Unit Meets for 1st Time as a Whole," *Buffalo Courier-Express,* 24 July 1980.

44. "Canal Buy-Out Intern Chief Is Appointed," *Buffalo Courier-Express,* 9 August 1980.

45. Bob Dearing, "Love Canal Agency Head Eyes Home in Canal Area," *Buffalo Courier-Express,* 15 May 1981; "Morris May Purchase Home in Love Canal," *Niagara Gazette,* 18 May 1981.

46. Jo Ann Kott, "Morris Canal Move Makes Light of Serious Problem," *Niagara Gazette,* 27 May 1981; Patricia Grenzy ,"Morris' Plans 'Shock' Former Canal Resident," *Niagara Gazette,* 7 June 1981.

47. Bob Dearing, "EPA Aide Raps 2 Decisions on Love Canal," *Buffalo Courier-Express,* 22 May 1981.

48. Bob Dearing, "Love Canal Agency Head Moves to Love Canal," *Buffalo Courier-Express,* 2 July 1981.

49. Ibid.; Fred Caso, "Aide Moves Family to Love Canal," *Buffalo Evening News,* 2 July 1981; "Morris Family Is Welcomed into New Love Canal Home," *Niagara Gazette,* 2 July 1981; "Agency Head's Home Damaged," *Niagara Gazette,* 1 July 1981; Dearing, "Love Canal Agency Head Eyes Home in Canal Area."

50. Dearing, "EPA Aide Raps 2 Decisions."

51. Dan McDonald, "Love Canal Agency Will Begin Planning without Federal Report," *Buffalo Evening News,* 5 August 1981.

52. Jerauld E. Brydges, "Quarrels among Agency Members Stall Love Canal Revitalization," *Niagara Gazette,* 23 November 1981.

53. Jerauld E. Brydges, "Voting Policy Hampers Canal Agency's Effectiveness," *Niagara Gazette,* 16 August 1981.

54. Brydges, "Quarrels among Agency Members."

55. Ilene Reid, "Tensions Halt Meeting on Love Canal," *Buffalo Courier-Express,* 11 November 1981; Ilene Reid, "2 Quit Love Canal Panel over Resolution," *Buffalo Courier-Express,* 19 November 1981; Ilene Reid, "Canal Unit Reshuffling Intended to Split Block, " *Buffalo Courier-Express,* 5 January 1982.

56. See Gibbs, *Love Canal,* 203–223; Mazur, *Hazardous Inquiry,* 216–217, 224.

57. For information about the backlash to the second-wave women's movement, see Rebecca E. Klatch, *Women of the New Right* (Philadelphia: Temple University Press, 1987).

58. Deborah Curry (formerly Cerrillo), transcript of telephone interview by author, 29 January 2002, Holley, N.Y., 8, 18; Patricia Grenzy, transcript of telephone interview by author, 12 June 2001, Lockport, N.Y., 19; Luella Kenny, transcript of telephone interview by author, 18 July 2001, Grand Island, N.Y., 16.

59. Lois Gibbs, transcript of telephone interview by author, 19 April 2002, Falls Church, Va., 14.

60. Kristine Moe, "Genetic Harm Tied to Canal," *Buffalo Courier-Express,* 17 May 1980.

61. Gibbs, *Love Canal,* 170–171.

62. According to the Office of Refugee Resettlement's 1999 report to Congress, refugee admissions from East Asia jumped from 20,574 in 1978 to a high of 163,799 in 1980. Similarly, the number of refugees from Latin America climbed from 3,000 in 1978 to 7,000 in 1979. Available at http://www.acf.hhs.gov/programs/orr/policy/99arc8.htm (accessed 1 December 2006).

63. "Gibbs Sends Message to the President," 18 May 1980, ETF Collection.

64. Letter from Eva Lynch to [William] Hennessey, 2 August 1979, ETF Collection.

65. Ann Hillis, "From the Love Canal to the Welland Canal—Petition to the Government of Canada," 17 October 1979, ETF Collection.

66. Lois Gibbs, "To the Editor," 14 October 1979, 1, Citizen's Clearinghouse for Hazardous Waste Collection, Tufts University Archives, Medford, Mass. This proliferation of citizenship language by the LCHA women may have been influenced by the well-publicized visit of Tom Hayden and Jane Fonda to the area in early October 1979. Hayden stressed his ideas about "economic democracy" and stated, "Americans have political rights but no economic ones." He "linked the nation's corporate structure to the political system in the Soviet Union." Bob Dearing, "Fonda Calls Love Canal 'Immense Tragedy,'" *Buffalo Courier-Express,* 5 October 1979.

67. Norman Cerrillo, transcript of telephone interview by author, 7 June 2001, Grand Island, N.Y., 9.

68. Curry interview, 37.

69. Gibbs interview, 6.

70. Joann Hale, transcript of telephone interview by author, 16 and 17 July 2001, Grand Island, N.Y., 5.

71. Grenzy interview, 20.

72. Kenny interview, 6.

73. Curry interview, 27.

74. Gibbs interview, 18; Edmund Pozniak, transcript of telephone interview by author, 4 June 2001, Grand Island, N.Y., 19.

75. Hale interview, 4.
76. Pozniak interview, 20.
77. Grenzy interview, 40.
78. Michael Levy, "Lois and Harry: Love Canal Has Changed Their Lives Forever," *Buffalo News*, 18 November 1979.
79. Gibbs interview, 18–19.
80. "Let's Avoid 'Witchhunt' Trap," *Buffalo Evening News*, 17 August 1978.
81. Bob Dearing, "Emotions Mixed as Mrs. Gibbs Goes to D.C.," *Buffalo Courier-Express*, 29 March 1981.
82. Ann Podd, "Possible Love Canal Backlash Worries Area Industrial Firms," *Buffalo Courier-Express*, 20 August 1978.
83. "Angry Crowd Greets Officials," *Niagara Gazette*, 4 August 1978; Eric Stutz, "Jail's Better Than This House," *Niagara Gazette*, 4 August 1978.
84. Jay Rosen, "Serenity of Area Belies Turmoil of Love Canal," *Buffalo Courier-Express*, 12 August 1978.
85. Mike Billington, "Love Canal Red Tape Snags One Woman's Plea for Help," *Buffalo Courier-Express*, 2 June 1980.
86. Ibid.
87. Mike Billington, "Love Canal Restaurant Owner Called 'Eligible' for Relocation," *Buffalo Courier-Express*, 8 September 1980.
88. Brenda Cawthon, "Mom: We've Been Raped," *Buffalo Courier-Express*, 2 May 1979.
89. Pozniak interview, 8.
90. David Koepcke, transcript of telephone interview by author, 29 May 2002, Troy, Mich., 6.
91. Gibbs interview, 20, 19. According to Gibbs, the unions were not concerned about retirement benefits. "They would always argue about health care benefits, salary benefits and survivor benefits [but] . . . they almost never argued about retirement benefits. Because most of the workers in a chemical plant knew that they would not retire." Gibbs interview, 20.
92. Roger Cook, transcript of telephone interview by author, 9 November 2001, Grand Island, N.Y., 10.
93. Ibid., 11.
94. "Union Donates to Homeowners," *Niagara Gazette*, 25 March 1979.
95. "UAW Offers Funds," *Niagara Gazette*, 17 August 1979.
96. Kenny interview, 31–32.
97. Koepcke interview, 5, 19.
98. "200 Protest Pollution in Falls March," *Buffalo Courier-Express*, 11 May 1979.
99. Unions also became involved in other environmental issues, spreading awareness in a variety of ways. For instance, several unions assisted residents near Hyde Park and Bloody Run Creek, another hazardous waste dump in the Niagara Falls area. The United Steelworkers of America, associated with the AFL-CIO, opened an investigation into residents' complaints at Hyde Park (many of

them were members of that union or others). Union leaders also testified before governmental committees about the illnesses of workers who lived in the Bloody Run area. The Hooker Employees Union, led by president Neil Hayes, sponsored an informational meeting about the health effects of chemicals in May 1979, but only 100 of the 800 members showed up. Hayes attributed the low turnout to the fear of possible retribution by the company. "Hooker Workers Told Health Hazards Hidden," *Buffalo Courier-Express*, 5 May 1979.

Playing into the renewal of cold war propaganda in the late 1970s, the United Auto Workers invited Soviet physician Yuri Kundiev to visit several sites in the Niagara Falls area. At Bloody Run, Kundiev noted with horror that the Soviet Union handled waste and worker health far better than the United States did. Stricter controls worked wonders, Kundiev bragged to the American press. Jean Westmoreland, "Russian 'Amazed' at Dump," *Niagara Gazette*, 18 May 1979; Judy Patterson, "Love Canal Peril Shocks Soviet Authority on Health," *Buffalo Courier-Express*, 20 May 1979. Kundiev's remarks were obviously calculated to embarrass U.S. corporations and the government into trying to "measure up" to perceived Soviet "advances" in waste management, however incorrect they were.

100. *Buffalo Workers Movement Newsletter*, May 1978 [probably 1979].
101. Gary Spencer, "Group to Plan March, Picket at Love Canal," *Buffalo Courier-Express*, 24 November 1978.
102. Adeline Levine, transcript of telephone interview by author, 7 June 2001, Buffalo, N.Y., 17.
103. David Shribman, "7 More Canal Pickets Arrested at Cleanup Site," *Buffalo Evening News*, 12 December 1978.
104. Cook interview, 10.
105. "Dioxin Is Confirmed," *Niagara Gazette*, 12 December 1978.
106. Gibbs interview, 17–18.
107. Donald G. McNeil Jr., "Study at Hooker Plant Found 75 Emissions Dangerous to Health," *New York Times*, 17 April 1979; Bob Silver, "Conscience Brought 'Bootstrap' Out," *Niagara Gazette*, 17 April 1979; "Plant Conditions Better: Workers," *Niagara Gazette*, 17 April 1979; Sabrina Porter, "Profit Concerns Caused Hooker Hazards: Bayliss," *Niagara Gazette*, 17 April 1979; "Hooker Workers Told Health Hazards Hidden." Bayliss later terrorized the Love Canal office, waving a shotgun at Gibbs and several others before being arrested.

CHAPTER 3: RACE AT LOVE CANAL
1. Approximately 660 of the 1,100 Griffon Manor residents were black. Memo from Dan Workman to James Jones, Governor's Office, 14 February 1980, Ecumenical Task Force (ETF) Collection, State University of New York–Buffalo Archives. The Love Canal neighborhood also housed a handful of Native American residents. The disaster prompted some reaction from neighboring tribes, including the Tuscarora, who had a reservation in nearby Lewiston. Richard Hill stated that

Love Canal "is a prime example of non-Indian irreverence to the land. When your ancestors came, our people were very friendly to them and tried to teach them a sense of the land. . . . Now we see the results of technology gotten out of hand. The earth is reacting badly. The earth is our last home. You could always go into the woods and renew yourself. It was prophesized that the world would be destroyed by non-Indians. . . . We're saying, remember your children and our children and all our grandchildren." Mary Ognibene, "Canal's Crisis Stirs Prophecy of Tuscaroras," *Niagara Gazette*, 16 August 1978.

2. "Black Family Harassed in Falls," *Buffalo Weekly Challenger*, 15 March 1979, 1.

3. Donna Ogg, transcript of telephone interview by author, 24 October 2001, Lewiston, N.Y., 18.

4. Ibid.; Deborah Curry (formerly Cerrillo), transcript of telephone interview by author, 29 January 2002, Holley, N.Y., 36. For additional comments on the racial tensions in the area, see Luella Kenny, transcript of telephone interview by author, 18 July 2001, Grand Island, N.Y., 17; Barbara Quimby, transcript of telephone interview by author, 6 June 2001, Grand Island, N.Y., 30–31; Sarah Rich, transcript of telephone interviews by author, 19 and 27 March 2002, Niagara Falls, N.Y., 8; James Brewster, transcript of telephone interview by author, 24 July 2001, Tonawanda, N.Y., 12–14.

5. Memo from Workman to Jones; Adeline Levine, *Love Canal: Science, Politics, and People* (Lexington, Mass.: D. C. Heath, 1982), 198.

6. Interview 111, Adeline Levine Love Canal Collection (C94-2), Buffalo and Erie County Historical Society, Buffalo, N.Y.

7. Joyce Sanders, "A Curse Just for Whites," *Niagara Gazette*, 1 May 1979.

8. Laurie Nowak, "Attack Uncalled For," *Niagara Gazette*, 9 June 1979.

9. Ibid.

10. Mike Billington, "Abandoning Homes Painful for Canal Families," *Buffalo Courier-Express*, 26 May 1980.

11. Mike Billington, "Ex–Griffin Manor Tenants Say State Ignoring Them," *Buffalo Courier-Express*, 9 June 1980.

12. Lois Gibbs, transcript of telephone interview by author, 19 April 2002, Falls Church, Va., 26.

13. Curry interview 25, 33–36; Gibbs interview, 27.

14. Patricia Grenzy, transcript of telephone interview by author, 12 June 2001, Lockport, N.Y., 21–22.

15. Interview 125, Levine Collection. Ironically, this couple could afford their home in Love Canal only because of significant government subsidies and limitations on their mortgage payments.

16. Interview 115, Levine Collection.

17. Levine, *Love Canal*, 196–199.

18. Diane Sheley, "Impasse on Relocation of Large Families at LaSalle Development," memorandum to the ETF Executive Board, 8 April 1981; Diane Sheley, "Report of

Advocacy and Direct Aid Program," memorandum to the ETF Executive Board, 6 May 1981, ETF Collection.

19. Interview 148, Levine Collection.

20. Certificate of incorporation of the Love Canal Homeowners Association Inc., 21 August 1978, Citizen's Clearinghouse for Hazardous Waste (CCHW) Collection, Tufts University Archives, Medford, Mass.; emphasis added.

21. Gibbs interview, 21.

22. Curry interview, 25.

23. Gibbs interview, 27.

24. Bylaws of the Love Canal Homeowners Association [spring 1979], ETF Collection.

25. Bylaws of the Love Canal Homeowners Association, Inc. [spring 1979], CCHW Collection.

26. Larry Perrault, "Canal Forum Becomes Bedlam," *Niagara Gazette,* 28 August 1978; Thad Komorowski, "LaSalle Contamination Scares Parents," *Niagara Gazette,* 28 August 1978.

27. Gary Spencer, "LaSalle Residents Remain Up Tight on Canal Cleanup," *Buffalo Courier-Express,* 1 September 1978.

28. Gary Spencer, "Love Canal Issue Splits Community," *Niagara Gazette,* 6 September 1978; Eric Stutz, "LaSalle Development Residents Hit Task Force," *Niagara Gazette,* 7 September 1978.

29. Ibid.

30. Henry D. Locke Jr., "Love Canal Investigators Overlooking Black Residents, Falls NAACP Claims," *Buffalo Courier-Express,* 10 September 1978.

31. Ibid.

32. Henry D. Locke Jr., "NAACP Urges Canal Area Medical Checks," *Buffalo Courier-Express,* 23 October 1978.

33. "Griffon Manor Residents Form Group to Learn of Love Canal Daugers [*sic*]," *Buffalo Courier-Express,* 27 September 1978.

34. David Shribman, "Cleanup—Court Action Delayed until Next Week," *Buffalo Evening News,* 11 October 1978.

35. Mary Ognibene, "Tenants Angry at Task Force," *Niagara Gazette,* 8 October 1978.

36. Francine Delmonte, "Study Finds Housing Defects," *Niagara Gazette,* 8 October 1978.

37. "LaSalle Group Plans Private Health Survey," *Buffalo Courier-Express,* 8 October 1978.

38. In addition, Agnes Jones and the tenants' association refused to support the CLCRA's decision to pursue litigation, further isolating the group of renters and splitting the black community.

39. "Canal Pre-Suit Claims Slated," *Niagara Gazette,* 4 October 1978; "3 Canal-Area Families' Relocations Extended by Additional Funds," *Niagara Gazette,* 6 October 1978.

40. "State to Argue against Injunction to Halt Work," *Buffalo Courier-Express*, 11 October 1978; Shribman, "Cleanup—Court Action Delayed."

41. "Justice Refuses Order to Halt Work on Canal," *Buffalo Courier-Express*, 19 October 1978.

42. Sarah Herbert was interviewed for this book, but she refused to allow the interview to be used. She feels that telling her story to scholars or others will diminish the monetary value of the memoir she is preparing.

43. Gibbs interview, 27–29. Gibbs stated that she had very little knowledge of any problems faced by the black renters until Sarah Herbert assumed leadership.

44. "Fonda Joins Relocation Fight," *Niagara Gazette*, 4 October 1979.

45. Paul McLendon, "Carey Proposes State Purchase All Canal Homes," *Buffalo Evening News*, 27 October 1979.

46. Bob Dearing, "Canal Residents Trade Tears for Cheers at Victory Party," *Buffalo Courier-Express*, 28 October 1979.

47. Ibid.

48. "LaSalle Unit Exclusion on Relocation Aid Hit," 12 October 1979.

49. "NAACP Head Charges Bias in Canal Plan," *Buffalo Courier-Express*, 24 October 1979.

50. Bob Dearing, "Love Canal Agency Names Final 3 Panel Members, *Buffalo Courier-Express*, 17 July 1980.

51. Jerauld Brydges, "Love Canal Unit OKs Renter's Relocation Aid," *Niagara Gazette*, 20 December 1980.

52. Minutes of the Board of Directors' Meeting (LCARA), 7 April 1981, ETF Collection.

53. Sheley, "Impasse on Relocation of Large Families at LaSalle Development."

54. Ibid.

55. Paul Westmore, "Smith Calls HUD Funding Requirement 'Blackmail,'" *Niagara Gazette* [April 1981].

56. ETF Executive Board Meeting Minutes, 8 June 1981, 1, ETF Collection.

57. Minutes of the Board of Directors Meeting (LCARA), 7 April 1981; Sheley, "Report of Advocacy and Direct Aid Program."

58. Rich interview, 14.

59. Sister Margeen Hoffmann, transcript of telephone interview by author, 3 April 2002, Rochester, Minn., 9.

60. "Renters Meeting with Arthur Yves [*sic*]," [16 November 1979], ETF Collection; Hoffmann interview, 34.

61. "House Fails to Approve Funds for Love Canal," *Criterion*, 4–10 July 1979, 3.

62. "Progressive" apparently failed to include tolerance for other minority groups or other historically oppressed groups. The *Challenger* had a reputation for anti-Semitism in some of its editorials (for which it was widely criticized). In addition, it expressed intolerant views of homosexuality. When Barbara Banks, the longtime editor of the paper, was told that ABC was planning a TV series with

homosexual characters, she stated, "There is no room for gay liberation. There is only room for Black liberation. We must teach our children the un-naturalness of homosexuality and set positive examples for them to follow. . . . They have to be taught to reject the madness. . . . Just in terms of survival of the race . . . no homosexual relationship has ever brought a child into this world. . . . There is nothing 'gay' about watching Black men give up their manhood. It is unnatural, destructive and suicidal at best." "The 'Not So Gay' Liberation of the Black Man . . . ," *Buffalo Challenger,* 3 July 1980, 2.

63. "The 'Other Side' of the Love Canal," *Niagara Falls Challenger,* 22 May 1980, 1.
64. William J. Bradberry, "The Other Love Canal," *Buffalo Challenger,* 24 July 1980, 10.
65. Abdullah Luqman, "Dumpsters Invite Plagues," *Criterion,* 15–24 August 1979, 1.
66. Some examples from the period include "Hoyt Calls for Senate Passage of Nuclear Waste Ban," *Criterion,* 2–6 August 1978, 5; Sherman Briscoe, "Learning Ability Slowed by Pollution," *Rochester Criterion,* 2 November 1978; "Report Released on Housing Conditions of Blacks," *Criterion,* 14–20 February 1979, 3; Mary White, "A Blightened Community," *Criterion,* 4–10 April 1979, 5; "Spring Cleaning 'In & Out,'" *Criterion,* 25 April–1 May 1979, 9; "Poisonous Time Bombs Criss-Cross State's Roadways," *Criterion,* 17–23 October 1979, 3; Congressman Frank Horton, "Toward a Nuclear Free World," *Criterion,* 28 April–4 May 1982, 7.
67. "Questions and Answers: Rodent Control," *Buffalo Challenger,* 28 September, 1978, 4; "Lead Poisoning," *Buffalo Challenger,* 12 October 1978, 4; Barbara Banks, "Nukes, Nuts and Black Folks . . . ," *Buffalo Challenger,* 17 May 1979, 2.
68. Fanne Fernow, "Love Canal Project Folks Feel Neglected," *Buffalo Courier-Express,* October 1978.
69. Interview 148, Levine Collection.
70. Joann Hale, transcript of telephone interview by author, 16 and 17 July 2001, Grand Island, N.Y., 12–14, 33–34.
71. Kenny interview, 17.
72. "Griffon Manor Residents Form Group to Learn of Love Canal Dangers," *Buffalo Courier-Express,* 27 September 1978.
73. David Shribman and Paul MacClennan, "Project Families Feel 'Ignored' in Canal Plan," *Buffalo Evening News,* 29 August 1978, quoted in Levine, *Love Canal,* 198.
74. Interview 114, Levine Collection.
75. Interview 148, Levine Collection.

CHAPTER 4: CLASS AT LOVE CANAL

1. The LCHA actually still exists and remains active in various Love Canal issues, notably the rehabilitation of the neighborhood.
2. I have a hard time calling the ETF members "outsiders," although many of the residents of Love Canal saw them that way. The term *nonresident* seems more accurate and descriptive. Ogg, Mudd, and Moore, for example, were all from

Lewiston—literally right next door to Niagara Falls. Roger Cook lived on Grand Island, directly across the Niagara River from the beleaguered neighborhood. Donna Ogg, transcript of telephone interview by author, 24 October 2001, Lewiston, N.Y., 2–3; Terri Mudd, transcript of telephone interview by author, 30 July 2001, Lewiston, N.Y., 4; Roger Cook, transcript of telephone interview by author, 9 November 2001, Grand Island, N.Y., 5.

3. James Brewster, transcript of telephone interview by author, 24 July 2001, Tonawanda, N.Y., 5.

4. Ogg interview, 8–9.

5. Brewster interview, 2–4.

6. Mudd interview, 4.

7. Cook interview, 3–5.

8. Sister Margeen Hoffmann, transcript of telephone interview by author, 3 April 2002, Rochester, Minn., 5–10; Margeen Hoffmann résumé [1980], Ecumenical Task Force (ETF) Collection, State University of New York–Buffalo Archives.

9. Ogg interview, 7.

10. Mudd interview, 4.

11. Cook interview, 3–5.

12. For a complete collection of the documents related to the Vatican II Council (which ran from 11 October 1962 to 8 December 1965), see http://www.vatican.va/archive/hist_councils/ ii_vatican_council/index.htm (accessed 1 December 2006).

13. Hoffmann interview, 5–10; Hoffmann résumé.

14. Joann Hale, transcript of telephone interview by author, 16 and 17 July 2001, Grand Island, N.Y., 2–4.

15. Brewster interview, 9.

16. Paul L. Moore, "The Land Is Cursed," letter from the pastor to Lewiston Presbyterian Church [mid-August 1978], Citizen's Clearinghouse for Hazardous Waste (CCHW) Collection, Tufts University Archives, Medford, Mass.

17. Ibid.

18. Paul L. Moore and Donna Ogg, "A Letter of Concern to the Religious Community," 22 February 1979, 1–2, ETF Collection.

19. Ogg interview, 11.

20. The organization was later formally incorporated as the Ecumenical Task Force of the Niagara Frontier, Inc.

21. Donna Ogg, "Minutes—Ecumenical Task Force to Address the Love Canal Disaster," 20 March 1979, 1, ETF Collection. The early subcommittees of the ETF clarified and further delineated these goals: direct aid, which provided assistance to the residents in various forms; advocacy, which used the members' contacts in the religious and political communities to disseminate information about Love Canal; and data gathering and interpretation, which analyzed and gathered the myriad scientific data being generated. Donna Ogg, "Minutes—Ecumenical Task Force to Address the Love Canal Disaster," 2 April 1979, 2–3, ETF Collection.

22. The ETF had several Jewish members, including Rabbi Lawrence Pinsker and a female rabbi, who served on its board. However, non-Christian influence was extremely limited. Although some African American church leaders and laypeople participated, nonwhite influence was also minimal.
23. Moore, "The Land Is Cursed."
24. Ibid.; Margeen Hoffmann, ed., *Progress Report of the Ecumenical Task Force of the Niagara Frontier, Inc.* (Niagara Falls, N.Y.: n.p., 1980), ii, iii, ETF Collection.
25. James Brewster, "Theological Reflections—Eden and the Love Canal," speech presented at ETF Evaluation Day, 12 January 1981, ETF Collection.
26. Margeen Hoffmann, "Model of Response," in *Progress Report*, 9; Hoffmann interview, 38.
27. Moore and Ogg, "A Letter of Concern to the Religious Community," 1–2.
28. Letter from Margeen Hoffmann to Chairman, Niagara County Legislature, 1 April 1980, 2, ETF Collection.
29. *Progress Report*, ii.
30. Carolyn Merchant, *Ecological Revolutions: Nature, Gender, and Science in New England* (Chapel Hill: University of North Carolina Press, 1989).
31. Donna Ogg, "God's Good Earth," 19 August 1979, reprinted in *Progress Report*, xv.
32. Chief Seattle, "The Earth Is Our Mother" [1854], quoted in *Earthcare: Lessons from Love Canal*, ed. Sister Margeen Hoffmann (Niagara Falls, N.Y.: ETF, 1987), 97–98.
33. Ibid.
34. Letter from Hoffmann to Chairman, Niagara County Legislature, 2. The rest of the speech dealt with the rationale of the churches' involvement, the ETF's works, and the scope of the problem. Interestingly, in a newspaper article covering the speech, journalists emphasized the maternalistic language more than anything else.
35. Mudd interview, 7.
36. Luella Kenny, transcript of telephone interview by author, 18 July 2001, Grand Island, N.Y.,35.
37. Lois Gibbs, transcript of telephone interview by author, 19 April 2002, Falls Church, Va., 44.
38. Deborah Curry (formerly Cerrillo), transcript of telephone interview by author, 29 January 2002, Holley, N.Y., 30.
39. Barbara Quimby, transcript of telephone interview by author, 6 June 2001, Grand Island, N.Y., 23.
40. Hale interview, 35.
41. Gibbs interview, 44.
42. Patricia Grenzy, transcript of telephone interview by author, 12 June 2001, Lockport, N.Y., 47. For similar sentiments, see Hale interview, 34–35; Kenny interview, 34; Adeline Levine, transcript of telephone interview by author, 7 June 2001, Buffalo, N.Y., 22.

43. Sabrina Porter, "Rally Adds Twist to Mothers' Day," *Niagara Gazette,* 6 May 1979.

44. "200 Protest Pollution in Falls March," *Buffalo Courier-Express,* 11 May 1979; Sabrina Porter, "200 Join Protest on Toxic Dumping," *Niagara Gazette,* 14 May 1979; Geoff Seal, "200 Turn Out for March in Falls," *Buffalo Courier-Express,* 14 May 1979.

45. Grenzy interview, 54.

46. Quimby interview, 27.

47. Paul MacClennan, "Residents Try to Halt Work on Cleanup," *Buffalo Evening News,* 11 December 1978.

48. Grenzy interview, 38–42; see also Curry interview, 28.

49. Gibbs interview, 32

50. Thad Komorowski, "Canal Pickets Explain Actions," *Niagara Gazette,* 17 December 1978.

51. "13 Busted at Love Canal as More Poison Is Found," *New York Daily World,* 13 December 1978.

52. Gene Grabiner, "Condemns Arrests at Love Canal," *Buffalo Evening News,* 29 December 1978.

53. "Canal Picket Charges Dismissed by Certo," *Buffalo News,* 19 December 1978.

54. Lois Gibbs, *Love Canal: The Story Continues . . . ,* 20th anniversary rev. ed. (Stony Creek, Conn.: New Society Publishers, 1998), 150–151.

55. Relocation Report, 8 September 1979, 1, ETF Collection; "A Special Thank You," *Common Ground,* October 1979, 2, ETF Collection.

56. Bob Dearing, "Hundreds of Canal Residents Face Eviction from Hotels," *Buffalo Courier-Express,* 12 August 1979.

57. Hoffmann interview, 29–30.

58. Ann Hillis, transcript of telephone interview by author, 29 May 2002, Florida.

59. "Stella Niagara Story," *Common Ground,* October 1979, 1, ETF Collection; "A Special Thank You," *Common Ground,* October 1979, 2, ETF Collection; "Thank You, Also," *Common Ground,* October 1979, ETF Collection.

60. Bob Dearing, "Evacuees Share Living, Giving," *Buffalo Courier-Express,* in *Progress Report* [December 1979].

61. Hoffmann interview, 14, 16–17.

62. Ibid., 15.

63. James Brewster, John Lynch, Bruce Stearns, and Paul Graeber, "Toward the Reality of Hope: A Response of the ETF Regarding the Carey Plan for Revitalization of the Love Canal Area," ETF Resolution, 26 August 1980, 1–2, ETF Collection.

64. Memo from Margeen Hoffmann to LCARA Chairman and Members, 23 October 1980, ETF Collection; Margeen Hoffmann, "A Tension of Vision and Reality," statement read to LCARA public meeting, 23 October 1980, 1–2, ETF Collection.

65. Angelo Massaro, from notes taken by Barbara Hanna at LCARA meeting, 5 March 1981, 1, ETF Collection.

66. Ecumenical Task Force Executive Board Minutes, 6 October 1981, 2, ETF Collection.
67. "Task Force Questions Morris' Plan of Moving into Vacant Canal Home," *Niagara Gazette*, 19 May 1981; Margeen Hoffmann and James Brewster, "Statement," released at LCARA meeting, 14 September 1982, 2, ETF Collection.
68. Hoffmann and Brewster, "Statement," 4.
69. Frank Nepal, "Statement," transcribed 20 May 1980, FBI File Buffalo 9-1498, 2–3 [in 22 May 1980 memo from SAC, WFO (9-4493) (RUC) (C-4) to Director, FBI].
70. Quimby interview, 25–26.
71. Grenzy interview, 50–55; Quimby interview, 20–28; Gibbs, *Love Canal*, 172–182.
72. Gibbs, *Love Canal*, 172–182.
73. Hale interview, 36.
74. Nepal, "Statement," 2–3.
75. Dr. James Lucas, "Statement," transcribed 20 May 1980, FBI File Buffalo 9-1498, 2–3 [in 22 May 1980 memo from SAC, WFO (9-4493) (RUC) (C-4) to Director, FBI].
76. Lee Colwell, Report from Buffalo Field Office to Director, FBI, 19 May 1980, 2–3 [in 20 May 1980 "Daily Attorney General Report" from William H. Webster (Director, FBI) to Benjamin Civiletti (Attorney General)].
77. Richard Lippes, transcript of telephone interview by author, 17 April 2002, Buffalo, N.Y., 16–17; Gibbs, *Love Canal*, 172–182; Quimby interview, 20–28; Mike Billington and Richard Schroeder, "Falls Crowd Angered by Release of Hostages," *Buffalo Courier-Express*, 20 May 1980; Tony Farina and Mike Billington, "Release EPA Hostages," *Buffalo Courier-Express*, 20 May 1980.
78. Memo from Buffalo office to Director, 20 May 1980; Billington and Schroeder, "Falls Crowd Angered by Release of Hostages"; Farina and Billington, "Release EPA Hostages."
79. Gibbs, *Love Canal*, 184–187.
80. Ibid., 185–186; David E. Lynch, "State, Federal Officials Agree on Canal Plan," *Buffalo Courier-Express*, 20 August 1980; "Canal Revitalization Agency to Open Office Right on Site," *Buffalo Courier-Express*, 20 August 1980.
81. Hoffmann interview, 35–37; Brewster interview, 10–11; Bylaws of the Ecumenical Task Force of the Niagara Frontier, 8 November 1979, ETF Collection. In some of the group's literature and papers (and on stationery it could not afford to discard), the earlier name still appeared even after the formal adoption of the new name.
82. Roberta Grimm and Margeen Hoffmann, "A Time to Risk," in *Earthcare*, 43–49; Hoffmann, "Model of Response," in *Progress Report*, 9.
83. Roger Cook, Ecumenical Task Force Executive Board Meeting Minutes, 8 June 1981, 1, ETF Collection.
84. Rich Donoughue, Report to Education Committee, 8 June 1982, ETF Collection.

85. "Toward a Christian Ethical Response to the Problem of Hazardous Waste," preliminary paper prepared by members of the ETF of the Niagara Frontier for the Peace and Justice Commission of the Diocese of Buffalo and for Bishop Edward D. Head," December 1983, 7, ETF Collection.
86. Roberta Grimm, "An Advocate Report," in *Progress Report*, 15.
87. "The Challenge of Response," in *Earthcare*, 31.
88. John A. Lynch, "Agency's Course Continues 'Past Excesses,'" *Niagara Gazette*, 29 May 1983.
89. Roger Cook, Ecumenical Task Force Executive Board Meeting Minutes, 24 March 1981, 5, ETF Collection.
90. Margeen Hoffmann, "An Appeal to the Parishes/Congregations of Niagara and Erie Counties from the Ecumenical Task Force of the Niagara Frontier" [April 1981], 1; emphasis in original.
91. Brewster interview, 24.
92. Margeen Hoffmann, "Article for OSHA/Environmental Network News," memo to Roger Cook, 19 January 1982, 2, ETF Collection; Joan F. Malone, OSF, "An American Tragedy: The Corporate Legacy of Love Canal," ICCR brief, *Corporate Examiner*, October 1981, 3A–3D, ETF Collection.
93. Jim Brewster, "After Love Canal: Redefining the Meaning of 'Disaster,'" *Toxic Substances* [Church World Service Domestic Disaster Office newsletter], 10 November 1981, 1, ETF Collection.
94. Brewster interview, 24.
95. Hoffmann, "Article for OSHA/Environmental Network News," 3–4.
96. Ibid., 2. The court granted amicus status to the ETF along with two Canadian environmental groups, Pollution Probe and Operation Clean.
97. Margeen Hoffmann, memo to ETF Public Policy Committee—Internal, "Telephone Conversation with Edward Lawrence, VEATCH program," 12 January 1982, 3, ETF Collection.
98. Hoffmann, "Article for OSHA/Environmental Network News," 5–6.
99. Barbara Hanna, ETF Board of Directors Meeting Minutes, 16 October 1984, 2–4, ETF Collection.
100. Gibbs interview, 35–36.
101. Ibid., 35.
102. Kenny interview, 18, 32, 40–41.
103. Quimby interview, 33.
104. Curry interview, 20, 38.
105. Quimby interview, 33.
106. Curry interview, 20, 38.
107. Grenzy interview, 57.
108. Gibbs interview, 15.
109. Quimby interview, 12.
110. Grenzy interview, 8.

111. Gibbs interview, 36.
112. Brewster interview, 12.
113. Gibbs interview, 29.
114. Letter from Lois Marie Gibbs to "fellow citizens of America," 2 August 1979, 2, ETF Collection.
115. Hoffmann interview, 19.
116. Gibbs, *Love Canal,* 161.
117. "Who We Are," in *Progress Report,* iv; Hoffmann interview, 30; Ogg interview, 15.
118. Ogg interview, 15.
119. Diane Zielinski, "Sister 'Picks Up the Pieces,'" *WNYCV Vocations Supplement,* 14 October 1979, ETF Collection.
120. Hoffmann interview, 23.
121. Ogg interview, 25.

CHAPTER 5: HISTORICAL IMPLICATIONS OF GENDER, RACE, AND CLASS AT LOVE CANAL

1. Michael C. O'Laughlin, "Revitalizing Love Canal," *Niagara Gazette,* 25 January 1982; Ilene G. Reid, "Waggoner Resigns from Canal Agency," *Buffalo Courier-Express,* 16 September 1982.
2. The literature on gender during the Progressive Era and later twentieth century has been developed by historians and other scholars over the past several decades. For some of the more important works on gender and women, see Glenda Elizabeth Gilmore, *Gender and Jim Crow: Women and the Politics of White Supremacy in North Carolina, 1896–1920* (Chapel Hill: University of North Carolina Press, 1996); Aileen S. Kraditor, *Ideas of the Woman Suffrage Movement, 1890–1920* (New York: Anchor Books, 1971); Marjorie Spruill Wheeler, *New Women of the New South: The Leaders of the Woman Suffrage Movement in the Southern States* (New York: Oxford University Press, 1993); Winifred Wandersee, *On the Move: American Women in the 1970s* (Boston: Twayne Publishers, 1988); Sara Evans, *Personal Politics: The Roots of Women's Liberation in the Civil Rights Movement and the New Left* (New York: Vintage Books, 1979). On masculinity in America, see Gail Bederman, *Manliness and Civilization: A Cultural History of Gender and Race in the United States, 1880–1917* (Chicago: University of Chicago Press, 1995); Kristin L. Hoganson, *Fighting for American Manhood: How Gender Politics Provoked the Spanish American and the Philippine American Wars* (New Haven, Conn.: Yale University Press, 1998); K. A. Cuordileone, "'Politics in an Age of Anxiety': Cold War Political Culture and the Crisis in American Masculinity, 1949–1960," *Journal of American History* 87 (September 2000): 515–545; Joe Dubbert, *A Man's Place: Masculinity in Transition* (Upper Saddle River, N.J.: Prentice Hall, 1979); Peter Filene, *Him/Her/Self: Gender Identities in Modern America,* 3rd ed. (Baltimore: Johns Hopkins University Press, 1998); Michael Kimmel, *Manhood in America: A*

Cultural History (New York: Free Press, 1996); Peter Stearns, *Be a Man! Males in Modern Society,* 2nd ed. (New York: Holmes and Meier, 1990).

3. Carolyn Merchant, "Women of the Progressive Conservation Movement: 1900–1916," *Environmental Review* 8 (spring 1984): 57–85. Women also conducted campaigns for pure water during the Progressive Era, based on assumptions about its health value. They conducted educational programs for both children and adults, established libraries devoted to material on the issues, and campaigned to clean up waterfronts. A Louisiana group, the Women's National Rivers and Harbors Congress, lobbied in support of the preservation of Niagara Falls and worked for more efficient water transportation. I also address the issues covered here in Elizabeth D. Blum, "Women, Environmental Rationale, and Activism during the Progressive Era," in *"To Love the Wind and the Rain": African Americans and Environmental History,* ed. Dianne D. Glave and Mark Stoll (Pittsburgh: University of Pittsburgh Press, 2006), 77–92; and "The 'Gunfighters' of Northwood Manor: How History Debunks Myths of the Environmental Justice Movement," in *Energy Metropolis: An Environmental History of Houston and the Gulf Coast,* ed. Martin V. Melosi and Joseph Pratt (Pittsburgh: University of Pittsburgh Press, 2007).

4. Mrs. Overton Ellis, "The General Federation of Women's Clubs in Conservation Work," First Conservation Congress, 150, quoted in Merchant, "Women of the Progressive Conservation Movement," 74.

5. Lydia Adams-Williams, "Conservation—Women's Work," *Forestry and Irrigation* 14 (June 1908): 350–351, quoted in Merchant, "Women of the Progressive Conservation Movement," 65.

6. Suellen Hoy, "'Municipal Housekeeping': The Role of Women in Improving Urban Sanitation Practices, 1880–1917," in *Pollution and Reform in American Cities, 1870–1930,* ed. Martin V. Melosi (Austin: University of Texas Press, 1980), 61.

7. Roberta Frankfort, *Collegiate Women: Domesticity and Career in Turn-of-the-Century America* (New York: New York University Press, 1977); Ellen Lageman, *A Generation of Women: Education in the Lives of Progressive Reformers* (Cambridge Mass.: Harvard University Press, 1979); Harold Platt, "Jane Addams and the Ward Boss Revisited," *Environmental History* 5, no. 2 (April 2000): 194–203.

8. Jane Addams, *Twenty Years at Hull House, with Autobiographical Notes* (New York: Macmillan, 1911), 65–88, 102–107; Daniel Levine, *Jane Addams and the Liberal Tradition* (Madison: State Historical Society of Wisconsin, 1971), 34–88; James Weber Linn, *Jane Addams: A Biography* (New York: D. Appleton-Century, 1938), 65–128.

9. Addams, *Twenty Years at Hull House,* 281, 283.

10. Ibid., 284–285; Linn, *Jane Addams,* 169.

11. Addams, *Twenty Years at Hull House,* 287–288.

12. Jane Addams, *Women and Public Housekeeping* (New York: National Woman Suffrage Publishing Company, n.d.), 2, 1.

13. Addams, *Twenty Years at Hull House*, 281; Addams, *Women and Public House-keeping*, 1.
14. Lillian D. Wald, *The House on Henry Street* (New York: Henry Holt, 1915), 165.
15. One of the earliest efforts on smoke pollution is R. Dale Grinder, "The Battle for Clean Air: The Smoke Problem in Post–Civil War America," in *Pollution and Reform in American Cities, 1870–1930*, ed. Martin V. Melosi (Austin: University of Texas Press, 1980), 181–203. Angela Gugliotta, "Class, Gender and Coal Smoke: Gender Ideology and Environmental Injustice in Pittsburgh, 1868–1914," *Environmental History* 5, no. 2 (April 2000): 165–193, notes that early smoke abatement efforts were led independently by both women's clubs and working-class men. Women's activism proved to be instrumental in changing ideas about smoke, especially in transforming what had once been considered amenities into necessities. David Stradling, *Smokestacks and Progressives: Environmentalists, Engineers, and Air Quality in America, 1881–1951* (Baltimore: Johns Hopkins University Press, 1999), identified three major periods in smoke pollution reform between 1881 and 1951. The transitions involved shifts in the dominant forces behind reform efforts and in the attitude toward smoke production itself. In the first period, from about the 1890s to the 1910s, members of the public—predominantly women—tried to change people's perception of smoke as indicative of progress and economic success, using health and cleanliness concerns to rail against smokestacks. By the 1910s, however, engineers and other experts touted smoke as the enemy of efficiency. These experts attempted to improve boiler-room technology to make the burning of fuel more efficient and therefore less smoky. The next shift occurred in the 1930s, when fuel sources became an issue. Experts generally noted that "bad fuel led to bad air." Health concerns came to the forefront again and remained there when attention shifted to other types of air pollution, particularly chemical pollution, in the late 1940s and early 1950s.
16. Elmer S. Batterson, "Progress of the Anti-Noise Movement," *National Municipal Review* 6 (May 1917): 372–378, quoted in Grinder, "Battle for Clean Air," 186.
17. Conversely, the lack of a strong women's group could lead to less interest in smoke pollution reform or even efforts to weaken smoke regulations. In Birmingham, no women's group emerged to fight for health, morality, and beauty when local businessmen discussed smoke regulation. Faced with a barrage of complaints and arguments in favor of lessening regulation to promote business, the legislation was basically gutted to complete ineffectiveness. Stradling, *Smokestacks and Progressives*, 131–140.
18. Gugliotta, "Class, Gender, and Coal Smoke," 171–172, states that technological change and the diversification of Pittsburgh's economy were major factors in the success of smoke pollution control efforts. Between 1884 and 1892, Pittsburgh industry substituted natural gas for coal, resulting in much clearer skies. Residents refused to accept the smoke when industry returned to coal in the 1890s.

19. Stradling, *Smokestacks and Progressives,* 43–44. For other smoke control efforts, see Grinder, "Battle for Clean Air."

20. Stradling, *Smokestacks and Progressives,* 119. Although Stradling attributes this loss of power to a takeover by experts (discussed later), Gugliotta ("Class, Gender, and Coal Smoke") identifies different sources. With the advent of germ theory, the links between environmental cleanliness and health protection loosened. Since women had based their arguments on health issues, this shift reduced their authority.

21. *Houston Daily Post,* 8 July 1881, 1.

22. Gugliotta, "Class, Gender, and Coal Smoke," 167–170; quote on 169.

23. William Rend, *Chicago Record-Herald,* 26 April 1909, quoted in Stradling, *Smokestacks and Progressives,* 15.

24. Stradling, *Smokestacks and Progressives,* 47.

25. Ibid., 71.

26. As experts took over, they defined the smoke issue differently, seeing it in terms of efficiency and better control of technology. These experts formed a professional organization, the Smoke Abatement Association, which tended to stress technological developments at the boiler level to make coal burn cleaner, rather than discussing alternative fuels. Stradling, *Smokestacks and Progressives,* 78.

27. Quoted in Gifford Pinchot, *Breaking New Ground* (New York: Harcourt, Brace, 1947), 190.

28. Gifford Pinchot, *A Primer of Forestry, Part II—Practical Forestry* (Washington, D.C.: Government Printing Office, 1905), available at http://www.forestry.auburn.edu (accessed 1 December 2006).

29. Samuel P. Hays, *Conservation and the Gospel of Efficiency: The Progressive Conservation Movement, 1890–1920* (Cambridge, Mass.: Harvard University Press, 1959).

30. John Muir, "The Endangered Valley: The Hetch-Hetchy Valley in the Yosemite National Park," http://www.sfmuseum.org/john/muir.html (accessed 1 December 2006).

31. John Opie, *Nature's Nation: An Environmental History of the United States* (Fort Worth, Tex.: Harcourt Brace College Publishing, 1998), 388.

32. Ibid., 389.

33. Adam Rome, "'Political Hermaphrodites': Gender and Environmental Reform in Progressive America," *Environmental History* 11 (July 2006): 440–463.

34. Ibid.

35. Lois Gibbs, transcript of telephone interview by author, 19 April 2002, Falls Church, Va., 18.

36. For some of the literature dealing with the pre-1980s history of African Americans in the environmental justice movement, see Andrew Hurley, *Environmental Inequalities: Class, Race, and Industrial Pollution in Gary, Indiana, 1945–1980* (Chapel Hill: University of North Carolina Press, 1995); Glave and Stoll, "*To Love the Wind and the Rain*"; Sylvia Hood Washington, *Packing Them In: An*

Archeology of Environmental Racism in Chicago, 1865–1954 (Lanham, Md.: Lexington Books, 2005); Kimberly Smith, *African American Environmental Thought: Foundations* (Lawrence: University Press of Kansas, 2007); and Jeffrey Myers, *Converging Stories: Race, Ecology, and Environmental Justice in American Literature* (Athens: University of Georgia Press, 2005).

37. The material presented in this section has also been developed in Blum, "Women, Environmental Rationale, and Activism during the Progressive Era," 77–92; and Blum, "The 'Gunfighters' of Northwood Manor."

38. M. S. Pearson, "The Home," *National Association Notes* 19, no. 4 (January 1917): 11, in Records of the National Association of Colored Women's Clubs, 1895–1992, consulting editor, Lillian Serece Williams (Bethesda, Md.: University Publications of America, 1993), microform (hereafter, NACW Records).

39. Paula Giddings, *When and Where I Enter: The Impact of Black Women on Race and Sex in America* (New York: Quill, 1984), 95–117.

40. Mary Church Terrell, "The Bright Side," *National Association Notes* 3, no. 8 (December 1899): 1–3, NACW Records.

41. Evans, *Personal Politics*, 133–153; see also Jack M. Bloom, *Class, Race, and the Civil Rights Movement* (Bloomington: Indiana University Press, 1987); James C. Cobb, *Most Southern Place on Earth: The Mississippi Delta and the Roots of Regional Identity* (New York: Oxford University Press, 1992); and Robert Bullard, *Dumping in Dixie: Race, Class, and Environmental Quality* (Boulder, Colo.: Westview Press, 1994). The project was also known as the Community Improvement Contest and the Home and Neighborhood Improvement Contest.

42. Irene Gaines, 1956 President's Address, 33, NACW Records.

43. Irene Gaines, "Dear Clubwomen," Community Project Contest, 1956–57 brochure, 2, NACW Records.

44. Gaines information sheet, n.d., NACW Records.

45. Irene Gaines, "Supplementary Report of President Gaines Made at the Miami Convention of the National Association of Colored Women's Clubs," president's report, minutes of the 1956 NACW convention, 40-A, NACW Records.

46. Gaines, 1956 President's Address, 33.

47. Ibid., 35.

48. "Scoring for Prizes," Community Project Contest brochure, 7, NACW Records; "Project Suggestions," Community Project Contest brochure, 4, NACW Records.

49. "Project Suggestions," 4–6.

50. Gaines, 1956 President's Address, 35.

51. Conference with Mr. Harry Osgood, Sears Roebuck Foundation, 21 November 1956, 1, NACW Records.

52. Press release, 5 December 1956, 1–2, NACW Records.

53. Memorandum from Ora Stokes Perry to Project Promoters and Contestants, 26 February 1957, 2, NACW Records.

54. Ibid., 1–2.

55. "Five Won and No One Lost," *National Notes* 44, no. 4 (summer 1957): 4, NACW Records.
56. Ibid.
57. *National Notes* 44, no. 4 (Summer 1957): 11.
58. "Five Won and No One Lost," 5.
59. Ibid.
60. Ibid., 6–7.
61. "Neighborhood Improvement Contests," in *NACWC—What You Should Know about It* (Washington, D.C.: National Association of Colored Women's Clubs, 1959), NACW Records.
62. Conference with Osgood, 3.
63. Letter from Ora Stokes Perry to Mrs. Harry B. Gaines, 27 November 1956, NACW Records.
64. Interview 114, Adeline Levine Love Canal Collection (C94-2), Buffalo and Erie County Historical Society, Buffalo, N.Y.
65. For its part, the NACW rarely confronted the problem of nuclear weapons either as a means of defense or as an environmental issue. Several sources indicate that the NACW supported civil defense measures taken by the government; in 1954, for example, it passed resolutions supporting both federal and state civil defense measures. At the same time, the group condemned communist activities. In 1960, *National Notes* published an article outlining measures women needed to take for effective civil defense. See Resolutions, NACWC Convention Material, 1954, July–August 1954, 2, 3, NACW Records; Jennetta B. Whitby, "Civil Defense," *National Notes* 16, no. 2 (March 1960): 18, NACW Records.
66. Lawrence Wittner believes that this rhetoric may have backfired on women to some extent. He observes that governmental leaders rarely cultivated the female disarmament leaders, as they did the men. This "should hardly come as a surprise," Wittner notes, given "the nearly universal exclusion of women from politics and, particularly, from the realm of national security policy." Leaders' indifference, Wittner continues, "may have been reinforced by the movement's emphasis on women protesters as politically unsophisticated wives and mothers. The 'feminine mystique' was certainly useful in charming reporters and overcoming charges of subversive activities. But it did nothing to ensure that women leaders were taken seriously in the national security apparatus, where top officials engaged in male bonding of a locker-room type." Lawrence Wittner, *Resisting the Bomb: A History of the World Nuclear Disarmament Movement, 1954–1970*, vol. 2 in The Struggle against the Bomb series (Stanford, Calif.: Stanford University Press, 1997), 469.
67. Amy Swerdlow, *Women Strike for Peace: Traditional Motherhood and Radical Politics in the 1960s* (Chicago: University of Chicago Press, 1993), 56–57, 83.
68. "The Women Protest," *Newsweek*, 13 November 1961, 22. Wilson omitted significant elements of the history and development of the group. The garden party

that became part of the legend of WSP actually resulted in little action, as the women present "seemed indifferent" to her concerns. Swerdlow, *Women Strike for Peace,* 17. Swerdlow, who participated in WSP activities during the 1960s and 1970s, provides a detailed look at the WSP movement and its pacifist background. Wittner also provides a description of WSP and other women's organizations; see *Resisting the Bomb,* 250–258.

69. Dagmar Wilson, *Introduction to Journal of Women Strike for Peace: Commemorating Eighteen Years of Conscientious Concern for the Future of the World's Children* (New York: Women Strike for Peace, 1979), 2, quoted in Swerdlow, *Women Strike for Peace,* 17.

70. Swerdlow, *Women Strike for Peace,* 17.

71. Testimony of Dagmar Wilson, in *Committee on Un-American Activities, Communist Activities in the Peace Movement (Women Strike for Peace and Certain Other Groups), Hearings before the Committee on Un-American Activities on H.R. 9944,* 87th Cong., 2nd sess. (1962), 2189 (hereafter, HUAC Hearings).

72. "For Survival of Mankind: Women Mass for 'Strike,'" *Washington Post,* 1 November 1961, D1; Marie Smith, "500 Women Picket for Peace," *Washington Post,* 2 November 1961, D1.

73. "300 Women Protest Here against Nuclear Testing," *New York Times,* 2 November 1961, L5; "The Women Protest," 21–22; "Rally across Nation," *Washington Post,* 2 November 1961, D1–D5.

74. "300 Women Protest Here against Nuclear Testing"; "The Women Protest," 21–22. In her research, Swerdlow found "strike actions" in Arizona, California, Colorado, Connecticut, District of Columbia, Florida, Illinois, Iowa, Maryland, Massachusetts, Michigan, Minnesota, Missouri, New Jersey, New York, Ohio, Oregon, Pennsylvania, Washington, and Wisconsin. Swerdlow, *Women Strike for Peace,* 247 n. 1.

75. "Integration: Signs Down," *Newsweek,* 13 November 1961, 22, 24.

76. Clemens Reimann, *Chemical Elements in the Environment: Fact Sheets for the Geochemist and Environmental Scientist* (New York: Springer, 1998), 322–325.

77. "The Women Protest," 22.

78. "Rally across Nation," D5.

79. Blanche Posner, HUAC Hearings, 2074. Concern over milk contamination had become prevalent by the November strike. Indeed, on the very day of the strike, the National Dairy Council and the Milk Industry Foundation issued a statement declaring, "any dairy food available for sale can be consumed without fear of harmful exposure to radiation." The two groups feared that abstaining from drinking milk would lead to "nutritional imbalance or malnutrition which could be more harmful than exposure to fallout under present circumstances." "Dairy Trade Deprecates Fallout Fear," *Washington Post,* 2 November 1961, B5.

80. Swerdlow, *Women Strike for Peace,* 81.

81. Ibid., 82.

82. Jeanne Bagby, "Report on Health Hazards from Fallout," 1 December 1961, quoted in ibid., 83.

83. Swerdlow, *Women Strike for Peace*, 84, 83.

84. Ibid., 80.

85. *Woman's Day,* November 1963, 37–39, 141–142.

86. Swerdlow, *Women Strike for Peace*, 94–96, 129–134.

87. WSP lacked significant participation by African American women, although Coretta Scott King played a visible role.

88. HUAC Hearings, 2083.

89. For more details about WSP members' appearance before the HUAC, see Amy Swerdlow, "Ladies' Day at the Capitol: Women Strike for Peace versus HUAC," *Feminist Studies* 8, no. 3 (fall 1982): 493–520.

90. HUAC Hearings, 2047.

91. Elizabeth Moos, HUAC Hearings, 2156–2157.

92. Blanche Hofrichter Posner, HUAC Hearings, 2074. WSP tried on a variety of levels to cultivate an image to present to the press and the public. It often explicitly and consciously molded a feminine, maternalistic image of middle-class propriety. Especially in the early years, female strikers emphasized their neat and stylish dress, as well as their amateur nature. Spokespersons for the group emphasized that WSP was "not an organization . . . not politicians . . . [but] housewives and working women . . . united around one theme: 'End the Arms Race—Not the Human Race.'" "Women Mass for 'Strike,'" *Washington Post,* 1 November 1961, D1. This image presented a counterpoint to their activism, justifying it on non-threatening, acceptable terms to a country that was still worried about communist infiltration and the enforcement of strict gender codes.

  This image cultivation worked to a great degree. Newspapers described the striking women in feminine, but also condescending, terms. *Newsweek* described the activists as "perfectly ordinary-looking young women, with their share of good looks; they looked like the women you would see driving ranch wagons, or shopping at the village market, or attending PTA meetings." In New York, the *Newsweek* reporters saw "an array of housewives, college girls, career women, and grandmothers," while in Chicago, "well-dressed women gathered." The *Washington Post* noted that the November strikers were "dressed in low heels and sneakers for marching." Importantly, *Newsweek* noted that the women "returned to their homes and families" after the strike. "The Women Protest," 21, 22; Smith, "500 Women Picket for Peace," D1.

93. Anna Mackenzie, HUAC Hearings, 2144.

SELECTED BIBLIOGRAPHY

ARCHIVAL COLLECTIONS

Adeline Levine Love Canal Collection (C94-2), Buffalo and Erie County Historical Society, Buffalo, N.Y.

Citizen's Clearinghouse for Hazardous Waste Collection, Tufts University Archives, Medford, Mass.

Ecumenical Task Force Collection, State University of New York–Buffalo Archives. (All newspaper clippings courtesy of this collection unless otherwise noted.)

FBI File Buffalo 9-1498 (obtained under the Freedom of Information Act).

Records of the National Association of Colored Women's Clubs, 1895–1992. Consulting editor, Lillian Serece Williams. Bethesda, Md.: University Publications of America, 1993. Microform.

INTERVIEWS BY THE AUTHOR

Brewster, James. Telephone interview, 24 July 2001, Tonawanda, N.Y.

Cerrillo, Norman. Telephone interview, 7 June 2001, Grand Island, N.Y.

Cook, Roger. Telephone interview, 9 November 2001, Grand Island, N.Y.

Curry (formerly Cerrillo), Deborah. Telephone interview, 29 January 2002, Holley, N.Y.

Gibbs, Lois. Telephone interview, 19 April 2002, Falls Church, Va.

Grenzy, Patricia. Telephone interview, 12 June 2001, Lockport, N.Y.

Hale, Joann. Telephone interview, 16 and 17 July 2001, Grand Island, N.Y.

Hillis, Ann. Tape-recorded telephone interview, 29 May 2002, Florida.

Hoffmann, Sister Margeen. Telephone interview, 3 April 2002, Rochester, Minn.

Kenny, Luella. Telephone interview, 18 July 2001, Grand Island, N.Y.

Koepcke, David. Telephone interview, 29 May 2002, Troy, Mich.

Levine, Adeline. Telephone interview, 7 June 2001, Buffalo, N.Y.

Lippes, Richard. Telephone interview, 17 April 2002, Buffalo, N.Y.

Mudd, Terri. Telephone interview, 30 July 2001, Lewiston, N.Y.

Ogg, Donna. Telephone interview, 24 October 2001, Lewiston, N.Y.

Pozniak, Edmund. Telephone interview, 4 June 2001, Grand Island, N.Y.

Quimby, Barbara. Telephone interview, 6 June 2001, Grand Island, N.Y.

Rich, Sarah. Telephone interview, 19 and 27 March 2002, Niagara Falls, N.Y.

Wattle, Susan. Telephone interview, 5 June 2001, New York.

BOOKS, ARTICLES, AND OTHER SOURCES

Addams, Jane. *Twenty Years at Hull House, with Autobiographical Notes.* New York: Macmillan, 1911.

———. *Women and Public Housekeeping.* New York: National Woman Suffrage Publishing Company, n.d.

Allie King, Rosen and Fleming. "Love Canal Education and Interpretive Center." http://www.akrf.com/Projects/Medical_Cultural_Ed/project_love_canal.html (accessed 13 November 2006).

Bederman, Gail. *Manliness and Civilization: A Cultural History of Gender and Race in the United States, 1880–1917.* Chicago: University of Chicago Press, 1995.

Berton, Pierre. *Niagara: A History of the Falls.* Toronto: McClelland and Stewart, 1992.

Bloom, Jack M. *Class, Race, and the Civil Rights Movement.* Bloomington: Indiana University Press, 1987.

Blum, Elizabeth D. "The 'Gunfighters' of Northwood Manor: How History Debunks Myths of the Environmental Justice Movement." In *Energy Metropolis: An Environmental History of Houston and the Gulf Coast.* Edited by Martin V. Melosi and Joseph Pratt. Pittsburgh: University of Pittsburgh Press, 2007.

———. "Pink and Green: A Comparative Study of Black and White Women's Environmental Activism in the Twentieth Century." PhD diss., University of Houston, 1985.

———. "Women, Environmental Rationale, and Activism during the Progressive Era." In *"To Love the Wind and the Rain:" African Americans and Environmental History.* Edited by Dianne D. Glave and Mark Stoll. Pittsburgh: University of Pittsburgh Press, 2006.

Boris, Eileen. "What about the Working Mothers?" In "Maternalism as a Paradigm." *Journal of Women's History* 5, no. 2 (fall 1993): 95–131.

Brewster, James. "After Love Canal: Redefining the Meaning of 'Disaster.'" *Toxic Substances* [Church World Service Domestic Disaster Office newsletter], 10 November 1981.

Brown, Michael. *Laying Waste: The Poisoning of America by Toxic Chemicals.* New York: Washington Square Press Publications, 1979.

Brown, Phil, and Lois Gibbs. *Toxic Exposures: Contested Illnesses and the Environmental Health Movement.* New York: Columbia University Press, 2007.

Brown, Phil, and Edwin J. Mikkelson. *No Safe Place: Toxic Waste, Leukemia and Community Action.* Berkeley: University of California Press, 1990.

Brush, Lisa. "Love, Toil, and Trouble: Motherhood and Feminist Politics." *Signs* 21 (winter 1996): 429–454.

Bryant, Bunyan, and Paul Mohai. *Race and the Incidence of Environmental Hazards: A Time for Discourse.* Boulder, Colo.: Westview Press, 1992.

Bullard, Robert. *Dumping in Dixie: Race, Class, and Environmental Quality.* Boulder, Colo.: Westview Press, 1994.

———. "Environmental Racism and 'Invisible' Communities." *West Virginia Law Review* 96 (1994): 1037–1050.

———. *Invisible Houston: The Black Experience in Boom and Bust* (College Station: Texas A&M Press, 1987.

————, ed. *Confronting Environmental Racism: Voices from the Grassroots*. Boston: South End Press, 1993.

————.*Unequal Protection: Environmental Justice and Communities of Color*. San Francisco: Sierra Club Books, 1994.

Capek, Stella. "The 'Environmental Justice' Frame: A Conceptual Discussion and an Application." *Social Problems* 40, no. 1 (February 1993): 5–23.

Cobb, James C. *Most Southern Place on Earth: The Mississippi Delta and the Roots of Regional Identity*. New York: Oxford University Press, 1992.

Colten, Craig E., and Peter N. Skinner. *The Road to Love Canal: Managing Industrial Waste before EPA*. Austin: University of Texas Press, 1996.

Corburn, Jason. *Street Science: Community Knowledge and Environmental Health Justice*. Cambridge, Mass.: MIT Press, 2005.

Crawford, Vicki, Jacqueline Anne Rouse, and Barbara Woods, eds. *Women in the Civil Rights Movement: Trailblazers and Torchbearers, 1941–1965*. Bloomington: Indiana University Press, 1993.

Cronon, William, ed. *Uncommon Ground: Rethinking the Human Place in Nature*. New York: W. W. Norton, 1996.

Crosby, Alfred R. *Ecological Imperialism: The Biological Expansion of Europe, 900–1900*. Cambridge: Cambridge University Press, 1986.

Cuordileone, K. A. "'Politics in an Age of Anxiety': Cold War Political Culture and the Crisis in American Masculinity, 1949–1960." *Journal of American History* 87 (September 2000): 515–545.

Davis, Elizabeth Lindsay. *Lifting as They Climb*. New York: G. K. Hall, 1996.

DeLaney, Kathleen. "Disaster at Niagara Falls: Love Canal: Neighborhood Crisis, Worldwide Legacy." *Mid-Atlantic Archivist* 31, no. 3 (summer 2002): 6–8.

Dubbert, Joe. *A Man's Place: Masculinity in Transition*. Upper Saddle River, N.J.: Prentice Hall, 1979.

Dunlap, Thomas. *Saving America's Wildlife: Ecology and the American Mind, 1850–1990*. Princeton, N.J.: Princeton University Press, 1988.

Dunn, Margaret. *Niagara Falls: A Pictorial Journey*. Photography by Michael D. Romanowich. Niagara Falls, N.Y.: M. Dunn, 1998.

Evans, Sara. *Personal Politics: The Roots of Women's Liberation in the Civil Rights Movement and the New Left*. New York: Vintage Books, 1979.

Filene, Peter. *Him/Her/Self: Gender Identities in Modern America*. 3rd ed. Baltimore: Johns Hopkins University Press, 1998.

Flanagan, Maureen A. "The City Profitable, the City Livable: Environmental Policy, Gender, and Power in Chicago in the 1910s." *Journal of Urban History* 22, no. 2 (January 1996): 163–190.

————. "Gender and Urban Political Reform: The City Club and the Woman's City Club of Chicago in the Progressive Era." *American Historical Review* 95, no. 4 (October 1990): 1032–1050.

Foreman, Christopher H. *The Promise and Peril of Environmental Justice.* Washington, D.C.: Brookings Institution, 1998.

Frankfort, Roberta. *Collegiate Women: Domesticity and Career in Turn-of-the-Century America.* New York: New York University Press, 1977.

Gibbs, Lois. *Love Canal: The Story Continues.* . . . 20th anniversary rev. ed. Stony Creek, Conn.: New Society Publishers, 1998.

Giddings, Paula. *When and Where I Enter: The Impact of Black Women on Race and Sex in America.* New York: Quill, 1984.

Gilmore, Glenda Elizabeth. *Gender and Jim Crow: Women and the Politics of White Supremacy in North Carolina, 1896–1920.* Chapel Hill: University of North Carolina Press, 1996.

Glave, Dianne. "'A Garden So Brilliant with Colors, So Original in Its Design': Rural African American Women Gardening, Progressive Reform, and the Foundation of an African American Environmental Perspective." *Environmental History* 8, no. 3 (July 2003): 395–411.

Glave, Dianne, and Mark Stoll, eds. *"To Love the Wind and the Rain": African Americans and Environmental History.* Pittsburgh: University of Pittsburgh Press, 2006.

Gordon, Linda. *Pitied but Not Entitled: Single Mothers and the History of the Welfare State.* Cambridge, Mass.: Harvard University Press, 1994.

Gottlieb, Robert. *Forcing the Spring: The Transformation of the American Environmental Movement.* Washington, D.C.: Island Press, 1993.

Greenhill, Ralph, and Thomas Mahoney. *Niagara.* Toronto: University of Toronto Press, 1969.

Grinder, R. Dale. "The Battle for Clean Air: The Smoke Problem in Post–Civil War America." In *Pollution and Reform in American Cities, 1870–1930.* Edited by Martin V. Melosi. Austin: University of Texas Press, 1980.

Gugliotta, Angela. "Class, Gender, and Coal Smoke: Gender Ideology and Environmental Injustice in Pittsburgh, 1868–1914." *Environmental History* 5, no. 2 (April 2000):165–193.

Hays, Samuel P. *Beauty, Health and Permanence: Environmental Politics in the United States, 1955–1985.* Cambridge: Cambridge University Press, 1987.

———. *Conservation and the Gospel of Efficiency: The Progressive Conservation Movement, 1890–1920.* Cambridge, Mass.: Harvard University Press, 1959.

Hennepin, Louis. *A New Discovery of a Vast Country in America* [1678]. Vol. 1. Edited by Reuben Gold Thwaites. Chicago: AC McClung, 1903. Available at http://www.americanjourneys.org/aj-124a (accessed 26 July 2006).

Higginbotham, Evelyn Brooks. *Righteous Discontent: The Women's Movement in the Black Baptist Church, 1880–1920.* Cambridge, Mass.: Harvard University Press, 1993.

Hofrichter, Richard, ed. *Toxic Struggles: The Theory and Practice of Environmental Justice.* Philadelphia: New Society Publishers, 1993.

Hoganson, Kristin L. *Fighting for American Manhood: How Gender Politics Provoked the Spanish American and the Philippine American Wars.* New Haven, Conn.: Yale University Press, 1998.

Hoy, Suellen M. *Chasing Dirt: The American Pursuit of Cleanliness.* New York: Oxford University Press, 1995.

———. "'Municipal Housekeeping': The Role of Women in Improving Urban Sanitation Practices, 1880–1917." In *Pollution and Reform in American Cities, 1870–1930.* Edited by Martin V. Melosi. Austin: University of Texas Press, 1980.

Hurley, Andrew. *Environmental Inequalities: Class, Race, and Industrial Pollution in Gary, Indiana, 1945–1980.* Chapel Hill: University of North Carolina Press, 1995.

Kendall, Martha. *The Erie Canal.* Washington, D.C.: National Geographic, 2005.

Kimmel, Michael. *Manhood in America: A Cultural History.* New York: Free Press, 1996.

Klatch, Rebecca E. *Women of the New Right.* Philadelphia: Temple University Press, 1987.

Kraditor, Aileen S. *Ideas of the Woman Suffrage Movement, 1890–1920.* New York: Anchor Books, 1971.

Krauss, Celene. "Women and Toxic Waste Protests: Race, Class and Gender as Resources of Resistance." *Qualitative Sociology* 16, no. 3 (fall 1993): 247–262.

Ladd-Taylor, Molly. "Toward Defining Maternalism in U.S. History." In "Maternalism as a Paradigm." *Journal of Women's History* 5, no. 2 (fall 1993): 110.

Lageman, Ellen. *A Generation of Women: Education in the Lives of Progressive Reformers.* Cambridge, Mass.: Harvard University Press, 1979.

Lasch-Quinn, Elisabeth. *Black Neighbors: Race and the Limits of Reform in the American Settlement House Movement, 1890–1945.* Chapel Hill: University of North Carolina Press, 1993.

Levine, Adeline. *Love Canal: Science, Politics, and People.* Lexington, Mass.: D. C. Heath, 1982.

Levine, Daniel. *Jane Addams and the Liberal Tradition.* Madison: State Historical Society of Wisconsin, 1971.

Linn, James Weber. *Jane Addams: A Biography.* New York: D. Appleton-Century, 1938.

Malone, Joan F., OSF. "An American Tragedy: The Corporate Legacy of Love Canal." ICCR brief. *Corporate Examiner,* October 1981.

Mazur, Allan. *A Hazardous Inquiry: The Rashomon Effect at Love Canal.* Cambridge, Mass.: Harvard University Press, 1998.

Melosi, Martin V. "Battling Pollution in the Progressive Era." *Landscape* 26 (1982): 36–37.

———. "Environmental Justice, Political Agenda Setting, and the Myths of History." *Journal of Policy History* 21, no. 1 (2000): 43–71.

———. *Garbage in the Cities: Refuse, Reform and the Environment, 1880–1980.* College Station: Texas A&M University Press, 1981.

————. *The Sanitary City: Urban Infrastructure in America from Colonial Times to the Present*. Baltimore: Johns Hopkins University Press, 2000.

————, ed. *Pollution and Reform in American Cities, 1870–1930*. Austin: University of Texas Press, 1980.

Merchant, Carolyn. *Ecological Revolutions: Nature, Gender, and Science in New England*. Chapel Hill: University of North Carolina Press, 1989.

————. "Women of the Progressive Conservation Movement: 1900–1916." *Environmental Review* 8 (spring 1984): 57–85.

Miller, Char, and Hal Rothman. *Out of the Woods: Essays in Environmental History*. Pittsburgh: Pittsburgh University Press, 1997.

Mills, Kay. *This Little Light of Mine: The Life of Fannie Lou Hamer*. New York: Plume, 1993.

Mink, Gwendolyn. *The Wages of Motherhood: Inequality in the Welfare State, 1917–1942*. Ithaca, N.Y.: Cornell University Press, 1995.

Muir, John. "The Endangered Valley: The Hetch-Hetchy Valley in the Yosemite National Park." Available at http://www.sfmuseum.org/john/muir.html (accessed 1 December 2006).

Muncy, Robyn. *Creating a Female Dominion in American Reform, 1890–1935*. New York: Oxford University Press, 1991.

Myers, Jeffrey. *Converging Stories: Race, Ecology, and Environmental Justice in American Literature*. Athens: University of Georgia Press, 2005.

Nash, Roderick. *Wilderness and the American Mind*. 3rd ed. New Haven, Conn.: Yale University Press, 1967.

Newman, Rich. "Making Environmental Politics: Women and Love Canal." *Women's Studies Quarterly* 29 (Summer 2001): 65–84.

Norwood, Vera. *Made from This Earth: American Women and Nature*. Chapel Hill: University of North Carolina Press, 1993.

Office of Refugee Resettlement. *Annual Report to Congress (1999)*. Available at http://www.acf.hhs.gov/programs/orr/policy/99arc8.htm (accessed 1 December 2006).

Opie, John. *Nature's Nation: An Environmental History of the United States*. Fort Worth, Tex.: Harcourt Brace College Publishing, 1998.

Pinchot, Gifford. *Breaking New Ground*. New York: Harcourt, Brace, 1947.

————. *A Primer of Forestry, Part II—Practical Forestry*. Washington, D.C.: Government Printing Office, 1905. Available at http://www.forestry.auburn.edu (accessed 1 December 2006).

Platt, Harold. "Jane Addams and the Ward Boss Revisited." *Environmental History* 5, no. 2 (April 2000): 194–203.

Reimann, Clemens. *Chemical Elements in the Environment: Fact Sheets for the Geochemist and Environmental Scientist*. New York: Springer, 1998.

Rome, Adam. "'Political Hermaphrodites': Gender and Environmental Reform in Progressive America." *Environmental History* 11 (July 2006): 440–463.

Runte, Alfred. *National Parks: The American Experience.* 3rd ed. Lincoln: University of Nebraska Press, 1997.

Scharff, Virginia, ed. *Seeing Nature through Gender.* Lawrence: University Press of Kansas, 2006.

Skocpol, Theda. *Protecting Mothers and Soldiers: The Political Origins of Social Policy in the U.S.* Cambridge, Mass.: Belknap Press of Harvard University Press, 1992.

Smith, Kimberly. *African American Environmental Thought: Foundations.* Lawrence: University Press of Kansas, 2007.

Smith, Susan L. *Sick and Tired of Being Sick and Tired: Black Women's Health Activism in America, 1890–1950.* Philadelphia: University of Pennsylvania Press, 1995.

Stearns, Peter. *Be a Man! Males in Modern Society.* 2nd ed. New York: Holmes and Meier, 1990.

Stoll, Mark. *Protestantism, Capitalism, and Nature in America.* Albuquerque: University of New Mexico Press, 1997.

Stradling, David. *Smokestacks and Progressives: Environmentalists, Engineers, and Air Quality in America, 1881–1951.* Baltimore: Johns Hopkins University Press, 1999.

Strasser, Susan. *Waste and Want: A Social History of Trash.* New York: Henry Holt, 1999.

Svejda, George. *Irish Immigrant Participation and the Construction of the Erie Canal.* Washington, D.C.: U.S. Office of Archeology and Historic Preservation, 1969.

Swerdlow, Amy. "Ladies' Day at the Capitol: Women Strike for Peace versus HUAC." *Feminist Studies* 8, no. 3 (fall 1982): 493–520.

———. *Women Strike for Peace: Traditional Motherhood and Radical Politics in the 1960s.* Chicago: University of Chicago Press, 1993.

Switzer, Jacqueline Vaughn. *Green Backlash: The History and Politics of the Environmental Opposition in the U.S.* Boulder, Colo.: Lynne Rienner, 1997.

Szasz, Andrew. *Ecopopulism: Toxic Waste and the Movement for Environmental Justice.* Minneapolis: University of Minnesota Press, 1994.

Sze, Julie. *Noxious New York: The Racial Politics of Urban Health and Environmental Justice.* Cambridge, Mass.: MIT Press, 2006.

Tarr, Joel. *Search for the Ultimate Sink: Urban Pollution in Historical Perspective.* Akron, Ohio: University of Akron Press, 1996.

Thompson, Linda. *The Erie Canal.* Vero Beach, Fla.: Rourke, 2005.

United Church of Christ Commission for Racial Justice. *Toxic Wastes and Race in the United States: A National Report on the Racial and Socio-economic Characteristics of Communities with Hazardous Waste Sites.* New York: Public Data Access, 1987.

U.S. Congress, House, Committee on Un-American Activities. *Communist Activities in the Peace Movement (Women Strike for Peace and Certain Other Groups), Hearings before the Committee on Un-American Activities on H.R. 9944.* 87th Cong., 2nd sess. (1962).

U.S. General Accounting Office. *The Siting of Hazardous Waste Landfills and Their Correlation with Racial and Economic Status of Surrounding Communities.* Pub. no. B-211461. Washington, D.C.: Government Printing Office, 1983.

Vogel, Michael. *Echoes in the Mist: An Illustrated History of the Niagara Falls Area.* N.p.: Windsor Publications, 1991.

Wald, Lillian D. *The House on Henry Street.* New York: Henry Holt, 1915.

Wandersee, Winifred. *On the Move: American Women in the 1970s.* Boston: Twayne, 1988.

Washington, Sylvia Hood. *Packing Them In: An Archeology of Environmental Racism in Chicago, 1865–1954.* Lanham, Md.: Lexington Books, 2005.

Wellin, Elaine S. "Women in the Grassroots Movement for Environmental Justice: A Gendered Analysis." PhD diss., University of Michigan, 1996.

Wheeler, Marjorie Spruill. *New Women of the New South: The Leaders of the Woman Suffrage Movement in the Southern States.* New York: Oxford University Press, 1993.

White, Deborah Gray. *Too Heavy a Load: Black Women in Defense of Themselves, 1894–1994.* New York: W. W. Norton, 1999.

White, Lynn Jr. "The Historical Roots of Our Ecological Crisis." *Science* 155 (10 March 1967): 1203–1207.

Wittner, Lawrence. *Resisting the Bomb: A History of the World Nuclear Disarmament Movement, 1954–1970.* Vol. 2 in The Struggle against the Bomb series. Stanford, Calif.: Stanford University Press, 1997.

Worster, Donald, ed. *The Ends of the Earth: Perspectives on Modern Environmental History.* New York: Cambridge University Press, 1988.

———. *Nature's Economy: A History of Ecological Ideas.* 2nd ed. New York: Cambridge University Press, 1994.

Zielinski, Diane. "Sister 'Picks Up the Pieces.'" *WNYCV Vocations Supplement,* 14 October 1979.

INDEX

Abrams, William, Sr., 73–74. *See also* National Association for the Advancement of Colored People

Adams-Williams, Lydia, 123

Addams, Jane, 123–125

AKRF, 14

American Forestry Association (AFA), 131

Anti-Smoke League, 126

Armagast, Fred, 112. *See also* Hyde Park landfill

Bagby, Jeanne, 145

Banks, Barbara, 81–82, 164n62

Barney, Kenneth, 103

Bayger, Frank R., 76

Bayliss, Michael, 60

Belk, Leotis, 42, 46, 77, 78

Billington, Mike, 68

Black Creek Village, 11, 14 (photo)
emergency declaration area, 12
LCARA and, 29
Love Canal 2000 and, 12
revitalization and, 47

Bloody Run. *See* Hyde Park landfill

Blueprint for Action Conference, 105

Borisov, Botislav, 143

Brewster, James (Jim)
background, 89
Hyde Park landfill and, 112
O'Laughlin and, 79
rationale of the ETF and, 93, 94
See also Ecumenical Task Force (ETF)

Brown, Edmund, 144

Brown, Michael
initial investigation and, 25
Lois Gibbs and, 26
Schroeders and, 25, 34
in standard story, 1

Brown, S. K., 14–15

Bryan, Charles
picketing and, 59, 100

Brzezinski, Stanley, 41

Buffalo Challenger, 80–82, 164n62

Buffalo Courier-Express, 36, 68, 78

Buffalo Evening News, 59

Buffalo State College, 88

Buffalo Workers Movement, 59

Calspan Corporation, 25, 28

Carborundum Company, 20

Carey, Hugh
criticism from African Americans, 84
formation of LCARA and, 41
health reports and, 29
inner-ring homes and, 28, 100
outer-ring homes and, 40, 76–77
remedial construction and, 100

Carson, Rachel, 95

Carter, Jimmy
chromosome study and, 49
emergency declaration area (1978) and, 28
emergency declaration area (1980) and, 12, 28
EPA hostage crisis and, 102, 107

Catholic Charities, 42

CCHW. *See* Citizens Clearinghouse for Hazardous Waste

Center for Health, Environment, and Justice (CHEJ), 114, 116

CERCLA. *See* Superfund

Cerrillo, Deborah (Debbie), 83
African Americans and, 66, 68, 73
after Love Canal, 115
early activism, 26, 28
emergency declaration (1978) and, 27
feminism and, 48
gender roles and, 51–52, 53
initial impression of neighborhood, 24
LCARA and, 71
media and, 98
picketing and, 101

Cerrillo, Norman
gender roles and, 51–52, 54, 121

CHEJ. *See* Center for Health, Environment, and Justice

Chief Seattle, 96. *See also* Native Americans

chromosome studies, 28, 49, 106–107. *See also* Environmental Protection Agency (EPA)

Citizens Clearinghouse for Hazardous Waste
(CCHW), 114. *See also* Center for
Health, Environment, and Justice
(CHEJ)
Citizens Smoke Abatement Association, 126
Clark, James, 38–39
CLCRA. *See* Concerned Love Canal Renters
Association
Clinton, Bill, 141
Community Project Contest (CPC)
Birmingham project, 136
Chicago project, 137–138
comparison with Love Canal activism,
139–141
Longview (Washington) project, 136,
138–139
Los Angeles projects, 136, 137
nomenclature of, 175n41
origins of project, 133–134
Tuscaloosa (Alabama) project, 137
winners of, 137–139
See also National Association of Colored
Women (NACW)
conservation and preservation movements, 123,
129–132
Concerned Area Residents, 46
Concerned Love Canal Renters Association
(CLCRA), 76, 163n38
criticism of, 84–85
demands of, 74, 75–76
ETF and, 79–80
Eves, Arthur and, 80
formation of, 74
Gibbs and LCHA, relationship with, 75,
77, 84
LCARA and, 77
maternalism and, 82–83
Cook, Roger
background, 89, 110
environmental views of, 111–112
picketing and, 59, 101
union involvement and, 58
See also Ecumenical Task Force (ETF)
Cook, Roger (Judge), 76
CPC. *See* Community Project Contest
Crane, Henry Hitt, 143
Criterion, 80–82
Cuddy, Michael
CLCRA and, 74
LCARA and, 43

Love Canal Task Force and, 28, 37
"motel people" and, 103
revitalization and, 37, 38, 56
Task Force II and, 38
views of Griffon Manor and, 68
violence towards, 104
Curry, Deborah (Debbie). *See* Cerrillo, Deborah
Curtain, John, 29, 113

Daly, John
Daly-Murphy Plan, 77
formation of LCARA and, 42
Daly-Murphy Plan, 77
Davis, Bruce, 54
Dearing, Bob, 78
Democratic National Convention (1980), 109
dioxin, 28
Dolson, Marilyn, 72
DuPont, 20, 104–105

Earthcare, 96
Eaton, Cyrus, 144
Ecumenical Task Force (ETF), 4–5, 58, 86, 109,
121
African Americans and, 65, 76, 79–80, 85,
103, 110, 141
compared to WSP, 141–142, 146–148
demise of group, 106
demographics of, 86–87, 88–90, 109–110
diversity of, 167n22
environmental views of, 111–112, 116, 121
EPA hostage crisis and, 106, 118
formation of, 91–93
habitability report and, 105–106
Hyde Park (Bloody Run) landfill and,
112–113
LCARA and , 42, 79, 105–106, 119
LCHA and , 91, 117–119
local corporations and, 104–105
March for Mother Earth and, 98
"motel people" and, 103–104
rationale of, 87–88, 93–97, 149
subcommittees of, 166n21
tactics of, 103–106
Edison, Thomas, 19
Edwards, John, 58
Ellis, Overton, Mrs., 123
emergency declaration (1978), 26–27, 28
effect on businesses, 55
emergency declaration (1980), 12, 28

Emerson, Fay, 143
Environmental Protection Agency (EPA)
    chromosome study and, 49, 106–109
    habitability study and, 45, 105–106
    hostages and, 5, 106–109
    initial sampling and, 25
    Morris's move and, 4
environmental racism movement, 141
EPA. *See* Environmental Protection Agency
ETF. *See* Ecumenical Task Force
Eves, Arthur, 80

Falcon Manor, 46
FBI. *See* Federal Bureau of Investigation
FDAA. *See* Federal Disaster Assistance
    Administration
Federal Bureau of Investigation
    EPA hostage crisis and, 99, 108
Federal Disaster Assistance Administration
    (FDAA), 35, 108
Filatov, Vladimir, 144
First Presbyterian Church (Lewiston), 91
Fonda, Jane, 159n66
Fort Frontenac, 16
Freeman, Victoria, 138–139
Frey, Thomas, 55
Frontier Fire Station, 10, 11, 27

Gaines, Irene, 133–134, 135. *See also* National
    Association of Colored Women
    (NACW)
General Motors, 57
Gibbs, Harry
    comparison to Progressive era concerns, 131
    divorce of, 53, 114
    emergency declaration (1978) and, 27
    gender roles and, 52, 53–54, 61, 121
    OCAW membership and, 57–58
Gibbs, Lois, 1, 2, 3, 11, 32 (photo), 72, 83
    African Americans and, 68, 74, 76, 164n43
    CHEJ and, 114, 116
    children's empowerment and, 98
    chromosome study and, 49, 106
    citizenship rights and, 49, 50
    criticism of, 54, 59, 67
    Daly-Murphy Plan, 77
    disillusionment with government and,
        115–116
    divorce of, 53, 114
    early activism and, 26, 27, 28, 34

economic concerns of, 35
emergency declaration (1978) and, 27
EPA hostage crisis and, 106–109
feminism and, 48
gender roles and, 52, 53–54
health concerns of, 36, 37
Heisner and, 36
Hoffmann and, 117–118
inclusiveness of, 33, 35, 37, 71
initial impression of neighborhood, 24
LCARA and, 29, 41, 42, 71
Lester, Stephen and, 114
local issues and, 113–114
March for Mother Earth and, 98–99
maternalism and, 31, 97, 100–101
media and, 63, 86, 97
O'Laughlin and, 41
proposals for future use and, 38, 39
relocation of, 114
remedial construction and, 75, 100–101
tactics of, 106
    See also Love Canal Homeowners
        Association (LCHA)
Gibbs, Melissa (Missy), 116
Gibbs, Michael, 24, 26, 116
Gogos, Maria, 55–56
Good Morning America, 109
Goodyear Chemical, 57
Granieri, Sam, 14
Grenzy, Ernest (Ernie)
    gender roles and, 52, 53
Grenzy, Patricia (Patti)
    after Love Canal, 115
    children's empowerment and, 98, 99
    disillusionment with government and, 115–116
    EPA hostages and, 99
    feminism and, 48
    gender roles and, 52
    Griffin Manor residents and, 68–69
    picketing and, 101
Griffon, 18
Griffon Manor, 4, 28, 63, 65 (photo), 76, 82, 132
    comparison with Progressive Era activism,
        139–141
    Concerned Love Canal Renters Association
        and, 74
    Daly-Murphy Plan, 77
    environmental racism movement and, 141
    Head Start program and, 70, 72
    health testing and, 68, 72–73, 74–75

Griffon Manor *(continued)*
  LCARA and, 78–80
  NAACP and, 73–74, 76, 77
  nomenclature of, 151n7
  problems with, 75
  racism towards, 51, 66–70, 72–73, 140
  remedial construction and, 72
  replaced by Vincent Morello Senior
    Housing Complex, 11, 47, 79
  Section 8 housing and, 78
Grimm, Roberta, 111

Hadley, Kathleen, 48
Hadley, Wayne, 97
Hale, Gary
  background of, 90
  reaction to role reversal, 53
Hale, Joann
  African American community and, 83
  background, 83, 90
  EPA hostage crisis and, 107
  gender roles and, 52
  media and, 98
  unions and, 58
Hall, Mrs. John P., 143
Hayden, Tom, 159n66
Hayes, Neil, 161n99
Hays, Sam, 129
Head Start Program, 70, 72
Heisner, Tom
  early leadership, 27, 33, 34–35
  economic concerns, 34, 35, 56, 131
  emergency declaration (1978) and, 34
  end of activism, 36, 97
  exclusionary attitude, 33, 35, 36, 47, 72
  health concerns, 34, 35
  LCHA and, 28, 36
  Schroeders and, 25
Hennepin, Louis, 16, 17, 20. See also *A New
    Discovery of a Vast Country in America*
Hennessey, William, 37
Herbert, Sarah, 69, 76, 77, 164n43
  LCARA and, 78
  See also Concerned Love Canal Renters
    Association (CLCRA)
Hetch Hetchy dam controversy, 130–131
Hicks, Gertrude Reece, 136, 137
Highland Avenue, 66
Hill, Richard, 161n1
Hillis, Ann, 2, 50, 103, 104

Hillis, Ralph, 104
Hillis, Ralph, Jr., 104
Hoffmann, Margeen, 87 (photo), 112
  African Americans and, 80
  background, 89–90
  corporations and, 104–105
  ETF and, 93, 94, 95, 96, 110, 146
  Gibbs and, 117–118
  "motel people" and, 103
  See also Ecumenical Task Force (ETF)
Hooker, Elon, 21
Hooker Chemical Company, 30, 42, 98. *See also*
    Hooker Electrochemical Company;
    Occidental Chemical Company
  chromosome study and, 49
  criticism from unions, 59
  criticism of emotion, 54
  employees union, 161n99
  The Killing Ground and, 39
  Love Canal neighborhood and, 21–23, 25
  Operation Bootstrap and, 60
  relationship with activists, 104
  in standard story, 1
  waste dumped and, 22
Hooker Electrochemical Company, 20, 21.
    See also Hooker Chemical Company;
    Occidental Chemical Company
Hooker Employees Union, 161n99
Hoover, Herbert, 134
House of God Church, 72
House Un-American Activities Committee
    (HUAC), 147–148
HUAC. *See* House Un-American Activities
    Committee
Hull House, 124
Hyde Park landfill, 112–113, 161n99

inner ring, 8 (map), 154n46
Iroquois Confederation. *See* Native Americans

Jackson, Jesse, 80
Jackson, Marion, 139
Javits, Jacob K., 84
Johnson, Brad, 41
Joncaire, Daniel, 18
Jones, Agnes, 72, 73, 163n38
Jones, James, 41

Kennedy, Jacqueline, 143
Kennedy, John, 142, 145, 146

Kenny, Luella, 87 (photo)
  African American community and, 83–84
  after Love Canal, 115
  background of, 83, 90
  feminism and, 48
  gender roles and, 52–53
  health fund, 114
  initial impression of neighborhood, 24
  media and, 97
Kenny, Norman
  gender roles and, 52–53
Khrushchev, Nikita, 143, 144
The Killing Ground, 39, 67
KKK. *See* Ku Klux Klan
Knowles, Richard, 104, 105
Koepcke, David
  LCHA and, 58
  union involvement and, 57
Ku Klux Klan (KKK), 66, 83
Kundiev, Yuri, 161n99

LaFalce, John, 25, 84
La Hontan, Baron, 15
Lake Ontario Water Works, 89
Lane, Donald, 76
LCARA. *See* Love Canal Area Revitalization Agency
LCHA. *See* Love Canal Homeowners Association
Lester, Stephen, 114
Levine, Adeline, 59
Lewis's Bar and Restaurant, 55, 77
Lippes, Richard
  EPA hostage crisis and, 108
  Gibbs and, 97
  LCHA and, 27, 70, 71
Longview Woman's Study Club, 138
Love, William T., 20–21
Love Canal Action Committee. *See* National Association for the Advancement of Colored People
Love Canal Area Revitalization Agency (LCARA), 72, 80
  comparison to Progressive era concerns, 131
  economic concerns of, 61, 120
  ETF and, 79, 105–106
  habitability declaration, 30
  habitability report and, 105–106
  hiring handicapped workers, 40
  initial name of, 41
  interpretive center and, 12
  marginalization of women, 121–122

opposition from residents, 43, 44, 121
origins of, 41–42, 43
residents and, 46, 78, 79
revitalization and, 33–34, 37, 46
Wattle and, 12
See also Love Canal Task Force; Task Force for the Future Land Use of the Love Canal (Task Force II)
Love Canal Homeowners Association (LCHA), 2, 4, 33, 165n1
  Action Committee, 59
  attempts at inclusion, 35, 36, 71
  children and, 98, 99–100
  CLCRA and, 74, 76
  Daly-Murphy Plan, 77
  demographics of, 87, 90–91
  economic concerns of, 55
  effects of Love Canal crisis on, 115–117
  EPA hostage situation and, 99, 102, 106–109, 149
  ETF and, 91, 102, 117–119
  exclusionary attitude of, 51, 69
  feminism and, 47, 121, 127
  gendered views of, 43, 131
  goals for future, 34, 37
  health concerns of, 61
  health studies and, 75
  Heisner and, 36
  labeled as "emotional," 54–55
  LCARA, 77–78
  local issues and, 113–115
  maternalism and, 47, 61, 96, 97–102, 120
  media and, 86, 97–98
  origins of, 27–28, 70–71
  picketing and, 59–60, 99–100, 100–102
  proposals for future use and, 38
  racism within, 66
  rationale of, 88
  renters and, 63, 72–73, 80
  tactics of, 98–99, 99 (photo), 106–109
  unions and, 58–59
Love Canal Task Force
  disregard of health concerns, 40
  initial formation of, 28
  See also Love Canal Area Revitalization Agency (LCARA); Task Force for the Future Land Use of the Love Canal (Task Force II)
Love Canal 2000, 12, 14–15
  community opposition to, 14–15

LoVerdi, Nunzio, 46
Lucas, James, 106, 107
Lynch, Eva, 50, 51
Lynch, John
    CLCRA and, 78
    environmental views of, 111
    LCARA and, 42, 46, 77, 105
    Morris's move and, 44–45
    O'Laughlin and, 43
    See also Ecumenical Task Force (ETF)

March for Mother Earth, 98–99
Massaro, Angelo, 41, 43, 105
maternalism, 3, 154n1
    during Progressive Era, 123–127
    by ETF, 96
    by LCHA, 47, 97–102, 120
Matsulvage, Albert, 44
Matsulvage, Eileen, 44
McCoulf, Grace, 43
McNichols, Steve, 144
Mineo, Joseph, 40
Moore, Paul
    background, 88, 89, 110
    ETF and, 92–93, 95, 96
    initial interest in Love Canal, 91–92
    stewardship and, 93
    See also Ecumenical Task Force (ETF)
Morris, Anne, 44
Morris, Richard, 45 (photo)
    beliefs in revitalization, 43–44
    decision to move to Love Canal, 44, 45, 106
    as executive director of LCARA, 43, 78
    habitability study and, 45
    opposition from residents, 43
    See also Love Canal Area Revitalization
        Agency (LCARA)
Morrison, Barbara, 113
Mudd, Terri
    background, 89
    ETF and, 96
Muir, John, 129–130
Murphy, Matthew, 77

NAACP. See National Association for the
    Advancement of Colored People
NACW. See National Association of Colored
    Women
National Association for the Advancement of
    Colored People (NAACP), 65, 73, 74

CLCRA and, 74, 85, 141, 149
Daly-Murphy Plan, 77
Love Canal Action Committee, 76
March for Mother Earth and, 98
National Association of Colored Women
    (NACW)
    civil defense activism and, 176n65
    Community Project Contest (CPC) and,
        133–141
    comparison with Love Canal activism,
        139–141
    during Progressive Era, 132–133
    maternalism and, 132–133
National Committee for a Sane Nuclear Policy
    (SANE), 142–143
Native Americans, 15, 16, 17–18
    environmental views of used by ETF, 95–96
    at Love Canal, 161n1
Nepal, Frank, 106, 107, 108
A New Discovery of a Vast Country in America,
    16. See also Hennepin, Louis
New Hope Baptist Church, 42
New Right, 122
Newsweek, 144
New York Public Interest Group, 101
New York State Department of
    Transportation, 37
New York State Health Department's Love
    Canal Health Studies Team, 68
New York State Industries for the
    Handicapped, 40
New York Times, 144
Niagara County Environmental Fund, 14
Niagara Falls School Board, 22–23
Niagara Gazette, 34, 59, 67, 72, 112
    initial investigation and, 25
    See also Brown, Michael
Niagara University, 103
Nichols, H. R., 138
99th Street School, 22–23, 23 (photo)
    closure and, 28
    Gibbs, Michael and, 26
    proposals for future use and, 38
Nowak, Laurie, 67

OCAW. See Oil, Chemical, and Atomic Workers
Occidental Chemical Company, 20
    legal action against, 29, 113, 114
    See also Hooker Chemical Company;
        Hooker Electrochemical Company

Oedipus the King, 91–92
Ogg, Donna
    background, 88–89, 110
    ETF and, 92–93, 95, 118
    Highland Avenue and, 66
    Lake Ontario Ordinance Works and, 89
    LCHA and, 117, 118
Oil, Chemical, and Atomic Workers (OCAW),
    57–58, 61
O'Laughlin, Michael
    comparison to Progressive era concerns, 131
    criticism of emotion, 54
    definition of revitalization, 38, 39, 46
    development of Love Canal Task Force
      and, 28
    disregard of health issues by, 40
    economic concerns of, 39, 40
    ETF and, 110, 118
    exclusionary attitude of, 41, 42, 47, 79,
      121–122
    Gibbs and, 39
    habitability study and, 45
    The Killing Ground and, 39–40
    LCARA and, 41, 43
    Morris's move and, 45
    opposition from residents, 43, 46
    Section 8 housing and, 79, 110
Olmstead, Frederick Law, 20
Operation Bootstrap, 60
Operation Clean, 170n96
Osgood, Harry, 137, 139–140
outer ring, 8 (map), 154n46

Paigen, Beverly, 75
Parker, Russell, 41
Pearson, M. S., 132
Perry, Ora Brown Stokes, 135–136
Phil Donahue Show, 109
Picciano, Dante, 49
Pinchot, Gifford, 129, 130, 131
Pino, Pat
    economic concerns and, 56–57
    picketing and, 100
    unions and, 58
Pinsker, Lawrence, 167n22
Pollution Probe, 170n96
Posner, Blanche, 145
Pozniak, Edmund
    comparison to Progressive era concerns, 131
    initial impression of neighborhood, 24

    reaction to role reversal, 53
    union involvement of, 57
Pozniak, Marie, 53, 87 (photo), 100, 101, 107
Primer of Forestry, 129

Quimby, Barbara
    after Love Canal, 114–115
    chromosome study and, 49, 106–107
    criticism of government, 115–116
    EPA hostage crisis and, 106–107
    gendered views of, 43
    initial impression of neighborhood, 24
    LCARA and, 42
    media and, 98
Quimby, James (Jim)
    reaction to role reversal, 53

Raymond, Michael, 41
Reagan, Ronald, 122
Ribicoff, Abraham, 145
Rich, Sarah, 75, 76, 79
Roosevelt, Theodore, 129
Roswell Park Cancer Institute, 52
Russell, Bertrand, 142–143

Sanders, Joyce, 67
SANE. *See* National Committee for a Sane
    Nuclear Policy
Schoellkopf, Jacob, 19
Schroeder, Karen
    Brown, Michael and, 25, 34
    end of activism, 36
    health problems of family, 34
    history at Love Canal, 22
    LCHA and, 28, 34, 36
Schroeder, Tim, 25
Sconiers, Lester, 76
Scott, Lawrence, 143
Sears Roebuck Foundation,
    Community Project Contest and, 133, 134,
      135, 136, 137, 139, 141
Section 8 certificates, 78–79
Seneca Nation. *See* Native Americans
Sergel, Annie, 126
settlement house movement, 123–125
Seven Years War, 18
Shredded Wheat (Nabisco), 20
Shribman, David, 59
Sierra Club, 111–112
Silent Spring, 95

Simon, John, 41–42
Smith, Barbara J., 76, 77
Smith, Joseph, 79
Smoke Abatement Association, 174n26
smoke pollution reform, 125–126, 128
Snyder, Gerald, 34, 35
Solidarity, 59
Spencer, Gary, 36
Starks, Vera, 72, 74, 82
Stella Niagara, 103–104
stewardship, 93–94
strontium 90, 143, 144–145
Superfund, 1, 78

Task Force for the Future Land Use of the Love
    Canal (Task Force II)
  goals for future use, 38
  initial formation of, 38
  marginalization of African Americans,
    72–73
  See also Love Canal Area Revitalization
    Agency (LCARA); Love Canal Task
    Force
Task Force to Stabilize and Revitalize the Love
    Canal Community. *See* Love Canal Area
    Revitalization Agency (LCARA)
Task Force II. *See* Task Force for the Future
    Land Use of the Love Canal
Terrell, Mary Church, 133
Tesla, Nikola, 153n21
Thoreau, Henry David, 94
Thornton, Elene, 74, 75, 76, 84
Torcasio, Eleanor, 104
Torcasio, Lauren, 104
Torcasio, Sam, 104
Tyson, Ray, 112

union involvement
  at Love Canal, 57–61
  outside environmental issues, 160n99
United Auto Workers (UAW), 57, 58, 59, 61,
    161n99
United Auto Workers Amalgamated, 57

United Cerebral Palsy Association, 40
United Steelworkers, 58
U.S. Soviet Treaty Banning Nuclear Weapons
    Tests in the Atmosphere, in Outer Space,
    and Underwater, 146

Vianna, Nicholas, 68
  and health testing at Griffon Manor, 74–75
Vincent Morello Senior Housing Complex, 9,
    11, 12 (photo)
Voorhees, Aileen, 22, 25
Voorhees, Edwin, 25

Waggoner, William, 42, 44–45, 46, 77
Wald, Lillian, 125
Washington, Booker T., 140
Wattle, Susan, 12
Wesley United Methodist Church, 92
West New York Council on Occupational Safety
    and Health, 58
West Valley Nuclear Waste Depository, 113–114
Whalen, Robert,
  emergency declaration (1978) and, 26–27,
    34, 100
Williams, Frank, 66
Wilson, Dagmar, 142, 145, 147
Wilson, Margaret, 72
Women's Health Protective Association, 126
Women Strike for Peace (WSP), 4
  anti-nuclear movement and, 142–146
  comparison with ETF and, 146–148
  effects of, 142, 146
  image cultivation, 178n92
  lack of race or class issues, 146–147
  maternalism and, 142
  origins of, 142–143, 147
  protests of, 143–146
  testimony to HUAC, 147–148
Workman, Dan, 80
WSP. *See* Women Strike for Peace

Yosemite National Park, 130